TO WAKE THE DEAD

ALSO BY MARINA BELOZERSKAYA

The Arts of Tuscany: From the Etruscans to Ferragamo

The Medici Giraffe and Other Tales of
Exotic Animals and Power

Luxury Arts of the Renaissance

Ancient Greece: Art, Architecture, and History
(with Kenneth Lapatin)

Rethinking the Renaissance: Burgundian Arts Across Europe

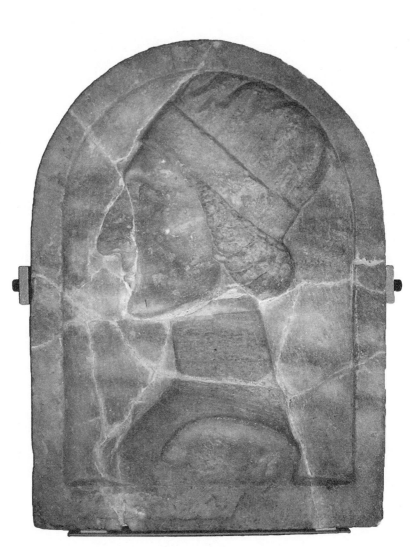

Presumed portrait of Cyriacus. Ancona, City Museum.
(Kenneth Lapatin)

TO WAKE
THE DEAD

*A Renaissance Merchant and the
Birth of Archaeology*

MARINA BELOZERSKAYA

W. W. NORTON & COMPANY

• NEW YORK • LONDON •

Francesco Scalamonti. *Vita Viri Clarissimi et Famosissimi Kyriaci Anconitani.*
Charles Mitchell and Edward W. Bodnar, eds. and trans. Transactions of the
American Philosophical Society, volume 86, part 4. Philadelphia: The
American Philosophical Society, 1996.

Reprinted by permission of the publisher from *Cyriac of Ancona: Later Travels,*
edited and translated by Edward W. Bodnar, The I Tatti Renaissance Library,
Cambridge, Mass.: Harvard University Press, Copyright © 2003 by the President
and Fellows of Harvard College.

For information about permission to reproduce selections from this book,
write to Permissions, W. W. Norton & Company, Inc.,
500 Fifth Avenue, New York, NY 10110

For information about special discounts for bulk purchases, please contact
W. W. Norton Special Sales at specialsales@wwnorton.com or 800-233-4830

Manufacturing by Courier, Westford
Book design by Brooke Koven
Production manager: Anna Oler

Library of Congress Cataloging-in-Publication Data

Belozerskaya, Marina, 1966–
To wake the dead : a Renaissance merchant and the birth of archaeology /
Marina Belozerskaya. — 1st ed.
p. cm.
Includes bibliographical references and index.
ISBN 978-0-393-06554-1 (hardcover)
1. Ciriaco, d'Ancona, 1391–1452. 2. Archaeology—History. 3. Italy—Intellectual
life—1268–1559. 4. Archaeologists—Italy—Biography. 5. Classicists—Italy—
Biography. 6. Travelers—Mediterranean Region—Biography. I. Title.
CC115.C57B456 2009
930.1—dc22

2009016582

W. W. Norton & Company, Inc.
500 Fifth Avenue, New York, N.Y. 10110
www.wwnorton.com

W. W. Norton & Company Ltd.
Castle House, 75/76 Wells Street, London W1T 3QT

1 2 3 4 5 6 7 8 9 0

For Ken,
companion of my travels

CONTENTS

favor the enterprise, having already filled the sail
of your servant, the blithe one from Ancona,
who unveils the noble ancient world to the new . . .

—Cyriacus of Ancona
February 1, 1446[1]

TO WAKE THE DEAD

Arch of Trajan in Ancona. (Kenneth Lapatin)

It is possible that some word of me may have come to you, though even this is doubtful, since an insignificant and obscure name will scarcely penetrate far in either time or space. If, however, you should have heard of me, you may desire to know what manner of man I was, or what was the outcome of my labors, especially those of which some description or, at any rate, the bare titles may have reached you.

—Petrarch, *Letter to Posterity*[1]

On the Threshold of History

IN THE AUTUMN OF 1421 something remarkable happened in Ancona, a port city on the Adriatic coast of Italy south of Venice.

A thirty-year-old clerk named Cyriacus Pizzecolli, responsible for helping to reform the port's disordered bookkeeping system at the behest of the new governor, was hurrying to work along the waterfront. He passed carracks swaying in the dirty water and creaking wooden cranes swinging between the quay and the ships, their loads dangling in the air. He exchanged greetings with merchants inspecting newly arrived shipments of spices, slaves, cotton, and wax from eastern markets, and scuttled out of the way of porters groaning under the sacks of nuts, jars of Apulian olive oil, bales of Florentine,

Lombard, Flemish, and Catalan cloth, local soap, and Balkan lead they were loading on outgoing boats.[2] As he scanned the inventory of goods passing through the port, he overheard brokers haggling with handlers, sailors singing and swearing as they scrubbed decks and adjusted rigging, boys laughing as they ducked in and out of crowds in search of adventure and mischief, and seagulls flying overhead.

Slight and wiry, Cyriacus was restless by nature, his small eyes ever scanning the scene for something interesting, his large aquiline nose seemingly pulling him forward, his pointy chin and dimpled cheeks hinting at coiled energy that could erupt at any moment into a charming chatter or a decisive dash toward some aim.[3] But the real motor within him was his hungry mind. Cyriacus was bored by his job of streamlining financial regulations and procedures, and unfulfilled by his daily reality of money and merchandise. He yearned for something bigger, a more meaningful life. Occasionally, in awkward poems he composed at night, he poured out his frustrations:

> Not to follow the style which urges us to lofty
> Parnassus . . .
>   do I shed the ink of my ampoules,
> but to follow my commercial labor;
> I write and cancel out, and in my books
> the debtor is nurtured instead of poetry.[4]

Alas, his father's premature death when Cyriacus was just a boy had left him little choice beyond earning a living through plain accountancy and trade.

As Cyriacus hastened along the quay, something caught his eye and caused him to look up at the Roman arch that rose over the port. He had passed it countless times since childhood. It had always been there, and while he had noticed with interest ancient buildings on his trips to Alexandria and Constantinople, he had paid little attention to this structure at home, its very familiarity making it blend into its surroundings. Yet now—did the light fall on the arch in a particular way, throwing into sharper relief traces of letters incised into the marble?—he seemed to see it for the first time. He slowed down, came closer, and peered at it with curiosity.

The gleaming white monument was astonishingly well preserved, considering it had been erected centuries ago. Its inlaid bronze letters had been pried out, leaving the inscriptions as ghostly cavities, but the rest of the structure was intact and appeared light and graceful. Two pairs of elegantly fluted columns flanked the portal. The upper story was articulated with a series of horizontal lines, still crisp, as if only recently carved. Cyriacus was struck by the beauty of the arch, all the more so compared to the coarse warehouses and port cranes around it. And it seemed to be speaking to him.

Like someone suddenly lovestruck, Cyriacus began admiringly to study the arch, examine it from every angle, puzzle out why it attracted him so suddenly and intensely. He could not read Latin, but managed to make out the name of the emperor Trajan and surmised that he was responsible for the structure. What had life in Ancona been like in Trajan's reign, over a millennium before? Had the place been a prosperous port or a small town, had it been handsome or humble? It must have possessed wealth and sophistication enough to erect such an elegant and enduring monument. As Cyriacus pondered the arch and the distant time to which it belonged, it dawned on him that what the arch was whispering to him was an invitation to uncover that long-ago history and bring it back from oblivion.

Cyriacus's contemporaries—like him, up to that moment—were largely indifferent to the scattered vestiges of the bygone civilizations amidst which they passed their lives. Of course, ancient texts—Virgil, Ovid, Cicero, Livy, and books by several other authors—were still read by boys in Latin schools and cherished by intellectuals. And many cities claimed Romans, Etruscans, and even Trojans as their founders. Some antique monuments had been given a Christian use or interpretation and were thus treated with veneration. In the course of the Middle Ages nearly all the bronze sculptures of gods, rulers, and athletes that once populated ancient cities and sanctuaries had been melted down for weapons and coins. But the equestrian statue of Marcus Aurelius escaped this fate and was given a place of honor in front of the church of St. John Lateran in Rome because it was thought to depict Constantine the Great, the emperor who recognized Christianity as an official religion. Countless ancient buildings, meanwhile, had been more or less haphazardly incorporated into churches, fortresses, and houses constructed into or around them. Cyriacus had seen such hybrids during his business trips around Italy and abroad. It was much cheaper and easier to add on to well-constructed old cores than to demolish them and start anew.

Yet it was not simply a matter of convenience. Medieval Europeans did not see a fundamental difference between their time and antiquity. They knew, of course, that the ancient Greeks and Romans had been pagans, but in retelling or depicting ancient stories, they turned the ancients into versions of themselves. In romances, tapestries, and illuminated manuscripts, Alexander the Great, Julius Caesar, and other classical rulers became medieval knights who behaved like contemporary men. When the thirteenth-century chronicler Ricordano Malespini, in his *Storia fiorentina* (History of Florence), narrated the tale of the Roman aristocrat Catiline, he recounted how his wife, Queen Belisea, attended church for Easter Mass. Never mind that Catiline was a Roman republican, and that he and his wife lived in the first century before Christ.

It seemed to Cyriacus's predecessors and contemporaries as if ancient monuments, too, had always just been there. No one gave much thought to how they had come about, when they were built, or why they looked different from newer buildings. People did view some old structures as "marvels" because of their size or fine carving, but that only made them suspect. The Pantheon, for example, was said to have been erected by demons who piled up dirt at its center as a core around which to construct the walls and the lofty dome. When the building was completed, the demons spread the rumor that they had buried coins in the soil. Locals rushed in to dig out the treasure and in the process carried away the dirt.

Ancient sculptures, too, were accused of being pagan idols and hosts to devils. The sculptor Lorenzo Ghiberti, in his *Commentaries*, recounted a story of an ancient statue of Venus discovered in Siena in the mid-fourteenth century during the construction of a house. At first, everyone came running to see the figure "made with such beautiful and marvelous artistic skill." The statue was solemnly set up in the main square before the town hall. But soon a member of the community sounded an alarm. "Fellow citizens," he proclaimed,

> having come to the conclusion that since we discovered this statue we have had nothing but bad luck, and considering how idolatry is abhorrent to our faith, we must conclude that God is sending us grief for our errors. Consider too how since we have been honoring this statue, things have gone from bad to worse, and we are going to continue to have bad luck. I am of the opinion of those who recommend that it be broken and smashed and the pieces sent to be buried in [the lands of our enemies in] Florence.

The Sienese shattered the Venus to bits and turned it into a kind of unconventional weapon, surreptitiously transferring its spiritual pollution to the foe.

The person who began to turn indifference, suspicion, and hostility toward ancient monuments into admiration was a poet, Francesco Petrarch, whom Cyriacus read with affection before he ever discovered his own affinity for the past. In his *Letter to Posterity* (ca. 1372), Petrarch had written:

> among the many subjects which interested me, I dwelt especially upon antiquity, for our own age has always repelled me, so that, had it not been for the love of those dear to me, I should have preferred to have been born in

any other period than our own. In order to forget my own time, I have constantly striven to place myself in spirit in other ages, and consequently I delighted in history.

It was Petrarch's aversion for his own era that had led him to postulate a sharp break between the golden age of ancient Rome and the following "dark ages," which, to his chagrin, continued into his own day.[5] To escape from "these regions, these times, and these customs," Petrarch wrote letters to classical authors—Homer, Socrates, Cicero, and Livy, to whom he declared:

> ... I should render thee thanks, for many reasons indeed, but especially for this: that thou didst so frequently cause me to forget present evils, and transfer me to happier times. As I read, I seem to be living in the midst of the Cornellii Scipiones Africani, of Laelius, Fabius Maximus, Metellus, Brutus and Decius, of Cato, Regulus ... It is with these men that I live at such times and not with the thievish company of today among whom I was born under an evil star.[6]

Like other medieval and Renaissance Europeans, Petrarch conveniently ignored the darker aspects of classical antiquity: ruthless conquests of foreign territories, bloodthirsty spectacles in Roman arenas, the corruption and cruelty of many an emperor.

Petrarch believed, or at least ardently hoped, that "Rome would rise up again if she but began to know herself." So he devoted himself to making his contemporaries aware and appreciative of the accomplishments of the ancient civilization, initiating what would come to be known as the Renaissance. Being a poet, he focused chiefly on ancient literature, though he was quite moved by physical remains. When he visited Rome for the first time in 1337, the sight of ancient monuments rendered him speechless. Returning to the city in 1341 to be crowned poet laureate by the Roman Senate, Petrarch went on numerous walks with a local friend, the friar Giovanni Colonna, and tried to imagine Rome's former glory by discerning in the ruins before his eyes the history which he had gleaned from his beloved ancient authors. In his poem "Africa," recounting the war between Rome and Carthage in the third century BC, Petrarch conjured up the splendor of the capital in its golden days.

Petrarch's antiquarian interests were slow to bear fruit. For the first couple of generations after his death only a handful of sensitive souls felt compelled to pore over ancient texts and imbibe from them the perfect usage of Latin and historical lessons for contemporary society. A still smaller number of humanists tried to coax life from inscribed blocks and coins, though they often did so for literary reasons rather than out of a desire to understand the monuments themselves. The Florentine Coluccio Salutati sought out and copied ancient inscriptions carved into Roman triumphal arches, temple facades, and grave markers in order to master proper Latin spelling.[7]

When Cyriacus saw the arch of Ancona in 1421, the "Renaissance," or wider interest in the classical world, was already under way, but curiosity about its physical vestiges was still negligible.[8] That he was captivated by the majesty and significance of this edifice in a city with no tradition of humanistic studies was all the more remarkable, for Ancona was squarely a merchant community. Nor did Cyriacus's basic mercantile training furnish him with the kind of education and mindset that disposed humanists to contemplate Roman remains. Yet his fascination with antiquity was no less keen or sincere than theirs. He was deeply touched by the arch. This living witness from the past beckoned him to step through its portal and travel to a distant culture that had so much to teach his own age.

Cyriacus's business trips to Byzantium, the Greek islands, Egypt, and Syria had introduced him to other lands and lifestyles and must have made him sensitive to this vestige of another society marooned in the middle of his own. His daily drill of record-keeping honed his habit of documenting what he saw. As he looked at the arch now, he felt the urge to scrutinize its every physical detail, to draw its architectural elements and to copy its inscriptions, even though he could not properly read them. He also recalled the ancient monuments he had seen in Alexandria, Damascus, and Constantinople. Who were the people who had carved them? What hopes and ambitions did they seek to commit to posterity? How could he find out more about their lives?

The stones themselves seemed to promise the answers. Unlike texts on the pages of books, handed from one generation to the next by more or less caring hands and prone to errors of transcription or misunderstanding, physical artifacts were direct links to the past. They reflected immediately and tangibly the preoccupations of the ancients, bore their fingerprints and traces of their breath. Ancient hands had carved these blocks, ancient eyes had read these inscriptions, ancient Anconitans returning from the sea had sought out this arch to welcome them home.

Though elated by this visceral connection with the past, Cyriacus also felt troubled. Throughout Italy and in the East he had seen ancient remains not merely disregarded by the locals, but regularly despoiled for building blocks and burned for lime. If they were not somehow safeguarded, they would be gone before people besides himself and a few other enthusiasts began to appreciate how much vital information they contained. How could he prevent this tragedy?

Standing before Trajan's arch in Ancona, Cyriacus sensed his life coming into focus. His curiosity, his hunger for travel, his quest for a meaningful existence, his need for intellectual enrichment would all be amply satisfied if he were to take on this new mission: to seek out, study, and preserve for future generations the material remains of classical cultures. How he would accomplish this he did not yet know, nor could he imagine where this journey would take him. He would probably have found it hard to believe, in that autumn of 1421, that his efforts to save from extinction thousands of remnants of Greek and Roman civilization would transform him from mundane merchant to friend of emperors, artists, humanists, a pope and a sultan; international diplomat and spy; and founder of a new and enduring science.

View of Ancona in the Renaissance in a fresco by Pinturicchio.
Piccolomini Library, Siena. From Augustin Boyer d'Agen,
Oeuvre du Pinturicchio, *Paris: Société d'éditions littéraires et*
artistiques, 1903.

he hath an argosy bound to Tripolis, another to the Indies;
I understand moreover, upon the Rialto, he hath a third at
Mexico, a fourth for England, and other ventures he hath,
squandered abroad. But ships are but boards, sailors but
men: there be land-rats and water-rats, water-thieves and
land-thieves, I mean pirates, and then there is the peril of
waters, winds and rocks.

—Shakespeare, *The Merchant of Venice*
(Act I, Scene iii)

An Unlikely Hero

I N THE EARLY 1400s a businessman from a provincial town, with just a rudimentary education in grammar and mathematics, seemed an improbable candidate for the role of the father of archaeology.

Cyriacus was born into a merchant family. His maternal grandfather, Ciriaco Silvatico (named, like his grandson, in honor of Ancona's patron saint), traded in various towns around Italy. His father, Filippo de Pizzecolli, exported Italian goods to countries around the Mediterranean and brought back lucrative wares from the East. As a child, Cyriacus probably learned from stories around the dinner table that Italy was a small hub in a vast commercial network that stretched from

China to England, from the Arabian Sea to the Baltic, from the Indian Ocean to the Pacific—places his young imagination likely conjured up as settings for the lives of saints and the exploits of knights, stories he'd heard recounted by street performers. Ancona, he discovered early on, was a major port in Italian trade with the East—not a match to Venice, to be sure, but a harbor favored by the papacy, under whose jurisdiction the city fell, and by the Florentines. From his house on the steep hill overlooking the port, Cyriacus could see Ancona's busy waterfront, ships coming in laden with spices, cloth, and human cargo, others setting out for the Levant full of goods and their owners' hopes of gain.

International trade was immensely profitable when it went well, as Cyriacus knew from his family's affluent lifestyle. Italians and other Europeans could not get enough of luxuries from the East, and Filippo Pizzecolli likely imported them as part of his business. Among the most prized commodities were spices, some of which would have perfumed the pantry of the Pizzecolli home.[1] Spices greatly improved the taste of food. In an age before refrigeration, once pastures dried in the autumn and livestock was slaughtered, meat was preserved for the long winter months by salting. From November until spring, dry, chewy, and salty flesh was the mainstay of the diet (of the better off, that is). Long boiling softened up and desalted the meat: sauces made with eastern spices turned it into enjoyable and varied dishes. During the numerous fast and Lenten days, fish was also rendered more flavorful by exotic seasonings. Wine, which tended to turn rancid soon after the barrel was opened, became drinkable owing to cloves and cinnamon, and quick-spoiling ale was preserved by nutmeg.

Spices also healed a host of ailments, from stomach problems to pestilence, or so Cyriacus's parents and contemporaries believed. Medical authorities advised that one should "eat a nutmeg in the morning, for the voiding of wind from the stomach, the liver, and the guts."[2] John of Eschenden, a fellow of Merton College, Oxford, credited his survival during the Black Death to a powder of cinnamon, aloes, myrrh, saffron, mace, and cloves. An elixir of ginger, pepper, galangal, cinnamon, and various herbs taken sparingly after lunch and dinner was said to cure impotence. And while ginger was meant to boost sperm, desire, pleasure, and fertility, pepper enhanced sexual performance. A Middle English guide to women's health promised that three ounces of powdered cloves mixed with four egg yolks would make a woman conceive, "God willing."[3] Indeed, spices did bend the ears of God and the saints. After all, the Magi brought frankincense and myrrh to baby Jesus. Chrism, the anointing oil used for various church ceremonies, was mixed with a combination of spices. And when tombs of saintly figures were opened, they emanated sweet aromas.

The spice trade was a truly global phenomenon, beginning in the Indian Ocean and ending on the Baltic Sea. Filippo and other Italian merchants braved countless dangers as they sailed to buy these fragrant substances in Alexandria, Damietta, or Beirut, carried them back home across the Mediterranean, and sold them to clients across Europe.[4]

Another must for rich Europeans were pearls and precious stones, which also traversed many a land and sea and possibly helped build Filippo Pizzecolli's fortune. Both small pearls, sewn on the clothes of the rich, and large ones, set into their jewelry, came from the Persian Gulf, the coast of Ceylon, and southern India. Brought to Ormuz, the primary distribution center (located in southern Iran, near the Strait of Hormuz), pearls were then sent on to Sultaniyeh and Tabriz in northwest Persia, and to Samarkand and Baghdad. The Europeans caught up with them, as well as with diamonds, emeralds, sapphires, and rubies from India and Ceylon, at the markets of Alexandria and Constantinople. These sparkling stones, too, were worth the risks and discomforts of overseas journeys, for princes, popes, and aristocrats could never satiate their desire for gems.[5]

Nor for silks, which Filippo and his wife, Masiella, probably wore on special occasions to show off their wealth and status attained through international commerce. Mulberry trees and silk were already cultivated in Italy, especially in Lucca, but European demand for damasks, brocades, and velvets was so great that Italian merchants made a handsome profit by importing raw silk and woven fabrics from markets in Asia Minor, such as Pera (a suburb of Constantinople), Chios, and Rhodes.[6] Silk cost ten times as much as pepper and was light to carry. So, to ballast their ships, Italians also loaded them with great quantities of alum and dyes. Dyeing was the most expensive component in the manufacture of quality fabrics, and a sure gauge of rank. Only elites could afford the beautiful saturated hues. Scarlet, produced from the Mediterranean insect kermes, was the costliest and thus was associated with the highest members of society, but lush blues, greens, and blacks were also luxuries. The deepest colors resulted from the most careful and labor-intensive dyeing processes, which, in turn, depended on alum, a mineral that bound pigment to cloth and had to be imported from mines on the western coast of Turkey.

The quest for spices, gems, dyes, fine textiles, and other products unavailable in Europe immeasurably expanded the geographical and intellectual horizons of Italians and their neighbors. Seeing these precious commodities on Ancona's wharf and in his own home made Cyriacus, too, curious about the faraway places which produced these exotic treasures.

Alas, alongside the promise of profit, trade carried with it the constant threat of ruin, as Cyriacus discovered early on. His father would load a vessel with Italian produce, textiles, and soap, send it out of Ancona, and pray for its safe journey and lucrative return from abroad. But the sea was unpredictable and treacherous. A storm could arise suddenly, even as a boat hugged the coast. If one was lucky, the wind merely blew the vessel to a shore it did not intend to visit, stranding it there as the crew appealed ardently to St. Nicholas or St. Christopher, patrons of merchants and travelers, and to the Virgin Mary, man's advocate at any time. If one's luck ran out, the ship might be wrecked and sunk, losing both cargo and crew. And then there were pirates forever combing the seas on the lookout for a poorly protected merchant vessel—quick gain for the brigands and quick and painful loss for the ship's owner and sailors. International trade was a nerve-racking business. But when it went well, one got nicely rich.

Cyriacus never described his home before disaster struck his family, but it was probably similar to the residences of other wealthy merchants: perhaps three stories high, with a central courtyard on the ground floor, public rooms on the *piano nobile* adorned with Egyptian carpets and engraved metal vases from Damascus, bedrooms upstairs furnished more simply with poster beds and chests safeguarding fine clothes of silk and velvet and family jewels, and a well-stocked pantry emitting the scents of nutmeg and ginger, cloves and cinnamon.[7]

This comfortable life was shattered in three blows. First, two of Filippo's ships were attacked by pirates. Private entrepreneurs, such as Filippo, could not afford a military convoy, the kind that the Venetian state sent out to protect its commercial galleys, particularly when they carried valuable silks and spices. And even the Venetians complained about the corsairs—some of them ruthless privateers who trolled the waves looking for any vulnerable vessel, others unofficially supported by rival maritime powers, such as Genoa or Catalonia. Soon thereafter, three more of Filippo's ships were wrecked at sea, sinking Filippo's wares and destroying his hopes of restoring his fortune. And then, when Cyriacus was only six years old, his father died. Was it of heartbreak, illness, an accident during a voyage? Cyriacus did not dwell on the cause in the account of his life which he later imparted to his biographer, Francesco Scalamonti. He only indicated that the demise of his father and his business plunged the family into poverty.

Gone were the silks and carpets, spices and decorative Oriental vessels, well-built furniture and other things that had made the family home beautiful—all probably sold to second-hand dealers to pay off Filippo's debts.[8] Masiella, left with Cyriacus and two younger children, had to roll up her sleeves and take on manual work. By working day and night she managed to educate her offspring in good manners and letters. But for the most part, Cyriacus would have to make it on his own wits. He would not have the security of a family firm behind him, nor the means to select a career that might nourish his eager mind. His options would be confined to what he could achieve by himself in the world of trade—a world in which he could still draw on connections through his grandfather. Yet he would forever strive for something more—more than being just a merchant, more than devoting his life to numbers and wares, more than remaining in Ancona.

When Cyriacus turned fourteen, his grandfather arranged for him to be apprenticed with a local merchant, "to raise the boy from poverty to wealth in that kind of enterprise." It must have struck Cyriacus as a mixed blessing. Of course, he needed to learn a useful profession, but he would be marooned in Ancona for seven years of training, quite likely under an abusive master, as was so often the case for young apprentices, his lot cast for a vocation with no wings.

Luckily, Cyriacus's master, Piero di Jacopo, owner of a local import-export firm, turned out to be a generous man, quick to notice and encourage his charge's abilities. Cyriacus had an enormous amount to learn: arithmetic, geometry, bookkeeping, and merchant manuals such as Francesco Pegolotti's *Practice of Commerce*—a compendium on international trade which began with a glossary of Italian and foreign terms and went on to describe nearly all the major trading cities; the goods sold there, their quality, packaging, and ways to preserve them en route; the imports and exports of various regions; business customs prevalent in each locality; and comparative values of coinages, measures, and weights.[9] Cyriacus worked day and night absorbing and applying all this information. Piero was so impressed with the boy's diligence and intelligence that within two years he entrusted to him the management of the entire office in Ancona plus his countryside estates. Cyriacus was only sixteen.

For the next five years, from 1407 to 1412, Cyriacus dealt with suppliers, shareholders, customers, and associated companies that did business with Piero. He organized various details of long-distance trade and kept the firm's books, gaining a reputation for competence and fairness among local businessmen and those from Venice, Florence, and Perugia who traded with Piero. Recognizing and fostering Cyriacus's abilities, Piero also pushed his apprentice to enter municipal government, and Cyriacus got elected to the post of *anziano* ("elder"), one of six who governed Ancona, and then to the Senate, even though he was under the age required for these positions. Yet what made Cyriacus happy was not success at the office—of which he was certainly proud—or in politics, but his escapes in the few hours of leisure. Whenever he had a moment, he read. Dante Alighieri's *Divine Comedy* was the source of inexhaustible inspiration for everyone in those days: scholars wrote learned commentaries on it, politicians cited its verses during civic debates, merchants copied pithy phrases from it into their account books and diaries. Cyriacus would later come to learn Latin through his love of Dante, following Dante's guide, Virgil, not to the Inferno, but to antiquity. Giovanni Boccaccio's poetry and prose offered a wider and lighter range of pleasures, from captivating and humorous stories with wonderfully realistic dialogue, to lessons in classical customs and myths. Of Francesco Petrarch's works, Cyriacus relished his collection of poems called *Canzoniere*, which spoke lyrically and passionately about love and art, politics and morality, and the author himself, who, though dead for several decades, came alive in his verses. These men opened for Cyriacus a window on a far richer world than the one he inhabited in Ancona.

Cyriacus finished his apprenticeship at twenty-one. Well versed in commercial practices and civic affairs, he was perfectly placed to begin a career as a merchant and a politician in the comfort of his native town. He could now obtain a post with a reputable firm, earn a good income, and build for himself the secure life he had lost when his father died. But was that what he wanted?

❧

When Cyriacus was a boy of nine, his grandfather had taken him along on a business trip to Venice. Ever since then, Cyriacus dreamed of seeing the wider world. Even before that journey, "the fates had already fired the boy's young mind with the fame of this great city,"[10] his biographer Scalamonti would write. So everything about the voyage must have felt exciting: boarding the ship and feeling it come alive under his feet as it rocked on the waves; pulling out of the port and seeing his home town from a whole new point of view—the bristling skyline of belfries and towers standing guard over private homes, the cathedral of St. Ciriaco perched on the lofty summit of Monte Guasco to the north, and the citadel echoing it from Monte Astagno to the south; sailing past coastal towns new

Mountebanks in Venice, from Habiti d'hvomeni et donne venetiane: con la processione della serma. Signoria et altri particolari cioè trionfi feste cerimonie pvbliche della nobilissima città di Venetia, *Venice: Forma in Frezaria al sol, c. 1600. (Research Library, The Getty Research Institute, Los Angeles, CA)*

to him—Fano, Pesaro, Rimini—and, at last, arriving at the renowned city on the lagoon.

Oh, what a wonder Venice was! Even though Cyriacus had heard stories about it from his grandfather, "he was filled with admiration for its marvelous splendor."[11] The piazzas and alleys around San Marco were packed with colorful crowds—a forest of locals and foreigners, merchants and pilgrims speaking a tangle of languages, mountebanks and charlatans hawking oils and salves, and vendors offering everything from bread to Murano glass.[12] Yet the streets were remarkably clean: no dust or mud, no horse droppings underfoot—in fact, no horses or mules anywhere—and though stagnant smells rose from the canals, perfumes burning at various corners sweetened the air. Cyriacus was surely beguiled by the luxuries of a kind his family once enjoyed beckoning from shop windows. "It seems as if the whole world flocks there, and that human beings concentrated there all their force for trading," wrote the Milanese canon Pietro Casola:

> Who could count the many shops so well furnished that they also seem warehouses, with so many cloths of every make—tapestry, brocades and hangings of every design, carpets of every sort, camlets of every color and texture, silks of every kind; and so many warehouses full of spices, groceries and drugs and so much beautiful wax! These things stupefy the beholder, and cannot be fully described to those who have not seen them.[13]

These riches hinted at other worlds—exotic, lush, fairy-tale places which Cyriacus knew only by name.

*Spoils from Constantinople at the Basilica of
San Marco in Venice. (Kenneth Lapatin)*

Venice itself felt like a foreign land. Its grand patrician
mansions, arrayed along the canals, vied with each other in
the extravagance of their marble windows and balconies. Colorful Oriental carpets hung over their windowsills. And the
Venetian women! What a spectacle they made in their opulent
dresses with shockingly low necklines, fortunes' worth of jewels, and foot-high platform shoes on which they strutted like
storks.

Still more astounding was the basilica of San Marco. Cyriacus was dazzled by the colored marble columns lining its
facade, the mosaics over the doorways, the four gilded horses

pawing the air over the main portal. How could so much splendor accumulate in one place? Inside, the church seemed to be the heavenly Jerusalem itself, its pavement composed of intricately patterned colored stones, its walls faced with veined marbles, a golden canopy of mosaics spreading overhead. The basilica's treasury, which the Venetians were not reticent about showing to visitors, glittered with agate and crystal vases and gold reliquaries thick with gems—all looted during the sack of Constantinople in 1204, as Cyriacus probably learned from his grandfather. The sight of these objects likely sparked Cyriacus's desire to see the legendary Byzantine capital, both admired and disdained by the Italians: approved for drawing to its markets all the material riches of the world and perpetuating ancient Greek language and literature, and reviled for refusing to submit to the Roman Catholic church and maintaining a centuries-long hostile distrust of the Europeans.

Meanwhile, the Arsenal—the dockyards where Venetian ships were built and outfitted for their voyages—may have ignited in Cyriacus the romance of maritime journeys. What nine-year-old boy would not wish to go to sea after watching a galley being prepared for its voyage? Pero Tafur, a Spanish visitor to Venice, recorded the thrill of seeing an empty vessel towed along a canal between warehouses and gradually filled with cordage and oars, ballast and arms, bread and wine, by men handing all these and many other supplies through the windows. By the time the galley reached the end of the street, all the provisions and sailors were aboard and ready to venture out to distant shores.[14]

Venice shaped Cyriacus's early imagination. As his biographer later wrote, "Destiny had decreed that this renowned and important Italian city should be the first starting point for a life of such great discoveries."[15]

⤚⤙⤚

Now, at twenty-one, his obligation to Piero discharged, Cyriacus was ready to make his own choices. Forsaking security, a steady income, and the comfortable and predictable life for which he had been preparing for seven years, he opted for uncertainty and adventure. He enlisted on a merchantman chartered by a kinsman, Ciucio Pizzecolli, taking a job as a minor clerk—a lowly and tedious position of copying registers, recording goods loaded and unloaded at various ports, and composing deeds and wills when storms imperiled the vessel or someone aboard neared death. On a raw, wintry day in 1412, he set sail for the exotic East.

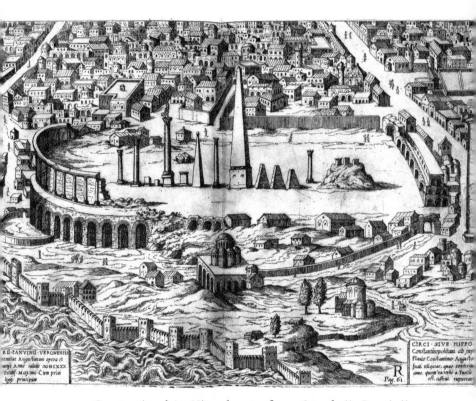

Constantinople's Hippodrome, from Onvphrii Panvinii
Veronensis, De lvdis circensibvs libri II; De trivmphis liber
vnvs: quibus vniuersa ferè Romanorvm vetervm sacra ritvsq.
declarantvr, ac figuris aeneis illustrantur, *Venice: Apud
Ioannem Baptistam Ciottum Senensem, 1600. (Research Library,
The Getty Research Institute, Los Angeles, CA)*

. . . his noble spirit, no longer content to risk stagnation in
these common involvements, now impelled him . . . to travel
and to see the world.

—Francesco Scalamonti, *Vita Viri Clarissimi et*
Famosissimi Kyriaci Anconitani[1]

From the Mundane
to the Sublime

THREE JOURNEYS SHAPED Cyriacus's outlook and laid the
foundation for his archaeological calling: that first trip to
Venice which ignited in him the urge to see the world; a visit
to Alexandria where ancient monuments caught his attention;
and a sojourn in Constantinople which taught him about the
vulnerability of the past in the face of human violence and
greed.

Cyriacus had probably heard tales about Alexandria from
international merchants at home: about bazaars brimming
with spices from Arabia, precious stones from India, Egyptian carpets, shimmering silks, and the finest cottons and linens; about traders gathering from across the world to haggle
over such wares and over slaves from Africa, the Black Sea,
and former Greek lands conquered by the Turks; about the

strange caste of Mamluks, who began as slave boys brought from the Black Sea region to serve in the Egyptian royal army and rose through the military ranks to become sultans. But it was another matter altogether to walk the streets of Alexandria, past men dressed in turbans and long robes and women covered in white mantles from the tops of their conical hats to the tips of their pointed shoes; to see itinerant cooks carrying portable stoves on which they prepared food to order, and peripatetic barbers with mirrors attached to their chests and blades at the ready, offering a shave on the go. It was astonishing how green the city was, with its numerous gardens full of fruit trees, from familiar oranges and lemons to dates, figs, and bananas, which Cyriacus had never seen before. And he was smitten by the sight of the strangest animals: camels and dromedaries swaying under their massive loads in the streets; ostriches, apes, elephants, and giraffes pacing their enclosures in the sultan's zoo; and "monstrous snake-engendered crocodiles" moving slowly on the banks of the Nile.[2]

Yet what Cyriacus found most magnetic, or so he later told his biographer, were the ancient monuments.[3] He strolled with pleasure along the two colonnaded avenues running the length and width of Alexandria and intersecting at its center. They dated back almost to the time of Alexander the Great. When the conqueror died in 323 BC, one of his Macedonian generals, Ptolemy, claimed Egypt and expanded Alexandria into a splendid metropolis—with elegant streets and a magnificent lighthouse, now sadly in ruins, that directed sailors to the new city. Cyriacus encountered another bit of history at the Caesareum—the sanctuary begun by Cleopatra in honor of Mark Antony: at its entrance, two Egyptian obelisks soared

*Giraffe from Alexandria, drawing by or after Cyriacus in
Bartolomeus Fontius, Bodleian Library Ms. Lat. misc. d. 85,
f. 73r, Bodleian Library, Oxford University.*

into the sky (one of them now stands in New York's Central
Park).[4] Journeying outside the city, probably on a tip from Italian merchants residing in Alexandria, Cyriacus sought out
the pyramids built by the pharaohs. He did not know why he
was drawn to these vestiges of the past, and it would be several years before he would grasp their significance for him—

years in which his mind was occupied chiefly by commerce, and sightseeing was just a diversion when time and occasion permitted. Still, on that trip to Egypt, seeing the remnants of distant civilizations stirred in him a craving to travel not just across the world, but in time.

As Ciucio's clerk, Cyriacus also visited Crete and Cyprus, Chios and Rhodes, and several cities on the western coast of Asia Minor (modern Turkey). Yet what he yearned to see the most kept eluding him. Constantinople, the city he had dreamed about ever since his trip to Venice, seemed perpetually out of reach. Only in 1418 did an opportunity to fulfill that longing appear on the horizon. Another relative, Pasqualino, needed a clerk for a ship he had chartered for a voyage to the Byzantine capital. Cyriacus seized this chance. In October of that year he finally sailed up the Hellespont (now the Dardanelles)—the narrow strait that flows from the Aegean to the Sea of Marmara, dividing Europe from Asia Minor and forming a crucial shipping channel that leads to Constantinople and the Black Sea ports beyond.

Constantinople looked as majestic at first sight as Cyriacus had likely imagined it: projecting into the sea, it was girdled by a massive and imposing wall, its base anchored to the rocks rising out of the water. Countless towers warned approaching vessels not to contemplate an attack. No wonder the Turks had failed to take the city, despite several attempts. Behind the wall a profusion of buildings, churches, and columns climbed the seven hills, and the mountainlike dome of Hagia Sophia reached for the sky.

But as Cyriacus disembarked and walked in from the waterfront to the center of town, his delight must have given way to dismay. The coastal district was fairly populous and lively, but further inland, grandeur quickly gave way to dilapidation. Run-down streets stood nearly deserted; fields and gardens grew in the middle of the city. Ruy González de Clavijo, a Castilian diplomat, recorded in 1401 that "there are within [the city's] compass many hills and valleys where corn fields and orchards are found, and among the orchard lands there are hamlets . . . Everywhere throughout the city there are many great palaces, churches and monasteries, but most of them are now in ruin."[5] Constantinople, Cyriacus quickly discovered, was not a lofty capital filled with magnificent buildings and precious artworks, but an assemblage of humble villages with a few grand structures rising here and there as islands of sunken glory. The inhabitants scurrying along looked as poor and sad as the city, "showing the hardship of their lot," commented the Spaniard Pero Tafur, "which is, however, not so bad as they deserve, for they are a vicious people, steeped in sin."[6] Westerners were deeply prejudiced against the Greeks, viewing them as wily, treacherous, and heretical. The feeling was mutual. Constantinople had been splendid before the Latins sacked it in 1204. As Cyriacus traversed the city, he probably struggled to discern what it must have looked like not only before the Fourth Crusade, but when it was first constructed by Constantine the Great.

Greeks had inhabited the town of Byzantion unremarkably for several centuries before the Romans took it over in the second century AD. The place remained a provincial backwater until 324, when Emperor Constantine decided that this spot, poised between Europe and Asia, would be the perfect location from which to control and draw on the resources of both the eastern and the western parts of the Roman Empire.[7] Constantine realized the amazing potential of the site: washed by the sea on two of its three sides, which made it easy to defend, and blessed with great harbors. He was already keen to project divine splendor by letting his tresses (some of them false) fall to his shoulders and covering himself with gold bracelets and jeweled robes. Now, godlike, he personally paced out the perimeter of his new capital, spear in hand, and set about transforming it into a metropolis in a mere six years. He more than quadrupled the area of the city, attracted immigrants by granting them land and food rations in perpetuity, spent enormous sums on erecting opulent new buildings, filled the city's libraries with Greek and Latin books removed from Rome, and dispatched agents across the Mediterranean to bring back every art object they could find. Artifacts wrought in silver and gold, vases carved from semiprecious stones, sculptures fashioned from ivory, bronze, and marble poured into the new capital, turning it into a museum of the whole empire. As St. Jerome noted, Constantinople was enriched by stripping bare almost every other city.[8]

Cyriacus observed some traces of that first flowering and of the following centuries of Constantinople's prosperity in the ancient Hippodrome, in the few beautifully carved ancient columns, and in the fabric of the imperial palace. When Robert de Clari, a French knight, saw the city in 1203, he recorded that the imperial palace alone contained five hundred halls, all connected together and adorned with gold mosaic, and thirty chapels, including a spectacular one dedicated to the Blessed Virgin at Pharos, "so rich and noble that there was not a hinge nor a band nor any other part such as is usually made of iron that was not all of silver, and there was no column that was not of jasper or porphyry or some other rich precious stone. And the pavement of this chapel was of a white marble so smooth and clear that it seemed to be of crystal."[9] Now Cyriacus faced only a shadow of that former splendor, a building "badly kept, except certain parts where the Emperor, the Empress, and attendants can live, although cramped for space."[10] The Fourth Crusade in 1204 had destroyed much of the city, denuded it of its ancient artworks, and created a permanent rift between Byzantium and Europe. Though the Greeks regained control over their shrunken empire in 1261, Constantinople never recovered from the ordeal inflicted upon it by the Latins and remained a battered and depopulated place.

Most visitors in Cyriacus's day devoted their attention to the numerous religious relics that had somehow escaped the clutches of the crusaders and gave the city a mystical appeal.[11] A modern observer would doubt their authenticity, but for believers of the day, they were the most valuable bits of matter in the world, embodying actual contact with the divine. Hagia Sophia preserved the great doors made from the wood of Noah's ark, the stone on which Christ had sat while conversing with the Samaritan woman at Jacob's well, fragments of the Cross, and the gridiron on which St. Lawrence and other saints had been roasted. In the church of the Holy Apostles pilgrims kissed the pillar to which Jesus had been bound while being scourged and another pillar at which the Apostle Peter had wept after he had thrice denied Christ. The monastery of the Pantocrator kept the cup in which Christ had changed water into wine at the wedding feast of Cana, and the slab on which Joseph of Arimathea and Nicodemus had laid out His body after taking it down from the Cross and on which the tears of Mary, His Mother, were still visible as white drops. At the monastery of St. John the Baptist in Pera one could peer at the chest enclosing the relics of the Passion: Jesus's purple robe for which the soldiers had cast lots on Calvary, the spear with which His side had been pierced, the vinegar-filled sponge, still moist, which had been given to Him when He asked to quench His thirst on the Cross, as well as a morsel of bread from the Last Supper which Jesus had offered to Judas, who was unable to swallow it. Such marvels dotted the city, although a Russian visitor, Stephen of Novgorod, commented that "Entering Constantinople is like [entering] a great forest; it is impossible to get around without a good guide, and if you attempt to get around stingily or cheaply you will not be able to see or kiss a single saint unless it happens to be the holiday of that saint when you can see and kiss the relics."[12]

Cyriacus paid little attention to the sacred treasures prized by most of his contemporaries. Instead, he sought out the remains of ancient Greece and Rome that survived around the crumbled capital. The Golden Gate, through which Byzantine rulers used to enter the city after military triumphs, had been stripped of the gold plate that once covered the structure and of its crowning bronze group of four elephants pulling the chariot of the victorious emperor Theodosius I. But the ancient reliefs above the entryway remained, and Cyriacus was so impressed by them that he believed a local guide who told him, falsely, that they had been carved by Phidias, the renowned architect and sculptor of the Parthenon in Athens. At Hagia Sophia, Cyriacus gazed in amazement at the vast dome, the colored marble columns and walls, and the intricate

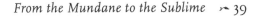

*Hagia Sophia, Sangallo's drawing after Cyriacus, from
Giuliano da Sangallo,* Il libro di Giuliano da Sangallo Codice
vaticanobarberiniano latino 4424 riprodotto in fototipia, *ed.
Cristiano Huelsen, Lipsia: O. Harrassowitz, 1910.*

inlaid floors. The colossal bronze equestrian statue of Justinian (which a local informant identified as Heraclius) rose atop a tall spiral column in front of the church and filled Cyriacus with delight. The emperor still looked commanding in his diadem, his left hand grasping an orb, symbolic of world rule, his right pointing toward the east.

At the ancient Hippodrome, as he scrutinized the noble curved structure adorned with two tiers of columns at one end of the racetrack, Cyriacus must have tried to imagine how the place had looked in its heyday. The *spina*—the elongated oval island in the center of the course around which the chariots used to gallop—had once been decorated with numerous ornate pillars and sculptures. They were there when the crusaders arrived in 1203, but not after they left. (The bronze horses crowning the entrance to San Marco in Venice had been carried away from the Hippodrome.) All that remained now were a few bases and two giant columns. One was a sixty-four-foot-tall monolithic obelisk, which had originally been erected at the temple of Karnak in Luxor by the pharaoh Thutmose III around 1450 BC, and had been transported to Constantinople around 390 AD and set up in the Hippodrome by Theodosius I. The other was a twenty-six-foot-tall bronze column composed of three intertwining snakes. Constantine had brought it from Delphi, where it had been erected in 478 BC in honor of Greek victories over the Persians at Plataia and Salamis. Numerous snake-related legends swirled around it now. Some locals claimed that the column could cure those bitten by snakes within the city walls; others said that it kept venomous reptiles out of Constantinople or rendered them harmless.

Cyriacus also admired the hundred-foot-tall spiral columns of the emperors Theodosius I and Arcadius and attempted to decipher the stories of their deeds carved in relief along the shafts. He may have even climbed up their internal staircases to look at Constantinople from above, as the statues of the emperors used to do before they were toppled by earthquakes and replaced in the Middle Ages by hermits who spent their lives in solitary prayer high in the sky. Combing the city further, Cyriacus spotted porphyry columns here, a few surviving stone and bronze statues there, some ancient fountains, and a great brick aqueduct that still carried water a millennium after its construction.

Soon after returning home from Constantinople, Cyriacus "discovered" the arch of Trajan—or, rather, saw it with new eyes. It led him to ponder more seriously his attraction to ancient artifacts. When he encountered them during his travels abroad, they had been, to some degree, an extension of the exoticism of those lands: novel, intriguing, diverting. Now it became clear to him that whether in the East or in the West, such monuments were more meaningful than mere curiosities. The ancient cultures which had produced them were foreign countries unto themselves, only what they offered was not material riches, but spiritual gains: lessons in writing and expressing oneself with eloquence and elegance, insights into nature and the human body, aesthetic ideals to inspire and reform modern arts. Physical vestiges of those distant civilizations provided an immediate connection with the people who created such models for thought and conduct; made their concerns, ideals, and accomplishments tangible; bridged the gap between the present and the past. The ghosts of the ancients hovered by their lapidary remains, inviting inquiry and proffering answers in carved inscriptions and reliefs.

Yet these messengers from faraway times were more vulnerable than their solid appearance suggested. Having seen Constantinople stripped of most of its monuments and thus robbed of its history, Cyriacus recognized that these precious relics must be preserved and recorded for future generations before greed and carelessness erased what remained— even if no one around him showed any interest in such an enterprise.

Cyriacus now saw in a new light the benefits of the career forced upon him by family circumstances: had he not been a merchant, he would not have traveled to Alexandria, Constantinople, and other places where the past mingled with the present in visible strata. Had he not trained as an accountant, he might not have paid such close attention to material details. Thanks to the layers of his own history, he found his calling; as he would write to Jacques Veniero de Racanati, bishop of Ragusa, he believed himself charged by the gods to resurrect the ancient world. One day, he would tell Racanati, as he explored the town of Vercelli in Piedmont, scrutinizing its Roman amphitheater, aqueduct, sarcophagi, and inscriptions, an ignorant priest asked him what he was doing. It is my profession, Cyriacus replied, to wake the dead.[13]

Yet in the autumn of 1421, when he came to this conclusion, he realized that he was not well prepared for his task. He knew practically nothing of ancient history, literature, or arts, and would have to educate himself if he were to take on this new mission—starting with learning Latin, so that he could understand the ancient voices issuing from the stones. It was a commitment to begin a new language at thirty, carving out time for study while working a busy job at the port. But this is what he would do for the next two years. He was eager for the

challenge—so eager that instead of gradually mastering grammar, syntax, and spelling, he dove at once into an ancient text.
At first with the help of a private tutor and then on his own,
Cyriacus read Virgil's *Aeneid*. Far from a common textbook for
learning Latin, the great Roman epic was more difficult that
the *Eclogues* and the *Georgics*, which were usually taught in
schools. But Cyriacus's fondness for Dante's *Divine Comedy*,
in which Virgil guides the author through the underworld,
spurred him to choose the ancient poet's magnum opus as
his entryway into the past. As he deciphered the *Aeneid* line
by line, Virgil's words came into focus and gradually arranged
themselves into vivid narratives of battles and ordeals, heroic
strivings and profound losses, visions of past and future history, and a gamut of emotions driving humans and gods.
Cyriacus also relished seeing nouns and verbs line up into
graceful sentences and convey the poet's meaning with pithy
mastery. Virgil was the best teacher he could dream of, and
when he began composing his own Latin prose and verse two
years later, his style would be clearly influenced by the Roman
writer. Cyriacus's politics, too, would come to be shaped in
part by Virgil, the preeminent bard of Augustus, Rome's first
emperor: he would advocate universal monarchy, extol Caesar
(admired as the founder of the empire and a great general who
subjugated more "barbarians" than anyone else), and eventually embrace a military solution to the preservation of ancient
heritage.

Cyriacus practiced his newly gained Latin skills by reading
the inscriptions on the arch in Ancona, learning that it was
Trajan who bestowed on the city its "life-giving port." Cyriacus
also tried to understand the original aspect of the structure

by comparing it with ancient coins, and deduced that it must have been crowned with a statue of the emperor flanked by his sister, Marciana, and his wife, Plotina, who were named in the inscriptions. The arch, Cyriacus's biographer would write, "was the first seminal inspiration to Ciriaco, as we often heard him say, to search and examine all the other worthy memorials of antiquity in the world."[14]

Indeed, he was ready to expand his knowledge—beyond Virgil and his lessons, beyond Ancona and its inspiring arch—to the treasure trove of monuments still standing across Italy and beyond. His next step was now clear. He must begin with Rome.

Rome in its dilapidated state, from Etienne Dupérac, I vestigi
dell'antichita di Roma, *Rome: Appresso Gottifredo de Scaichi
1621. (Research Library, The Getty Research Institute,
Los Angeles, CA)*

> *If one of the early citizens of the ancient city should come back to life, he would exclaim that he had long ago dwelt in another city. For its appearance and the city itself are so demolished that he would recognize almost nothing which represented the city as it was.*
>
> —Poggio Bracciolini, *On the Mutability of Fortune*[1]

At the Crumbling Epicenter of the Past

CARDINAL CONDULMARO, who oversaw the port renovation at Ancona on which Cyriacus has been working when he discovered the arch, left for another post in the summer of 1423. Cyriacus at once tendered his resignation.

It was November 1424 when he left Ancona for Rome, probably on foot, horse being a luxury. Raw wind must have pierced his clothes as he walked and hitched rides on occasional carts, cold rain sending him for cover in abandoned barns or under the thin foliage of autumnal trees, his feet throbbing from sloshing along chilly, muddy paths. It was a wretched time for travel. But he was on his way to a new adventure.

However Cyriacus may have pictured the eternal city—once grand with imposing palaces and temples, marble and bronze heroes and statesmen populating its well-paved squares and streets—what he walked into, on December 3, was a maze of twisting alleys filled with stinking rubbish and rambling dwellings whose crumbling masonry threatened passersby. Churches with caving walls gaped at the sky through broken roofs. Sheep and goats grazed in the squares. The areas between the Colosseum and the Porta Maggiore, the Quirinal and the Porta Salaria, the Caelian and Aventine hills, were a wilderness interrupted only occasionally by ecclesiastical structures and hulks of ancient ruins. The Forum, the Capitoline, and the Palatine appeared derelict.

Six years earlier, when Martin V took the papal throne, he had lamented that Rome was so "dilapidated and deserted that it bore hardly any resemblance to a city. Houses had fallen into ruins, churches had collapsed, whole quarters were abandoned; and the town was neglected and oppressed by famine and poverty."[2] Small wonder: for over a century the popes had forsaken the city. From 1309 seven pontiffs in a row resided in Avignon. The Great Schism (1378–1417), during which up to three popes contended for the highest church office, plunged Rome into further disarray. Even after the election of Martin V ended the discord and returned the papal court to the Eternal City, improvements came slowly. In a bull issued five years into his tenure, Martin complained that

> many inhabitants of Rome . . . have been throwing . . . entrails, viscera, heads, feet, bones, blood, and skins, besides rotten meat and fish, refuse, excrement, and other fetid and rotting cadavers into the streets . . . and have dared boldly and sacrilegiously to usurp, ruin, and reduce to their own

use streets, alleys, piazzas, public and private places both ecclesiastical and profane.[3]

Cyriacus was in good company in discovering the dismal state of the former capital of the world. Petrarch, who first saw the city in 1337, lamented the tumbling walls, falling temples, sanctuaries on the verge of collapse, and St. Peter's standing without a roof, exposed to wind and rain. The poet found the natives shockingly indifferent to their heritage: "Who today are more ignorant of Roman history than the citizens of Rome? Nowhere is Rome less known than in Rome." When he revisited it in 1341, he was reminded in a still more unpleasant way of how low the city of his dreams had fallen: he was robbed by brigands outside the walls and had to beg the authorities for an armed escort.[4]

A local observer painted a bleak picture of Rome in those days: the place

> had no rulers; men fought every day; robbers were everywhere; nuns were insulted; . . . wives were taken from their husbands in their very beds; farmhands going out to work were robbed; . . . pilgrims, who had come to the holy churches for the good of their souls, were not protected, but were murdered and robbed; even the priests were criminals.[5]

The ongoing struggles between old baronial families, with their armed retainers, further exacerbated this lawlessness.

A contemporary of Petrarch's, the politician Cola di Rienzo, promised to address and ameliorate this situation. He used the traces of Rome's former glory to rally fellow citizens behind his ideal vision of what the city could once again become. Bright and ambitious, Cola claimed to be a natural son of the Holy Roman Emperor Henry VII (though he was actually the child of a Roman tavern-keeper and a washerwoman). Having learned Latin as a teenager, he read avidly Roman historians, orators, and poets, and resolved to restore his native city to its bygone greatness. Ablaze with his utopian dream, Cola fired up his fellow citizens with eloquent and vehement speeches. "Lord, how well he spoke!" his biographer sighed, "He would exert all his skill in declamation, and would speak so effectively that everyone would be stupefied by his beautiful speeches; he would lift each man off his feet."[6] Even Petrarch endorsed the young revolutionary who drew his inspiration from Cicero, Seneca, Livy, and Valerius Maximus and proposed, through their lessons on law and civics, to usher in a new age of liberty, justice, and peace.

Cola used not only texts, but physical monuments as his sources of inspiration and political tools. "Every day he would gaze at the marble engravings which lie about in Rome. He alone knew how to read the ancient inscriptions. He translated all the ancient writings; he interpreted those marble shapes perfectly."[7] Cola's biographer probably overstated the singularity of his hero's competence, but it was true that few contemporaries could read or cared to understand ancient blocks, and none made them come to life with such urgency.

One day, in the church of St. John Lateran, Cola spotted a bronze tablet leaning with its face against the altar. Turning it over, he discovered that it was inscribed with the *Lex de imperio Vespasiani* ("Law regulating Vespasian's authority")—

an act of the Roman Senate, dated to December of 69 AD, by which Vespasian received his imperial powers. Vespasian apparently took to heart the words incised on the plaque: "whatever he decides will be in accordance with the advantage of the republic and with the majesty of things divine, human, public, and private, he shall have the right and power so to act and do." Industrious rather than ostentatious, Vespasian had ruled Rome as an efficient administrator, replenishing the treasury depleted by Nero and ending the civil wars. He also restored the Capitol and built a new Forum, a Temple of Peace, and began the Colosseum. According to the historian Tacitus, unlike all his predecessors, he was the only emperor who was changed for the better by his office.

On May 20, 1347, Cola summoned the Romans to St. John Lateran to make his great find public. Contrasting the glorious past with the miserable present, he read his translation of the *Lex de imperio Vespasiani* as a proof that supreme power belonged to the Roman people, who delegated it to the emperors, and urged his contemporaries to reclaim their authority. It was the first time a classical object served as the basis for a political summons to action.

Impressed by Cola's speeches and rosy visions, his fellow citizens elected him their ruler, bestowing upon him the title of tribune, a Roman republican official representing the people. Alas, Cola's actual governance failed to match his rhetoric. His luxurious lifestyle and the inordinate taxes he imposed to pay his troops and finance other expenditures quickly eroded his support. Even his admiring biographer wrote that "Cola changed his earlier habits drastically. He used to be sober, temperate, and abstinent; now he became an intemperate drinker.

He drank wine continually; at every hour he ate sweets and drank. He observed neither order nor time . . . His expression would change suddenly, and his eyes become inflamed. His mind and will would change like fire . . . He levied a tax on wine and other commodities, which he called a 'subsidy.' "[8] Cola also offended the pope and the Holy Roman Emperor by proposing a new Roman empire whose sovereignty would rest on the will of the people.

Finding that he went too far and fearing for his life, Cola abdicated and fled the city. After months on the run, he was imprisoned by Pope Clement VI in Avignon, but pardoned by Innocent VI and sent back home to fight against the Roman nobility who opposed the papacy. Cola resumed power and proceeded to rule even more arbitrarily, tyrannically, and ineffectively. He "began arresting people; he arrested one man after another, and released them for ransom. The murmuring sounded quietly through Rome. Therefore to protect himself he enlisted fifty Roman infantrymen for each region of the city . . . He did not give them pay. He promised it."[9] Before long, people lost patience. Within two months of his return to the city, on October 8, 1354, the Romans rose up in revolt. Crying "Death to the traitor who made the tax! Death!" they set fire to his residence, and murdered him as he tried to flee disguised as a peasant—the golden rings and bracelets that in his haste he forgot to take off giving him away.[10]

Cola's overreaching ambition and enormous failings undercut his aspirations to restore Rome, and his radical antiquarianism spawned few followers. During the 1390 jubilee, pilgrims arriving to venerate the relics scattered among the city's churches were still dismayed at the undignified aspect of the capital of Christendom: the sorry state of sacred buildings, the cattle grazing by the altars, the overgrown and rat-infested ruins of the Campo Marzio. They shuffled around in groups, hoping for safety in numbers against bandits lurking in the narrow alleys, and at night were kept awake by the howls of wolves fighting with stray dogs under the walls of St. Peter's. "O God, how pitiable is Rome!' one English visitor exclaimed, "Once she was filled with great nobles and palaces, now with huts, thieves, wolves and vermin, with waste places; and the Romans themselves tear each other to pieces."[11]

Little had changed by the time of Cyriacus's visit. He would have probably concurred with Pero Tafur, who commented in 1435 that

> there are parts within the walls which look like thick woods, and wild beasts, hares, foxes, wolves, deer and even ... porcupines breed in the caves ... I found no one in Rome who could give me any account of those ancient things concerning which I enquired, but they could, without doubt, have informed me fully as to the taverns and places of ill-fame.[12]

When not fighting or carousing, the natives spouted all manner of tall tales about the crumbling antiquities around them, some based on popular guidebooks such as the *Mirabilia urbis Romae*, written in the twelfth century and still in circulation, others probably invented on the spot. The Colosseum, they said, had been the temple of the sun; the substructures of baths—often the only surviving portions of these complexes—underground chambers used to heat imperial palaces in the winter and to chill them in the summer; the equestrian statue of Emperor Marcus Aurelius, a monument to a peasant who had saved Rome from invaders.[13]

Such ignorance was not the worst of it. The Byzantine scholar Manuel Chrysoloras, who came to Italy to teach Greek in the last years of the fourteenth century, denounced Romans for using statues as blocks to which to tie criminals. As Cyriacus picked his way through filthy streets, he, too, probably came across heads and limbs of quartered men displayed in public squares and perpetrators of major crimes punished at the Lateran under the ancient bronze statue of the she-wolf who had suckled Romulus and Remus.[14] At the Saturday market on the Capitoline hill—once the center of the Roman Empire, but now a desolate wasteland where "vines have replaced the benches of senators"—minor transgressors were placed astride an ancient marble lion devouring a horse (medieval Romans interpreted it as a symbol of punishment of crimes). There the culprits sat, their heads crowned by a paper miter, faces smeared with honey, hands tied behind their backs, and placards describing their misdeeds dangling on their chests.[15] These dispiriting spectacles, profaning the venerable monuments, must have reinforced Cyriacus's mounting urgency to save the precious vestiges of antiquity from human depredation and oblivion.

The use of ancient remains as props of justice was better than dispersing or destroying them entirely. Chrysoloras wrote of how the Romans heedlessly embedded carved stones in house foundations or turned them into mangers in stables.[16] Cardinal Alberto degli Alberti, uncle of Leon Battista—humanist, architect, and art theorist—visited Rome in March

1444 and noted that "There are many splendid palaces, houses, tombs and temples, and other edifices in infinite number, but all are in ruins. There is much porphyry and marble from ancient buildings, but every day these marbles are destroyed by being burnt for lime in scandalous fashion."[17]

Ironically, just as Cyriacus and a few others were beginning to notice and cherish these irreplaceable traces of Rome's past, they were becoming more endangered by the city's very revival.[18] With the return of the papal court to Rome, pontiffs and cardinals began renovating the dilapidated capital—widening the streets, clearing away the rubble, initiating new construction. In the process, they tore down the crumbling ruins, or dismantled them for building materials. As the new churches, palaces, and squares took shape, the old structures melted away. In the course of the fifteenth century the *Zecca vecchia* (old mint) disappeared forever, as did the arches of Gratian, Valentinian, and Theodosius. During the pontificate of the humanist Pope Nicholas V alone (1447–55), the region between the Caelian and Capitoline hills, as well as the Aventine, the Forum, and the Colosseum, were stripped of much of their ancient stones.[19]

Cyriacus witnessed this transformation as he explored Rome that winter. He stayed in the city for forty days as a guest of Cardinal Condulmaro—a great honor and an indication of the esteem he had earned from his employer through his dedicated work, keen intelligence, and personal charm. Every day, ignoring the winter chill and damp, Cyriacus rode out on a white horse kindly lent to him by the cardinal, "closely and diligently inspecting, examining and taking notes of whatever venerable antiquities survived in that great city—

temples, theaters, vast palaces, marvelous baths, obelisks and arches, aqueducts, bridges, statues, columns, bases and historical inscriptions. These he faithfully recorded exactly as they were written."[20] That winter Cyriacus began the first of his diaries—he called them *Commentaries*, probably in imitation of Caesar and Cicero—which he would keep for the rest of his life. Through them he would do his best to preserve the monuments that so touched him by describing the ancient sculptures and structures he encountered, drawing their notable features, and transcribing as many inscriptions as he could.[21] Inscriptions in particular brought the ancients to life by conveying directly their emotions and desires: pride in erecting a building, satisfaction at surviving and winning a military campaign, gratification at gaining a political office or civic distinction, grief at losing a beloved one, hope of being remembered beyond one's brief life span. In focusing on these traces of the past, Cyriacus was turning his sharp merchant's eye for detail and his accountant's habit of careful record-keeping to a new, and to him infinitely more profitable use.

❧

Cyriacus was not the only one to prowl around Rome in search of such fragments. During his sojourn in the city he probably met Poggio Bracciolini, the pioneering archaeologist of ancient texts who brought back to light numerous classical writings that had been lost for centuries, including Vitruvius's treatise on art and architecture, which profoundly shaped Renaissance aesthetics. While aware of the value of classical monuments,

Poggio and his colleagues focused chiefly on recovering ancient texts, which they saw not merely as enlightening reading and models for perfect literary style, but as potential remedies for modern ills. For Europe was in dire need of curing. It had been torn by the Hundred Years' War between England and France, by the Great Schism within the church, by political upheavals in individual cities and states, and by the Ottoman onslaught from the east. Its culture had declined pathetically over the centuries, as Petrarch had bemoaned, and its usage of Latin—the official language of law, diplomacy, university education, and the church—had become impoverished, not to say ugly. By reading and emulating Cicero and Caesar, Livy and Tacitus, Plato and Aristotle, Demosthenes and Plutarch, Poggio's generation and its followers hoped to revitalize learning in fields ranging from literature to science, to gain a better understanding of history and their own times, and to foster a new tribe of judicious rulers and responsible citizens.

Exploring Rome in 1423, the year before Cyriacus came to the city, Poggio sought out ancient inscriptions, "copying them word for word, for general use, and digging up some that lay hidden amid the bushes and brambles, so that others might have access to them."[22] Studying the old gates of Rome, he distinguished between building materials of different ages and used epigraphic evidence to date the structures. Alas, his efforts and sympathies were no match for the ambitions of the popes and cardinals to leave their lasting marks on the city by erecting handsome churches and palazzi in place of decrepit ruins. In his own lifetime, Poggio grieved, such important ancient buildings as the Temple of Concord—once the main shrine of Rome, dedicated to the goddess Concordia and gracing the western end of the Forum—went from being a nearly intact structure to a heap of lime.

Alongside Poggio and a few of his peers, several artists also tried to learn from what still survived of ancient Rome. Brunelleschi and Donatello, whom Cyriacus would meet a few years later and with whom he would discuss their mutual love of antiquity, journeyed from Florence to Rome to "rediscover the excellent and highly ingenious building methods of the ancients and their harmonious proportions."[23] They climbed all over the ruins; scrutinized their foundations, columns, capitals, cornices, and sculptural decorations; took measurements; and drew sketches in their notebooks. Absorbed in these pursuits, they cared little for how they ate or dressed (they supported themselves by making goldwork, in which both had been trained) and spent what money they had on porters and laborers who helped them excavate buried blocks. The Romans, watching the two poorly kempt young men digging excitedly in the dirt, took them for treasure-hunters. Which they were, only what they sought was not gold, but marble, and inspiration for a vibrant new art.[24] Brunelleschi would apply the lessons he learned in Rome to the construction of his majestic dome over Florence's cathedral, while Donatello would create sculpture of extraordinary eloquence and visual impact.

❧

Cyriacus's Roman sojourn proved equally formative, but in a different way. Rome confirmed his dedication to studying classical civilization, and the imperative of doing so immediately. It also solidified his belief that ancient monuments were more crucial than texts. As he examined "the great remains left behind by so noble a people . . . [it occurred to him] that the stones themselves afforded to modern spectators much more trustworthy information about their splendid history than was to be found in books."[25] In the first half of the fifteenth century, this was a wholly novel perspective. Cyriacus was a generation ahead of the first wave of antiquarians, men such as Flavio Biondo and Leon Battista Alberti, who would make a habit of reading ancient objects as thoroughly as texts. For the moment, he would make his own way through the foreign land of classical ruins, gaining insights from the stones. But he had a still more pioneering idea.

If ancient remains were perishing before his very eyes in Rome, what was happening to them in Greece and Asia Minor, where no antiquarian had set foot and where old monuments stood orphaned and imperiled not only by the lackadaisical scavenging of locals, but also by the territorial expansion of the Ottomans? Cyriacus made an extraordinary leap from Rome to the rest of the Mediterranean: he "resolved to see for himself and to record whatever other antiquities remained scattered about the world, so that he should not feel that the memorable monuments, which time and the carelessness of men had caused to fall into ruin, should entirely be lost to posterity."[26]

Cyriacus's plan was unique. Most contemporary aficionados of the past were armchair travelers, their noses stuck in the musty pages of books. They might travel around Italy to look at a few antiquities, but often they were reluctant to do even that. Poggio's deeply learned friend Niccolò Niccoli hesitated to journey from Florence to Rome for fear of the hardships of the road and the extremes of cold and heat. When he finally decided to endure such a trip, in 1424, the same year as Cyriacus, he brought along his mistress, Benvenuta, to minister to his comforts. Poggio, who helped organize Niccoli's visit, did his best to reassure him: "You will have a good room either alone or with her and she will rub your feet if you are tired . . . You shall have a mule or a horse which will carry you gently and not shake you, so that even on horseback you will be free of all care."[27]

Cyriacus, alone among Italian antiquarians, was not put off by the privations of sailing across the seas, walking and riding along dusty roads in foreign lands, sleeping in bad inns or under the open sky, eating strange or meager meals, risking attack by brigands. He had done it all before, many times, for the sake of his commercial career. He would gladly do it for a far nobler cause.

Mercury, protector of merchants and travelers, whom Cyriacus adopted as his patron deity, drawing by or after Cyriacus in Bartolomeus Fontius, Bodleian Library Ms. Lat. misc. d. 85, f. 68r, Bodleian Library, Oxford University.

Nurturing Mercury, father of the arts, of mind, of wit, and of speech, best lord of ways and journeys, who by your most holy power have long blessed our mind and heart, just as you have made safe and easy our most pleasant travels by land and sea though Italy, Illyria, Greece, Asia, and Egypt . . . Bless us with a favoring sea and a chorus of nymphs and nereids and, in your kindness, make our voyage a blessed and happy one.

—Cyriacus of Ancona, prayer to his patron deity[1]

An Antiquary Born of Trade

T HE ROMAN EXPERIENCE ignited Cyriacus's commitment to seek out the monuments of ancient Greeks and Romans throughout the Mediterranean, where no other Italian, or any other European, had troubled to go for that purpose before. But he had to square his self-chosen mission with the pragmatic reality of having to earn a living and support his aging mother. Unlike other humanists, who had wealthy benefactors, landed property, or curial ties, he needed a paycheck.

For two years Cyriacus remained moored in Ancona, working for various merchants and serving in city government—all the while itching to follow his new calling. Then, one day a letter arrived from his Venetian kinsman, Zaccaria Contarini. Zaccaria had numerous trade interests in the Levant, and Cyriacus must have torn the seal with impatient fingers, anticipating an offer. As he scanned the lines, his heart fell. Zaccaria was asking him to serve as his commercial representative either in the Marches, the province of Ancona, or in Apulia, the heel of Italy.

Emboldened by his passion, and "always more interested in grander pursuits than simply financial gain," Cyriacus went to Venice to negotiate with Zaccaria. He would gladly work for him, but only "in Greece or elsewhere, which would give him an opportunity to learn Greek and better understand Homer."[2] Zaccaria, keen to have the reliable and hardworking Cyriacus as his employee, readily agreed. His office on Cyprus was badly run by his brother, so he would be happy if Cyriacus would set it back on course, as well as do some trading at several markets around the Mediterranean. Cyriacus was jubilant. He hastened back to Ancona, packed his belongings, said goodbye to his anxious mother, and, early in 1428, boarded the first ship to leave harbor—its course set for Byzantium.

Any travel in those days was a trial, and if surface journeys by foot or mule, along bad roads, under constant threat from bandits and marauding soldiers, were bad enough to discourage Niccolò Niccoli and his colleagues, voyages by sea, as Cyriacus knew from his previous trips, were usually worse. If the weather cooperated, sailing went relatively smoothly, and the ship proceeded along the coast from one recognizable landmark to another, following written portolans—texts that described the markers en route. But calm waters were not always a gift. When the wind died, the vessel might be stranded mid-voyage, or even within sight of land. "When the ship stands still," wrote Felix Fabri, a Dominican friar on a pilgrimage to the Holy Land in 1480, "everything on board becomes putrid and foul and moldy; the water begins to stink, the wine becomes undrinkable, meat even if dried and smoked becomes full of maggots, and a profusion of flies, gnats, fleas, lice, worms, mice and rats assault you. Men become lazy and sleepy or untidy, envious, and angry."[3]

Strong winds were no friends either. Rising with fury, they boiled the sea around the ship, drenched it with lashing waves, and blew it off course. During Fabri's voyage storms kept ambushing his ship, tossing it amidst flashes of lightning, terrifying thunderclaps, and sheets of rain. Fierce squalls struck the galley, beating it "as hard as though great stones from some high mountain were sent flying along the planks," threatening to break them into splinters. The ship shook so violently that "no man could lie in his berth, much less sit, and least of all stand. People hung on to pillars which stood in the middle of the cabin supporting the upper works, or crouched on bent knees beside their chests, grabbing onto them with arms and legs." Water swamped the deck and splashed into the cabins, soaking mattresses, clothes, and food stores. "On the lower deck was terror and misery; on the upper deck toil and trouble."[4]

As Cyriacus knew well, storms also diminished provisions, by keeping a ship away from the coast and preventing it from resupplying. Fabri recorded that "when water got short, the sheep, goats, mules, and pigs kept aboard for food, stood around perishing of thirst, their rations having been given to men. During those days I often saw these creatures licking the planks and the spars, sucking off them the dew which had gathered in the night." When the ship finally reached shore and the crew took on fresh water, everyone turned giddy from joy:

> All the passengers ran from their berths and beds, carrying dishes, pots, basins, flasks, glasses and bottles, to beg water from the sailors. There was more struggling and pushing to get water than I ever saw for wine and bread, and the men were revived by the taste of that fresh water and seemed to come alive again, as if they had been plants and trees wilted and yellowed by heat and sprinkled by dew grown green again. The whole galley was exhilarated by the taste of water and people broke into song, water making them drunker than wine.[5]

Even when the voyage went fairly well, life on board was trying. Cyriacus had to share cramped sleeping quarters with other passengers in a suffocating cabin that trapped and amplified bodily odors, the chatter of voices, and snores. "When [passengers] go below to take their rest," wrote Fabri,

> there is a tremendous disturbance as they make their beds, all bumping against each other: the dust is stirred up, great quarrels arise between neighbors, especially at the outset, before they get used to it all—for one blames his neighbor for overlapping a part of his berth with his bed, and they argue back and forth for a while. Sometimes, when people

take sides of others, a general quarrel ensues and men pull out swords and daggers. There is shouting, shoving, and a great racket.[6]

The crew overhead added to the incessant noise, bellowing over the wind, singing lewd ditties, yelling orders and responses. Any change of sail sent them thudding across the deck, sounding like a massive hail to the ears of passengers below. The ship itself creaked and rattled, its wood squealing and throbbing under the assault of water and wind. Constant discomfort and fatigue made everyone irritable. If Cyriacus lingered on deck too late and woke others as he descended into the sleeping quarters, he risked getting his flickering oil lamp extinguished and himself splattered with the contents of someone's chamber pot.

Hygiene was an endless struggle, and vermin a constant torment. One traveler griped that the lice aboard ship grow "so large that some of them get seasick and vomit up pieces of flesh from apprentice seamen . . . [The ship] has an enormous profusion of game birds—cockroaches . . . and a great abundance of game—rats—many of which will turn and challenge their hunters like wild boars."[7] Fabri recalled that "as mice and rats multiply in the course of a voyage, they run about all night long, nibble at men's private larders, gnaw and befoul the food, spoil the pillows and shoes, and fall on men's faces while they sleep . . . The damp on board ship breeds fat white worms which crawl everywhere and come by stealth upon men's legs and faces when passengers sleep."[8]

Mealtimes created still more stress. "When dinner time comes," noted Fabri, "four trumpeters rise up and sound a call to the table. All who sit at the captain's table [as Cyriacus probably did] run with great haste to the poop to get a place where they can sit comfortably, or else end up with a bad seat—not at the tables set out in the poop, but on the galley slaves' [and rowers'] benches, in the sun, rain, or wind."[9]

When not fighting parasites or one another, passengers had to fill the long days at sea. Many gambled. The Venetian Benedetto Sanudo advised his younger brother Andrea, about to sail to Alexandria in 1473: "You know as well as I do that everyone on board ship gambles, whether playing cards or backgammon . . . if you care for your honor, never gamble . . . with anyone . . . [instead] set about reading one of the books that you will take with you. And if sometimes you want to spend time doing something else other than reading and writing, you may play backgammon with the priest."[10] Some passengers occupied themselves by writing. As Francis Bacon observed, "It is a strange thing that in sea voyages, where there is nothing to be seen but sky and sea, men should make diaries: but in land travel, wherein so much is to be observed, for the most part they omit it."[11] After Rome, Cyriacus kept diaries throughout his voyages, both on land and at sea, though, sadly, only those from his later journeys, in the 1440s, survive.

Remarkably, he never complained about the miseries of travel. Fabri, like many others, bemoaned that "a journey by sea is subject to many hardships. The sea itself is very injurious to those who are unaccustomed to it, and very dangerous on many accounts; for it strikes terror in the soul; it causes headache, it provokes vomiting and nausea; it destroys appetite for food and drink; it excites the passions and produces many strange vices; and it often brings men to a most cruel death."[12] If the sea did not get you, pirates might. Fabri warned future pilgrims that "when at port, be careful when wandering on the seashore, especially in lonely places, lest you be suddenly seized by pirates and made a miserable slave for all your days, or be robbed of all your money and valuables by the locals."[13]

All these perils and travails would be Cyriacus's constant companions as he sailed around the Mediterranean on his quest for vestiges of ancient civilizations. No wonder there were few takers for this job. Yet Cyriacus, buoyant by nature, weathered such hardships undaunted, and perceived opportunities where others saw setbacks. In one letter he described to a friend his unsuccessful attempt to sail from Chios to Lesbos:

> We labored our way at a moderate speed through the liquid deep within sight of your famous colony [Chios], finally at sunrise there was a struggle between the nymphs of Lesbos, who pulled us on, and those of Chios, who fought back, breasting the waves against them. Through the day and night we plowed the sea when, on the next day the north wind, becoming bolder . . . drove back the sails and forced our stern towards Lesbos and our prow toward Chios. The holy Nereid nymphs of Chios ended up getting what they wanted and they brought us into . . . port . . . where . . . [they] revealed why they had driven us into this gulf . . .[14]

It was in order to allow Cyriacus to see an ancient temple nearby. "Immediately I was enthusiastic," he exclaimed. Fabri and other travelers would have focused on the dread of being tossed back and forth by the wind, risking an imminent wreck. Cyriacus cast the experience in the poetic light of a contest between sea nymphs, with a reward at the end. As he continued in another letter, a few days later,

> the Nereids of Lesbos, roused by their anger and by the north wind, had blockaded us with swelling waves for about a hundred hours in that safe port [of Kardhamyla, on Chios], roaring from outside and threatening fiercely, when finally, by order of his king [Aeolus], the north wind Boreas was enchained in his immense Thracian prison and the deep sea grew quiet. Since we still had a strong desire to sail to Lesbos . . . our beautiful Calliope ["beautiful-voiced," the muse of heroic poetry] interceded with the nymphs of Kardhamyla and the other blue-green gods of the sea, the southeast wind we had hoped for increased in intensity, and . . . we set sail from the port at sunrise. So happy was our crossing of the sea, that, with the help and guidance of all the nymphs of Chios and Lesbos, we finished our course before Phoebus [the sun god, who measured the course of the day by riding the chariot of the sun across the sky] finished his.[15]

Cyriacus tended to look on the bright side: the word "joy" erupts frequently from his letters and notebooks. He praised nymphs for assuring him safe passage, and viewed delays as chances to discover and learn more.

Nymph holding up a galley, detail of Sangallo's drawing after Cyriacus. From Giuliano da Sangallo, Il libro di Giuliano da Sangallo Codice vaticanobarberiniano latino 4424 riprodotto in fototipia, ed. Cristiano Huelsen, Lipsia: O. Harrassowitz, 1910.

Cyriacus landed in Constantinople and inquired about the next boat for Cyprus. He was told that there would be none going that way for some weeks. He decided to use the time to begin learning ancient Greek, as he had hoped to do on this trip.

Few Italians, even among humanists, pursued classical Greek in those years. The language had all but disappeared in Italy. Petrarch had owned Greek copies of the *Iliad* and Plato, but had never managed to master the language, even though he took lessons from a Byzantine scholar. In the next half a century, fewer than a dozen Italians made the effort. And certainly no merchant bothered to cloud his brain with such an arcane pastime.

But the ancient language remained alive in Byzantium. Boys from good families studied classical grammar and literature and read Greek poets, historians, dramatists, and philosophers. At the turn of the fourteenth century, the leading scholar in Constantinople, Manuel Chrysoloras, a nobleman with close ties to court, hosted discussions of Greek literature and philosophy in his beautiful house with a hanging garden.[16] In 1391 Chrysoloras traveled to Italy as an envoy of the Byzantine emperor to seek Western assistance for the imperial capital threatened by the Ottomans. During his sojourn in Rome, he described eloquently the despoliation of its monuments. In Venice, he gave Greek lessons to the Florentine humanists Roberto Rossi and Jacopo Angeli da Scarperia. The two men, impressed and inspired, praised him extravagantly to Coluccio Salutati, the chancellor of Florence, and urged Salutati to invite Chrysoloras to teach in Florence.

Chrysoloras returned to Italy in 1397 for a five-year lectureship. In his late forties, he looked distinctive with his large aquiline nose, piercing deep-set eyes accentuated by bags below and arched eyebrows above, long hair tied in a pony-tail, and a beard flowing halfway down his chest (Florentines shaved their faces). A great teacher, he had a gift for simplify-ing the complicated Greek grammar and Byzantine method of instruction to make both accessible to Italians. In the words of one of his pupils, Leonardo Bruni, Chrysoloras restored to the Italians a knowledge of classical Greek which had been lost for seven hundred years. More accurately, it had been inaccessible for a whole millennium. His instruction inspired a whole gen-eration of students (still a very small group) to take classical studies to a new level by translating Greek texts into Latin and bringing them to European readers for the first time.

Though Chrysoloras's teaching sparked an enthusiasm for ancient Greek among Italian humanists, only three men risked a voyage to Constantinople to pursue it further: Gua-rino da Verona, Giovanni Aurispa, and Francesco Filelfo. Each returned home with the language implanted in his head and trunks full of Greek books. As Guarino sailed back to Italy in 1408 with two crates of priceless volumes, his ship was wrecked and one of the cases went down to the bottom of the sea. Guarino survived but was so distressed by the loss that his hair turned gray apparently overnight. Aurispa, in his turn, hunted so assiduously for ancient texts in Constantino-ple that the Byzantine emperor accused him of despoiling the city of books—which, in an age of only handwritten codices and thus relatively few books, was not such an unlikely claim. Aurispa's luggage, on his return journey in 1423, contained

238 volumes, including all the surviving works of Plato, most of them unknown in the West for over a thousand years, as well as Homer's *Iliad*, Demosthenes, Xenophon, and the celebrated "Codex Laurentianus" with seven plays of Sophocles, six of Æschylus, and Apollonius's *Argonautica*, along with other treasures. Aurispa had gathered these books not merely for intellectual profit. With the keen demand for ancient manuscripts among his Italian colleagues, he aimed to resell them at advantageous prices. Cyriacus, too, would combine his passion for the past with commercial acumen, acquiring books and artifacts both for himself and for such clients as Poggio Bracciolini, Niccolò Niccoli, and Cosimo de' Medici.

While moored temporarily in Constantinople, Cyriacus probably sought out a private teacher for his Greek lessons, as Guarino, Aurispa, and Filelfo had done. This time he began more traditionally, by learning grammar, rather than diving straight into an ancient text. But what he would do with the language would be new. While the humanists studied Greek in order to read ancient books, Cyriacus would use it to make audible ancient voices carved into stones. Thereby he would revive old monuments and make them known to Europeans for the first time in a thousand years.

Cyriacus's Greek reverie was interrupted by reality. He got word that an Anconitan ship had just docked at Chios, en route to Syria. Zaccaria had asked him to do some trading in Damascus, a great market for spices, silks, and other eastern luxuries. So it was time to get to the work that was financing his antiquarian education in the East. Catching the first boat to Chios, Cyriacus did not anticipate that this quick stopover would lead to a lifelong bond.

❧

The island of Chios, which claimed to be the birthplace of Homer, was a major commercial hub of the Mediterranean. It was ruled by the Genoese merchants who controlled the production of mastic, a resin from a tree grown only on Chios and vital to Renaissance medicines, perfumes, and painting varnishes. The island was also a key shipping center for alum, a mineral indispensable to the European textile and leather processing industries, mined by the Genoese in Old and New Phocaea on the Asia Minor coast, five miles away.[17]

A prominent member of this island community was Andreolo Banca Giustiniani—merchant, aspiring poet, and a man of elegant tastes.[18] Cyriacus met him through the Anconitans whose Syria-bound ship he came to join, and instantly recognized in the Genoese a soulmate: a businessman by trade, but a humanist by aspiration. Only Andreolo had better means to indulge his interests. He had constructed for himself a "Homeric villa" in a pine forest near the so-called "School of Homer," where he gathered an enormous library of some two thousand manuscripts.[19]

Cyriacus and Andreolo connected at once over their shared love of antiquity, and obviously found each other personally appealing as well. From that day on they would write frequently to each other (often monthly, occasionally as many as four times a month), and it is thanks to their correspondence that we know so much about Cyriacus's subsequent travels in the East. In his letters he would recount to Andreolo his adventures, archaeological discoveries, and embroilment in political events. Cyriacus would also make Chios a hub of his journeys and a storage depot for his wares. During this stay on Chios, Andreolo helped Cyriacus buy, for twenty gold pieces, a copy of the New Testament—his first Greek book. Later the Genoese would assist his friend in acquiring and reselling to clients in Italy many ancient objects and texts.

Collecting ancient artifacts was becoming increasingly popular in Italy. Carlo de Medici, Cosimo's illegitimate son, would comment in one of his letters that as the artist Pisanello lay dying in 1455, a long line of contenders stood outside his chambers negotiating with the servants for his ancient coins and medals. Cyriacus could supply especially rare objects—antiquities from the Eastern Mediterranean, largely unavailable in Italy. And he was dependable, respected for fair dealing ever since he was an apprentice running Piero's business in Ancona. True connoisseurs, wary of fakes, could rely on his honesty as well as his expertise, which could not be said of some of the other purveyors who told tall tales and cheated their clients out of promised goods.[20] Poggio Bracciolini complained to Niccoli in 1421 that he had commissioned a certain monk traveling in the Aegean to look for Greek statues, but was unsure of what he was getting:

> I gave some . . . errands to Master Franciscus of Pistoia. . . . Among them . . . was to look for any marble statue, even if it were broken . . . he informed me [from Greece] that he was holding in my name three marble heads by Polycleitos and Praxiteles . . . I do not know what to say about the names of the sculptors; as you know, the Greeks

are very wordy and perhaps they have made up the names in order to sell the heads more dearly.[21]

Bracciolini was enraged when Franciscus not only failed to send him the sculptures, but rerouted them to another customer. In contrast, when the humanist Francesco Filelfo asked Cyriacus to send from the Aegean specimens of Attic Greek script—capital letters used on ancient inscriptions—he knew that Cyriacus would obtain accurate copies.[22]

But that lay ahead. For now, Cyriacus and Andreolo said their good-byes, for the Anconitan ship was ready to sail. Cyriacus concluded whatever trading he had done for Zaccaria on Chios and proceeded to the next leg on his assignment.

∼§∾

"They set course through the clustered Aegean islands for Syria," Cyriacus recalled of the ship's itinerary, "landing first at the once-renowned Asiatic island of Rhodes, and thence continuing their voyage without delay before a favorable west wind to Beirut."[23] Beirut was Damascus's port on the Mediterranean, and all merchandise arriving here was unloaded and either sold at local markets or transferred onto donkeys and taken inland along a long, narrow, and fertile plain called the Valley of Noah, because Noah was said to have built his ark there.

In Damascus, likely on Zaccaria's advice, Cyriacus looked up the learned merchant Ermolao Donato, a member of a sizable Venetian community residing in the city and conducting a lucrative trade between Syria and Italy. Cyriacus probably solicited Ermolao's help in buying and shipping to Zaccaria a consignment of spices, fabrics, inlaid metalwork, and other merchandise in demand in Europe. But he also asked the Venetian for a personal favor: a tour of the city and "all the important ancient and modern monuments."[24] Ermolao happily obliged, for Damascus was a pleasure to share.

One of the oldest cities in the world, its layers of time and successive cultures were visible everywhere.[25] Its central landmark, the Great Mosque, stood on the site of a Roman temple of Jupiter that had been converted into a Christian church dedicated to St. John, and then, in 706 AD, transformed into a Muslim shrine.[26] The interior was off limits to Christians, but Cyriacus could glimpse a row of ancient columns within and ancient blocks built into the structure. Ancient, Christian, and Islamic strata shared space throughout the city and all around it. On the slope of nearby Mount Qassioun, a church built by St. Helena marked the spot where Cain had slain his brother Abel, Ermolao told Cyriacus. Inside the city walls, Damascus's Roman heritage was apparent in two main, bisecting streets. In each quarter nestled labyrinthine residential neighborhoods built by the Muslims, each a microcosm with its own mosque, baths, markets, and religious schools endowed by wealthy and pious patrons, for the Muslims were great supporters of learning.[27] Damascus's population, Cyriacus could see, was also a rich mix of cultures: Arabic-speaking Christian sects such as Jacobites and Nestorians lived next to the Jews and the Muslims. European pilgrims en route to and from the Holy Land stopped here to revere biblical sites. And merchants from Italy, France, Spain, and all over the Levant flocked to Damascus to conduct a lively trade.[28]

This gem in the desert had something for everyone. It was said that when the Prophet Mohammed passed Damascus on a journey from Mecca, he refused to visit it because he wanted to enter paradise only once, when he died. A Florentine pilgrim, Giorgio Gucci, stopped and recorded his impressions in 1384. Damascus, he gushed, was full of "notable and marvelous things, and in almost everything excels all the others subject to the Sultan; and to say Damascus for them is like saying Paris for us."[29] Bertrandon de la Broquière, a spy gathering intelligence for a Crusade plotted by the Duke of Burgundy, Philip the Good, paid a visit in 1432 and was enraptured by the spaciousness of the town, the profusion of beautiful gardens growing a myriad of fruits, and fountains in nearly every house. A network of canals, fed by the river Barata, which lapped the city to the north, crisscrossed Damascus to irrigate its vegetation and supply the countless fountains that filled the air with the refreshing murmur of water.

The city was no less fascinating by night. "When night comes they light many glass lamps in every street," marveled an Italian visitor, "and the light of the night is seen like that of day, so many are the lamps they light . . . in every street there are watchmen to guard the shops, and nobody dares go about at night without a lamp in hand, and if one is perhaps found without a light, he is taken and led before the admiral, and he pays the fixed fine. And so in this way no harm is ever done."[30]

During the day Damascus pulsated with activity. Situated at

the intersection of the main north–south route through Syria and the east–west caravan routes linking the Mediterranean coast with the Persian Gulf, the Red Sea, and the Silk Road, it was a great trade emporium. As Simone Sigoli, another Florentine pilgrim, wrote in 1384, "Really all Christendom could be supplied for a year with the merchandise of Damascus . . . [one finds here] such rich and noble and delicate works of every kind that if you had money in the bone of your leg, without fail you would break it to buy these things."[31] Sigoli and his companion on the journey, Giorgio Gucci, were entranced by the locally manufactured silks of every kind and color, cotton so fine, bright, and delicate that it could be taken for silk, gold and silver creations of exquisite workmanship, every kind of glass vessel, and brass basins and pitchers adorned with figures and foliage inlaid with silver and gold.[32] Cyriacus, too, fell in love with the famous Damascene metalwork, and bought several pieces for himself. He also thrilled at the "sight of the enormous number of camels that had come from Arabia Felix, Saba and Gedrosia, laden with many kinds of spices to be marketed in that remarkable city."[33] Dusty and worn out from their arduous journey across the desert, the animals were weighed down by aromatic resins, pearls and precious stones, exotic birds and cats.[34] Bertrandon de la Broquière witnessed in astonishment as some three thousand camels poured into the city over the course of two days.[35]

Nor did this exhaust Damascus's marvels. Its delicious sweets, concocted by master confectioners from sugar, apples, ginger, and other ingredients, were irresistible. Its flowers—violets, roses, and others varieties sold in specialty shops—

smelled stronger than in Europe. Its rose water was the best in the world. And the Damascenes were skilled at conserving snow from the surrounding mountains year-round (probably by building underground icehouses, in which snow and ice were packed in straw or sawdust), so that one could refresh oneself with cool drinks and chilled fruit in the summer heat.

Not satiated with everything he had seen in the city, and hungry for more ancient sights, Cyriacus asked Ermolao to take him to Sidon, a port town some twenty-eight miles south of Beirut. It had been famous in antiquity for producing the most prized purple dye used to color royal robes. The pigment was obtained from murex, a mollusk found in abundance off the coast. To extract the initially greenish liquid from the mollusk's vein and to turn it into a beautiful dye was a messy, smelly, and time-consuming business. Each animal yielded only a few drops of the precious liquid, and to obtain a mere 1.5 grams of purple—just enough to dye one dress—took 12,000 creatures, which made the price of purple garments truly regal, and Sidon very rich.[36]

Sidon first rose to preeminence under the Phoenicians, between the twelfth and tenth centuries BC. It continued to thrive as a vassal of the Persian Empire, providing ships and seamen to Persian kings waging wars against Egypt and Greece. But in 351 BC the Sidonians decided to rebel against their Persian overlords, and when King Artaxerxes III brought his vast army to their gates, they chose death over surrender. They set fire to their city, and more than 40,000 inhabitants perished in the conflagration. Yet Sidon's location and natural resources saved it from extinction. The city was rebuilt. The

Romans embellished it with a theater and other major public buildings, and in Cyriacus's day it prospered as a second port of Damascus.

Medieval buildings now covered what remained of the ancient structures, but Cyriacus could still see Roman columns and carved capitals built into the crusader castle erected on the site of the ancient temple to Melkart. Just south of the castle rose the Murex Hill, some 330 feet high and 165 feet long, formed of countless crushed mollusk shells left over from ancient dye-making. Outside the city Cyriacus probably visited the vestiges of the Persian temple of Eshmoun, god of medicine and patron of Sidon, and the adjacent Roman colonnade. And he may have peered at a few sarcophagi, grave stelae, and tomb sculptures peeking out between the weeds in the old cemeteries.

His curiosity satisfied and his business in Syria completed, Cyriacus found a Genoese ship heading for Cyprus and sailed on to his main job for Zaccaria.

꧁

Zaccaria's business was located in Nicosia, the capital of Cyprus, where its king, Janus, held court. Cyriacus would spend over a year (1428–9) working there (after a two-month stint as the lieutenant to the *podestà*, or chief magistrate, at Famagusta, where he first landed on the island and awaited Zaccaria's instructions).[37] Since the chief Venetian activity on Cyprus was the production and export of sugar and salt, he probably regularized the operations of Zaccaria's plantations. But he recorded almost nothing of his commercial activities, focusing instead on his antiquarian pursuits and the time spent in the company of the king. It was his first exposure to royalty and Cyriacus was smitten, writing exuberantly that one "had only to see and hear the king speak to recognize that his impressive personality outshone the renown of his name."[38]

Janus—tall, fat, strong, and good-looking with his blond beard—was, indeed, a man of culture and refinement who kept a splendid court and especially patronized music. As Khabil Dhabeir, chronicler to the Egyptian sultan Barsbay, reported: "The palace was richly furnished with costly beds and with particularly tasteful and expensive furniture. The walls were hung with splendid paintings and crosses of gold and silver. However, what my master admired most was a large organ that produced the most wonderful tones whenever its keys were pressed."[39]

Alas, Janus's troubled reign hampered his contemplative pleasures. He warred with the Genoese, who maintained a stranglehold on the island's commerce and his treasury, and became embroiled in a disastrous conflict with the Mamluks.[40] For many years the two states carried on a simmering war, motivated by economic interests rather than their religious divide. Janus regularly dispatched to Egypt either his own galleys or those of pirates, whom he tacitly encouraged to capture whatever resources they found. In one particularly bold raid, in 1403, Cypriot ships entered the port of Alexandria, ran fifteen miles up the Nile, and took some 1,500 prisoners to work on Janus's sugar plantations. The Mamluks sent retaliatory expeditions to pillage and burn what they could on Cyprus and to carry off its inhabitants. In 1414 the two sides negotiated a peace treaty, but the truce lasted for less than ten years, and

Cypriot piracy continued. Eventually Sultan Barsbay decided to squelch it for good. In late June 1426 he sent a force of some 180 ships to Cyprus, sacked Nicosia, and captured Janus, taking him to Cairo and holding him prisoner for ten months.

Janus returned to Cyprus in May 1427 broken in spirit and health; some said that he never laughed again. But Cyriacus seems to have set him at ease, for Janus listened to his "words of praise and his eloquent discussion of the king's recent misfortunes, cheerfully and graciously welcomed him and regally admitted him to the company of his principal courtiers."[41] The king also offered whatever help Cyriacus might need in executing his business in Nicosia. The relationship profited both men. Janus may have seen in the flattery of the merchant an opportunity to improve his image after his recent dishonor. Cyriacus gained free rein to investigate the antiquities of Cyprus and elevated his status through association with the king. Janus was the first in a series of rulers Cyriacus would befriend, and the king's benevolence boosted his confidence: he was able, he discovered, to transcend his modest roots and further his archaeological mission by charming powerful men.

As a welcomed guest at Janus's court, Cyriacus was invited to royal festivities and hunts. While the king and his retinue galloped through the meadows and woods, "startling the birds as he chased his panther prey," Cyriacus explored the island and stopped at local monasteries in search of ancient manuscripts. In one old religious house, "among its squalidly kept and long neglected manuscripts, he was overjoyed to discover an ancient codex of Homer's *Iliad*, which he persuaded an illiterate monk, not without difficulty, to let him have in exchange for a Gospel book."[42] In Nicosia itself, from another monk, he acquired the *Odyssey*, several tragedies of Euripides, and a book of antiquities by the Alexandrian grammarian Theodosius. Poring over these volumes, he puzzled through ancient Greek, just as a few years earlier he had mastered Latin through Virgil. The *Iliad*, Cyriacus recorded, "afforded him his first great help in overcoming his ignorance of Greek literature."[43]

This Cypriot sojourn proved profitable for both Cyriacus and his employer, whose business he administered "so diligently and skillfully . . . that he completed the whole task within a year, having made an accurate list of debtors and creditors and having reduced them to a very small number."[44] Zaccaria, delighted, asked him to proceed on his behalf to a new location: Adrianople, the capital of the Ottomans, the archenemies of Christendom. Little did Cyriacus anticipate that this posting would alter his life and propel him into a new, and far more dangerous, career.

Vittorio Carpaccio, The Stoning of St. Stephen, *1520, depicting turban-clad Muslims. From Pompeo Molmenti,* The Life and Works of Vittorio Carpaccio, *London: John Murray, 1907.*

The Ottoman Threat

FOR MUCH OF his life, Cyriacus had heard Western calls for a new Crusade against the infidel. Ever since they had established their dynasty a century earlier, the Ottomans had been gaining strength and expanding their territory from their original seat in Eskişehir, in western Anatolia, to Asia Minor, the eastern Mediterranean, and the Balkans. In 1396 the Ottomans defeated the Christians at Nikopolis and proceeded to make inroads into eastern Europe. But European princes and popes were too preoccupied with domestic wars and power struggles to expend time and resources on a confrontation in the East. The French and the English were fighting their Hundred Years' War, the Italian princes jostled with each other for control over the peninsula, the Bohemians battled against the Hussite heretics. Meanwhile, the Byzantines, distrustful of the Europeans, as often as not sought Ottoman help to solve domestic crises. In 1341, in a civil war between two claimants to the Byzantine throne, both sides asked Turkish rulers for troops and support.

Italian merchant states, Cyriacus knew from his trading in the East, were also ambiguous about fighting the Turks. The Genoese, who had extensive commercial dealings with the Ottomans, preferred to come to mutual accommodations with them. In 1351, when the Venetians attacked the Genoese colony of Pera, opposite Constantinople, the Genoese begged Sultan Orhan for aid in return for vast sums of money and perpetual gratitude. The sultan helped them expel the Venetians, and over the following century the Ottomans granted the Genoese a monopoly over alum production at Phocaea—for a price, of course. The Genoese reciprocated by transporting Turkish troops across the Dardanelles in 1421, when Sultan Murad II tried to attack Constantinople, and they would render him a similar service in 1444, much to Cyriacus's distress.[3]

Venice had a more fraught relationship with the Ottomans. Both wanted to retain and expand their markets and shipping routes around the Mediterranean. As the Venetians watched the Turks gain territory in the course of the fourteenth and fifteenth centuries, they grew increasingly more anxious about their commercial position in the East and fought them over key places in Albania, Morea (the Peloponnese), and the Greek islands. But they also had to tread carefully. As a maritime power rather than a land state, Venice depended on such vital eastern commodities as grain—grown in Ottoman-occupied Anatolia, Macedonia, Thrace, and Thessaly—and thus had to come to periodic compromises with the Turks in order to assure their supplies.

Cyriacus was probably aware of these complicated political maneuvers—from a distance. It was another matter actually to set foot in the heart of Ottoman territory, and as the representative of a Venetian firm. For, at this very moment, relations between Venice and the sultan stood at an especially low point.

Cyriacus arrived in Adrianople (now Edirne, in northwestern Turkey) some time in December of 1429, along with a camel caravan carrying his wares from the Turkish port of Gallipoli. He must have been surprised and relieved at what he found. Despite the Turks' fearsome reputation, their capital looked inviting: vibrant, cultured, cosmopolitan. Founded by the emperor Hadrian around 125 AD and contested for centuries due to its strategic position, it had been captured by the Turks in 1360 and prospered under the reigning Sultan Murad, who fostered economic development in his empire and encouraged commerce with other nations. Merchants from Italy, Spain, and Asia Minor traded briskly in Adrianople.[3] Bertrandon de la Broquière, the spy sent by the Duke of Burgundy to reconnoiter for a Crusade, reported that the Ottoman annual revenue was 2,500,000 ducats, and that if Murad had used all available resources, he could easily have invaded Europe.[4]

Close up, Cyriacus saw, the Turks were not nearly as threatening as they were described in the West. Pero Tafur, who passed through Adrianople in 1435, noted that "The Turks are a noble people, much given to truth. They are very merry and benevolent, and of good conversation, so much so that in those parts, when one speaks of virtue, it is sufficient to say that anyone is like a Turk."[5]

From stories told around the city, Cyriacus could gather that the sultan was also a more benevolent figure than he had anticipated, spoken of admiringly not only by his own subjects but also by the Europeans who observed him in person, and even by the Byzantines, whose territory he was shrinking by the year. Bertrandon described Murad as

> a fat, short man with a wide face . . . His nose is rather large and curved, his eyes rather small. His face is dark-skinned with fat cheeks and a round beard. He is said to be a gentle person, benign and free with land and money. He hates war, which seems to me to be true, for if he wanted to use his power and money, given the slight resistance to be found in Christendom, it would be an easy thing for him to conquer a large part of it.[6]

The Byzantine chronicler Laonicus Chalcocondylas concurred. Murad, he wrote,

> loved law and justice . . . He waged war only in self-defense. He attacked no one unjustly. But when he was attacked by others he took up arms. If no one provoked him, he took no pleasure in campaigns, but the reason for this is not to be sought in laziness. For when it was necessary to defend the empire, he did not fear to set out even in winter, nor did he measure the dangers and difficulties attending his undertakings.[7]

Murad, it seemed, was far from devoted to boundless expansion. He did what was necessary to consolidate his empire and secure it against enemies, but preferred to resolve conflicts with peace treaties. The Greek chronicler Doukas emphasized the loyalty with which Murad observed his accords with the

Christian powers, who, in their turn, failed to exhibit the same virtue.

In fact, Murad would repeatedly try to hand over the throne to his son so as to retire to a life of reading, hunting, and revelry. Bertrandon commented that the sultan loved to hunt and to hawk, and kept over a thousand dogs and two thousand birds for this purpose. He also relished drinking parties.

> His great pleasure is drinking and he likes people to drink well. He is said to drink easily ten or twelve cups of wine, that is six or seven quarts. When he has been drinking, there is nothing that he won't give away. His people are very happy when he drinks, for it is then that he makes great gifts.[8]

Unlike many rulers, Murad apparently recognized the cost of war to his soldiers and sought to avoid unnecessary bloodshed. A contemporary Ottoman chronicler recorded how in 1450 Murad tried and failed to take the Christian stronghold of Krujë, in Albania, defended by his former vassal and general Skanderbeg. The sultan's advisers suggested that he return in the winter to finish the job. "If I attack," the Sultan replied, "many men will be killed. I would not give one of my soldiers for fifty such fortresses."[9]

So this was the chief enemy of the West. Observing the sultan from a respectful distance at court entertainments, Cyriacus could not help admiring him "riding on his horse up and down the field in all splendor, accompanied by his magnificent, mounted bowmen."[10] Yet, genial and benign though

Murad might be, the Ottomans were at this very moment in open conflict with Venice over Thessaloniki, a formerly Byzantine city in northern Greece, and it was not the best time for a Venetian to come to Adrianople.

An important economic and cultural center, Thessaloniki had been ruled by the Turks from 1387 to 1403, when it was reclaimed by the Byzantines. Since 1411 the Ottomans have been attempting to get it back. The city refused to return to its former masters. The sultan tried to break its resistance by a lengthy blockade. The constant threat of invasion and the depletion of food stores fanned strife among political groups within Thessaloniki, and some citizens began to defect to the Turks. Those who remained were too weak to last much longer, let alone to fight if it came to it. The city officials faced a tough choice: to surrender to the enemy, or to ask the Venetians, ever keen to acquire another commercial base in the Aegean, to assume control of Thessaloniki in exchange for defending it against the Ottomans. The pro-Venetian faction won, and the Italians took over the beleaguered city in 1423. But life under them proved no better, and over the next seven years, as the Turkish assaults continued,

> most inhabitants of the neighborhood had fled and surrendered to the godless, others had become exiles in other people's islands, countrysides, and towns, others were known to have been taken prisoner, others had been slaughtered, while those who remained in the city had either already succumbed to starvation or were so worn out by privations that they had the fear of death from inside as well as from outside ever present before their eyes.[11]

The Venetians tried to strike against the enemy by attacking Turkish ships inside and outside the Dardanelles and by blockading the Bosporus Strait so as to cut communication between the two halves of the Ottoman Empire. But this did nothing to relieve Thessaloniki.

The relationship between Murad and Venice went from bad to worse in 1424, when the sultan imprisoned the Venetian ambassador, Niccolò Giorgio, who had come to Adrianople to try to resolve the conflict. Four years later, Giacomo Dandolo, dispatched by the Venetian Senate to negotiate peace with Murad, was arrested as well. At the time of Cyriacus's arrival in late 1429 or early 1430, relations between the Ottomans and the Venetians deteriorated further, as the sultan prepared to make a big push and take Thessaloniki once and for all. Given his Venetian employer and his travels around the Mediterranean, Cyriacus must have fit the profile of a likely spy, or at least an agent of Venetian interests, destined to cool off in Murad's dungeon. He had hoped to explore antiquities in Ottoman-held lands with the sultan's safe-conduct. But if he were to make such a request now, would Murad believe that he was looking merely for ancient stones, rather than for strategic information? No one had ever heard of a European merchant in the East chasing after old blocks with the sole purpose of recording them. It was better to lie low and to focus on trade until relations between the Venetians and the Ottomans improved.

In March 1430 the sultan and his great army marched on Thessaloniki. Making camp below the walls, Murad sent out emissaries with an offer of peace to the inhabitants of the city if they would voluntarily open the gates. The defenders on the ramparts greeted the approaching ambassadors with a shower of arrows. Murad ordered his troops to prepare for attack, but made a second attempt at a nonviolent solution. Again his peace-seekers were barraged with missiles. The third time, to spare the heralds' lives, the Sultan sent messages of peace by attaching them to arrows which his archers shot into the city. This time, seeing the Turk's words with their own eyes, the Greeks, according to an eyewitness, were inclined to accept his deal, but fear of their Venetian overlords, who threatened all those contemplating betrayal with the death penalty, spurred them to resist. And so they prepared for battle.[12]

The Venetians, meanwhile, got word that Murad was preparing to burn their galleys anchored in the harbor, and promptly moved their archers to the port. But they neglected to explain their actions to the Greeks, who, demoralized by the impending Turkish attack and the departure of the Venetian archers from the walls, abandoned their posts and fled to their houses. Left unprotected, the ramparts became a much easier target for the well-rested and more numerous Turks. At the same time, the Ottoman general in charge of undermining the walls brought loads of costly silk garments to the fortifications and promised each soldier a garment in return for each removed block.

The news of the drama enfolding at Thessaloniki had not yet reached Adrianople, so life in the capital continued much as before, if under a shadow of anxiety over the progress of the war. Cyriacus was putting his time in the city to productive and profitable use: buying leather, carpets, and other goods for his employer, and apparently wax for himself—a vital commod-

ity for the Anconitan candle-making industry, which supplied
the whole papal state. Wax candles burned cleaner and gave
off better light than tallow ones. They also cost much more,
but the demand for them was such that beeswax gathered in
Italy did not suffice and had to be augmented by imports from
Russia—where it was plentiful—via Ottoman and Genoese
intermediaries.[13]

Cyriacus also found a way to continue his classical education—with a Greek grammarian, Lio Boles, who gave public
discourses on Homer's *Iliad* and Hesiod's *Works and Days*.
Under Lio's tutelage, Cyriacus resumed the studies he had
begun in Constantinople and made progress in reading Greek
literature. The presence of a Greek school in Adrianople testi-
fied to Murad's support of learning. Not only did he sponsor
educational institutions in his larger cities, he also gathered
scholars around him twice a week to discuss religion, science,
and literature.[14]

Meanwhile, the assault on Thessaloniki raged on. With the
defense of the city weakened by years of privation, and now
by the defection of guards on the ramparts, Murad began his
onslaught on the fortifications. It took three days of struggle,
but once the walls were breached, an eyewitness described the
Turkish soldiers

> entering like bees or wild animals, howling and breathing
> out our murder, and they went through the city on foot
> or horseback . . . When they had entered the city . . . and
> had attacked us like oppressive wolves, they hastened to
> plunder everything . . . They were dragging off together

men, women, children of all ages, fettered, like senseless animals, and they led them all off to the camp outside the city.[15]

Some six thousand citizens were killed, many during the siege, others during the herding of the vanquished out of the city, as those who could not keep up with the soldiers had their heads cut off on the spot. About seven thousand weeping and lamenting survivors were enslaved. Once they had been brought to the Turkish camp, "everything in the city was taken away and overturned, and nothing, neither holy church nor monastery nor house of even the humblest was left undisturbed." Soldiers ransacked private homes as well as churches in search of money and hidden treasures, having pried information about their location from the captives by false assurances of freedom or by torture. Murad had promised his fighters this plunder, to spur them on, and now they were garnering their reward. When they were done, Thessaloniki stood depopulated, partially destroyed, and thoroughly looted. Murad's army marched home weighted down by ancient blocks from its buildings, manuscripts from its libraries, and thousands of slaves taken both in the defeated city and in northwestern Greece, where the Ottoman army headed for further conquests.

After the heat of the sack cooled off, Murad felt pity at Thessaloniki's devastation and resolved to bring the city back to life. He had a vested interest in making it again a vibrant commercial metropolis. So he ordered that the more illustrious citizens be freed—personally paying their ransom—and settled back in their homes; he sent messengers across his domains to tell those who had fled during the Venetian occupation to return promptly and reclaim their property. The sultan also decreed that all the structures damaged during the assault be restored to the same condition as before. Some were, but others remained in ruins because Murad was, at that time, building a splendid new bathhouse in Adrianople and his deputies had carted off to his capital stones from the despoiled churches and monasteries. Still, according to John Anagnostes, a citizen of Thessaloniki who witnessed the sack,

> From the time of the city's enslavement Murad honorably bestowed in words and letters everything, i.e. buildings, property, holy churches, monasteries and the sources of their revenues upon us at the time of our return from slavery from wherever. And everywhere he proclaimed freedom to those returning, and all took their houses and their real property, and every order and every nation of the city began to progress toward a second growth and renewal.[16]

Remarkably, Anagnostes spoke favorably of the sultan even though he had wrought such suffering on the city. When, two years later, Murad reversed some of his generous policies, Anagnostes would still lay the blame on his advisers. Meanwhile, Cyriacus must have hoped that with the end of the war at Thessaloniki, the victorious sultan, no longer concerned about Venetian espionage, would grant him his hoped-for safe-conduct.

∾

Cyriacus inadvertently profited from Murad's war even without the coveted passport. Among the captives the Ottomans herded home was a young girl called Chaonia. Cyriacus found and purchased her at a slave market in Adrianople, probably for well under forty florins—the price such girls fetched in Italy, after going through several middlemen (in comparison, Francesco Datini, the merchant of Prato, paid sixteen florins for "a good horse, which traveled 1,400 miles from Barcelona to Flanders without being any the worse for it").

Slaves were a normal part of life in the Mediterranean in this era. In Italy slavery had disappeared for a few centuries during the Middle Ages, but the Black Death had killed so much of the workforce that the Italians began to replenish it with human cargo imported from the East. Every prosperous nobleman and merchant had a couple of slaves—Mongolian girls with black hair, high cheekbones, and dark, slanting eyes, or else tall, blond Circassians or Russians with blue eyes and round faces (there were very few African slaves in Europe at that time). Even priests, small shopkeepers, and sailors often had one.[17] Most of the slaves brought to Italy were women employed as domestics. Men tended to be sent to labor on the Venetian sugar plantations on Crete and Cyprus, in the Genoese alum mines at Phocaea, and on war galleys.

Cyriacus grew up seeing such foreigners around his hometown and probably in his own house before his father died, for Ancona was a major slave bazaar. So were Venice, Genoa, and Pisa, where boatloads of miserable, barely clothed women and girls were unloaded from ships arriving from Alexandria and the Black Sea, Constantinople and Pera, Adrianople and Bursa, Chios, Rhodes, and Cyprus. Exhausted from long voyages in the stifling holds, where many of their fellows died from malnourishment and disease, confused and frightened by alien surroundings, the poor creatures were prodded and displayed like cattle and sold to middlemen who supplied clients across Italy. In the decade between 1414 and 1423, more than 10,000 slaves were traded in Venice alone. And Cyriacus very likely purchased slaves for Zaccaria in Adrianople and other emporia, for they were lucrative merchandise. Children under ten fetched between twenty and thirty florins, girls aged ten to fifteen went for forty florins, and fifteen to twenty-five-year-olds might cost up to fifty florins. Especially pretty and civilized girls sold for sixty-five to seventy-five florins. A Medici agent reported to his employer from Venice in 1459: "I have found for you one of the Circassian nation, between seventeen and eighteen years old . . . and not too delicate in face, but of good appearance and handy and lively and intelligent, so I think she will do very well."[18]

All too often these young women become their masters' mistresses, whether they wanted to or not.[19] Two early fifteenth-century Florentines, the silk merchant Gregorio Dati and the successful woolen cloth manufacturer Paolo Niccolini, noted in their *ricordanze* that they had fathered children by their slave girls. So did Cosimo de' Medici, who had four slaves in his household. Since babies born of such unions were often brought up alongside the legitimate children as free citizens, the supply of slaves had to be continuously replenished—and it was, thanks to constant wars waged by the Ottomans, the Latins, and other contenders for power in the East.[20]

Cyriacus's Chaonia—whom he would rechristen Clara— had been captured by Murad's army in Epirus, in northwestern Greece, right after the battle of Thessaloniki. She was not the most desirable kind. Those who could afford them preferred Russians and Circassians, or Mongolians, prized for their loyalty and hard work.[21] But Cyriacus's choice may not have been simply economic. He was infatuated with Greece, and he would refer to his girl as *koré*, the ancient Greek word for maiden. Quite likely she, too, became his concubine.

Cyriacus never married, apparently unwilling to be hampered by a wife who would tie him down to Ancona and curtail his travels (though he forever dreamed of Muses and nymphs). He was not unique: Brunelleschi and Donatello remained single, and Niccoli chose to keep a mistress instead of a spouse. There were good reasons to avoid matrimony. "Nothing in the world leads a man to poverty so speedily as taking a wife," wrote Giovanni della Casa in his pamphlet "Whether It Is Good to Take a Wife." "One must feed her and clothe her and give her money to adorn herself—one expense after another, without end." Giovanni concluded that it is entirely unnecessary to take "a permanent wife" and advocated the much less encumbering option of a concubine.[22] Leonardo Bruni complained to Poggio Bracciolini: "I have not just spent money on my marriage but almost entirely used up my patrimony on one wedding."[23] And Ludovico Carbone, a humanist at the Este court in Ferrara, in his oration on marriage, lamented how money impinged on one's choice of a spouse in the first place:

> The reason why so many naturally suited youths avoid marriage is that they see young girls who are worthy to embrace the greatest orator and to kiss a divine poet given to those who are not even deserving of life . . . A young

virgin like Venus or Pallas Athena is married off to a rough and foolish idiot, who snores night and day. But I, a lover of the Muses, on account of my hard work will get a freckled redhead with an upturned nose and weasel-like complexion, whom you would not want to meet in the middle of the night. If only I had never read literature! O the great ignorance of parents who do not understand the saving advice of Ennius, who preferred to give his daughter to a man lacking money rather than to money lacking a man.[24]

Cyriacus did not accumulate much wealth and was seemingly unwilling to sink whatever resources he had into a wife.[25] A slave girl had many advantages: she required no expensive upkeep, he could choose as pretty and clever a one as he wished, enjoy her during his stays in Ancona, and have her serve his mother the rest of the time.[26] Although he would later free his *koré*, she would remain in his household for the rest of her life and be buried together with him and his mother.[27] Meanwhile, to accompany him on his travels, Cyriacus purchased a black slave, Niccolino, who, for a reason Cyriacus did not elaborate on, would be later succeeded by a Greek, Hermodoros.

From the spoils of Thessaloniki Cyriacus also acquired (in addition to several other Greek manuscripts) a book that would accompany him on his travels as well: the *Geography* of Ptolemy, the Greek mathematician who lived and worked in Alexandria in the second century AD.[28] Ptolemy's book—the first attempt to map the known world—consisted chiefly of lists of places with their longitude and latitude, with occasional brief descriptions of important topographical features. Of Cyriacus's home region, for example, Ptolemy wrote: "The

Appennine mountains are located not far above Liguria beginning at the Alps, and from Liguria extending as far as Ancona,
then turning they approach the Adriatic, and extend as far
as the Garganus mountains, then turning they extend toward
the south to Leucopetra promontory." The book became
immensely popular when it was first translated into Latin by
Manuel Chrysoloras in the early fifteenth century, because
it revealed to the Europeans the "new" geographical science
of delineating the breadth and the length of different regions
through the use of coordinates. It also instructed the reader
on how to construct usable maps. It did not constitute a particularly useful guidebook for the kind of travel Cyriacus was
doing because he moved around largely on foot and by ship,
along well-trodden routes around the Mediterranean, finding
his way not by geographical measurements but by word-of-
mouth directions. Besides, many of the place names listed by
Ptolemy had changed since antiquity. Yet there was no better guide in existence—in fact, none at all. At least *Geography*
would give him some information about the sites he wanted to
visit. But he would rely most on the evidence of ancient stones
themselves.

❧

Murad's triumphant return from Greece put him into a kindly
mood. In the summer of 1430 he concluded a peace treaty with
Venice and granted permission to her subjects and merchants
to travel and trade freely throughout his territories, in exchange
for annual tribute. Cyriacus must have breathed a sigh of relief.
Now he could dare approach the sultan with his request. He

did not receive a private audience, observing Murad from a distance "holding court in his hall," but, whatever officials he had to charm, cajole, and bribe, Cyriacus obtained what he desired. Taking his goods to Gallipoli, he found an Anconitan ship in the harbor, loaded onto it a consignment of hides and carpets to be delivered to Zaccaria, and Chaonia, insured together with his other merchandise, to be taken to his mother, Masiella. His professional obligations thus discharged, he set out for his next date with the past.[29]

Cyriacus's itinerary on this journey was inspired in part by books and in part by recent events. He wanted to tour Macedonia, the birthplace of Alexander the Great, and to visit Philippi, the site of a defining moment in Roman history. At Philippi in October 42 BC Octavian and Mark Antony, who had declared a civil war to avenge the death of Caesar, won a decisive battle against Brutus and Cassius, his assassins. Their victory paved the way for the demise of the Roman Republic and the rise of imperial rule under Augustus (who changed his name from the humbler Octavian). Later, Philippi became a crucial place for Christian history: in 49 AD Paul established there the first Christian church in Europe, and in his famous letter to the Philippians, composed as he languished in a Roman prison, he laid out his thoughts on theology and apostolic love, his converts and the gospel, the joy of faith, and the salvation of all who followed Christ.

Cyriacus mentioned nothing of the Pauline history of Philippi in his diary, nor spoke of its magnificent, if crumbled, Christian churches. Instead, he devoted all his attention to the ancient monuments of the deserted town, trying to conjure up the noble fortifications of the city from the ruined marble remains, the plays performed in the theater, whose surviving circular orchestra and remnants of the stone proscenium suggested its former elegance, and the inhabitants of the town who were buried in large tombs on the outskirts.

Then he directed his steps to Thessaloniki, to see for himself the vanquished city and to record what remained of its antiquities.[30] As he would recount to his biographer, he examined admiringly

> the marvelous arch of Aemilius Paulus in the main square, and the ruined temple of Diana with numerous marble statues of the gods on its architraves [in fact, an elaborate colonnaded portico that stood in the ancient forum]. He also inspected many splendid Christian churches, delighting particularly in the big one dedicated to the warrior martyr, St. Demetrius; the turreted brick walls built by Lysimachos; and many inscriptions relating to heroes and poets, including an inscription on a tripod of the Muses [at Delphi that had been copied and] brought to Salonika from Mount Helicon, with its extraordinary reference to the date when Homer and Hesiod lived.[31]

As was becoming his habit, he also hunted for more books, buying manuscripts, probably on the cheap, from inhabitants reduced to destitution by the Turkish siege and conquest. He dispatched them on a Chios-bound galley to his friend Andreolo, who would store them until Cyriacus was ready to return home—where he could resell the prized volumes at a good profit to the humanists in Rome, Florence, and Venice.

Cyriacus did not elaborate on the destruction of Thessaloniki by Murad's soldiers, at least not to his biographer, but its effects would have been visible everywhere around him, giving him a preview of what would happen to other Greek cities if the Ottoman conquests continued. True, Murad had treated him generously, approving his safe-conduct, and, at least after taking Thessaloniki, was relatively lenient to that city. The next sultan might not be so benevolent—either to Cyriacus or to the ancient heritage spread across Asia Minor and Greece. Of course, back home, Italians were not taking very good care of classical remains either, but at least there a few humanists were awakening to their value. In the East, irreplaceable vestiges of the past stood orphaned and imperiled by the Ottoman expansion, and no one but Cyriacus was doing anything to safeguard them for the future. After his visit to Thessaloniki, the tone of his diaries changed, as did his plans: from a mere recorder of physical vestiges of classical civilization, he became a warrior on their behalf. His self-assumed mission and its fearless pursuit had been tinged with zealotry all along. So it is not altogether surprising that Cyriacus, by nature easily excitable and readily engulfed by a cause, decided to expand his purview from simply gathering information about the past to protecting it from those who, in his view, threatened it—by force.

*Temple at Cyzicus, drawing by or after Cyriacus in Bartolomeus
Fontius, Bodleian Library Ms. Lat. misc. d. 85, ff. 133v–134r,
Bodleian Library, Oxford University.*

completely committed to you as I am and being a long-time
faithful observer [of events] and primarily eager for your
glory, I might stir you, faithful and deeply Christian princes,
to support this campaign against a barbaric foe.

—Cyriacus of Ancona, *letter to*
Emperor John VIII Palaeologus[1]

Spy and Diplomat

CYRIACUS HAD INTENDED, after his trip to northern
Greece, to undertake an extended tour of Asia Minor and
Persia in the company of a learned Genoese merchant, Niccolò
Ziba, whom he had met at Adrianople and who regularly traded
in Persia, Parthia, and the territories around the Caspian Sea.
Ziba was interested in antiquities and would have made a perfect guide for Cyriacus. But the visit to Thessaloniki drastically
altered Cyriacus's course, and a letter that awaited him upon
his return to Gallipoli affirmed his new sense of purpose.

The dispatch contained momentous news: his former
employer at the port of Ancona, Cardinal Condulmaro, had
been elected pope on March 3, 1431, taking the name of Eugenius IV. Cyriacus was thrilled, writing to various friends:

I reckoned that the death of so good a Pope as Martin would be unfortunate for the Church and disastrous for virtually everyone in Italy; but now in the event I see that it was in a sense quite fortunate and timely, rather, in that so responsible, humane, clement, wise and wholly devout a man, as I now learn, has been elected his successor.

For if almighty God wills that Italy and our religion shall be restored by any priest, I am convinced that so excellent a Pope, Eugenius, is the very man to further this great task, because we have already seen how providently, firmly, justly, devotedly and large-mindedly he has always conducted the important affairs of the Church.[2]

Eugenius seemed to be a godsend, a natural ally to Cyriacus's new plan. He knew and liked Cyriacus from Ancona, and had hosted him for forty days in Rome. As the new pope, he had to prove his authority and create a legacy, and what Cyriacus had in mind would benefit them both. For, as Scalamonti records:

his plan now was to get clear of his commercial business, and then, having collected all the intelligence he could concerning a union with the Greeks and the whole Eastern Church and on an effective crusade against the Turks, to hasten home to Italy and to visit the pope in Rome in order, both orally and by written report, to lay before him whatever of importance in his view he had discovered on these matters.[3]

Cyriacus was determined, if Eugenius would support him, to instigate a new Crusade against the Turks.

Such a Crusade was not a novel idea. It had been current in the West for decades, both before and after the campaign mounted by the king of Hungary in 1396 which ended in the disastrous defeat of the Christian army at Nicopolis. During his travels in the East, Cyriacus may well have met Bertrandon de la Broquière, the Burgundian spy gathering intelligence for Duke Philip the Good—a vociferous, if ineffectual, proponent of the cause. This may have ignited Cyriacus's notion of mounting an offensive against the Ottomans, and his experience in Thessaloniki would have reinforced the idea. Cyriacus's adulation of Julius Caesar, who had been praised by the ancients for slaughtering scores of barbarians and vastly extending Rome's dominion, likely inspired him further. As a man of action, accustomed to organizing and carrying out international ventures, Cyriacus devised a strategy that he hoped would prove more successful than previous attempts.

The problem with launching a Crusade, to date, had been the lack of effective central organization. If he were to galvanize the pope, who would rally western princes, it would have a better chance of victory. Condulmaro's ascension to the throne of St. Peter and the Ottomans' recent gains in northern Greece made the time ripe for a new and concerted action. Since Cyriacus knew both the pope and the East, he took it upon himself to collect and deliver personally to Rome the information Eugenius IV would need to plan the war.

Cyriacus was not motivated by religion in this venture. His letters and diaries do not mention anything about a spiritual impetus for the Crusade, but are filled with feverish records of the monuments he was striving to preserve in the face of peril. He was not a religious man—not in the manner of most of his contemporaries. He never invoked Jesus, Mary, or saints. Instead, he referred to Christ as Jove and called upon Mercury, the ancient god of merchants, as his guardian. As he wrote in one letter, describing a crossing from Chios to New Phocaea: "All of us arrived safely thanks to supreme Jove's help, our most holy protector Mercury's guidance, and the favor of white-clad, learned Cymodocea, the brightest of Nereus' sea-nymph daughters, who kept the deep sea calm."[4] In advocating the Crusade, Cyriacus seemed to think not so much of restoring Christianity to the territories occupied by the Turks as of expelling them from the lands of classical antiquities. It was an unusual position for his time, but his whole archaeological enterprise was an innovation.

Cyriacus first needed to ascertain the state of the sultan's forces in his domains, then get the Byzantine emperor on board with the Latins. Then he would present his findings to the pope so that he could get the war under way. Having formulated this plot, Cyriacus must have corresponded with Eugenius and asked permission to act as his unofficial agent. As a merchant, he would not have had the authority to negotiate with the Greek ruler. Long ago he had proven to Gabriele Condulmaro his perseverance at whatever job he took on, as well as his charm, so the pope could trust him to negotiate diplomatically. Besides, Cyriacus was already perfectly positioned for this task. He still had Murad's safe-conduct, so he could travel through Ottoman lands under the guise of commerce and archaeology. Poking around ancient sites would give him an opportunity to snoop in places unfrequented by merchants or pilgrims; and conducting surveillance for a Crusade would give him a chance to see more antiquities.

༺ৡৡ৵

International merchants made natural spies: their success depended on knowing up-to-date information not only on goods and prices, but also on political conditions in the places they traded. Still, to spy among the Turks, Cyriacus needed a trustworthy guide who knew the system from within. He chose Memnon, whom he must have met at Murad's court. This illegitimate son of the recently deceased Carlo I Tocco, Count of Cephalonia (an island in western Greece) and ruler of Epirus (in the southwestern Balkans, straddling modern Albania and Greece), had become disenchanted with the sultan and seemed like a promising escort.

Carlo I Tocco had been a vassal of Sultan Murad's father, and as part of his obligation had sent his five sons (all of them illegitimate) to be brought up at the Ottoman court. When Carlo died in July 1429, he willed most of his domains not to his natural offspring, but to his nephew Carlo II. Memnon and his brothers appealed to the young Sultan Murad, in whose entourage they had been raised, for help in gaining a bigger share of the inheritance. Murad, who had just taken Thessaloniki, used this plea as a pretext for conquering more of Greece—without sharing his spoils with Memnon and his siblings. Disgruntled, Memnon was more than receptive to Cyriacus's request for help. "After a thorough discussion of eastern affairs," he agreed to accompany the Anconitan on an undercover tour of the "principal cities and centers of Asia that were under Turkish domination."[5] Having spent many years among the Turks, he knew the Ottoman army, strategic centers, and powerful officials. And so, in his company, Cyriacus—merchant and antiquarian—began his third career as a spy.

The two men left Gallipoli some time at the beginning of 1431, sailed through the Hellespont to Asia, and made their way to Bursa—"a populous and very wealthy place embellished by remarkable ancient and modern buildings," Cyriacus recorded.[6] Formerly a Byzantine city, Bursa had been conquered and made a capital by the Ottomans in 1361. Later supplanted in that role by Adrianople, it remained a thriving commercial and cultural center, blessed with a lovely climate and setting. As Bertrandon de la Broquière described it,

> It is a very large city, situated at the foot of a high mountain called Olympia . . . From the mountain comes a river which passes through the city in several places. Because of this, the city seems even bigger than it is, for it is made up of villages separated by the river. The Lords of Turkey are buried here. There are very nice palaces, like hospitals. In three or four of these, meat and wine are distributed to those who want to take them in God's name . . . There are all sorts of silk materials for sale . . . , precious stones, a very large number of pearls at good prices, and cotton cloth, among other things too numerous to mention. Nearby is another bazaar . . . It is there that I saw Christians sold, men and women, in a very high hall. It was a pity to see.[7]

Pero Tafur commented on Bursa's strategic importance:

> The city is unwalled, but greater and better than any in
> Turkey . . . It is situated very close to Greece, and since the
> Turks have owned it they have much improved the place,
> for it is a stepping-stone for the Turks from Greece to their
> own country. They have placed great stores here, for they
> use the city as a half way port.[8]

Bursa served as the Ottoman political and economic hub in
western Anatolia, and an entrepôt for East–West trade where
merchants from Arabia, Iran, and Syria exchanged goods with
their counterparts from Italy, France, and Spain. Bursa was
especially famed as a silk market, and the cloth manufactur-
ers of Venice and Lucca depended on its offerings.[9] Cyriacus
used trade as his cover and did some business for Zaccaria,
perhaps buying porcelain, musk, gems, and silks. But, espionage being his real goal, he consigned most of his affairs
to the Genoese merchant Bibilano Pallavicini, and together
with Memnon surveyed the town. They also paid a visit to the
Turkish governor of the province and commander of sultan's
armies, Canuza Bey, a brave and energetic vizier prepared to
supply his lord with twenty thousand armed warriors at his
own expense.[10]

Cyriacus, having apparently chosen a conversation about
local Greek and Roman monuments as an ice-breaker, found
himself unexpectedly impressed by the governor's manner
and erudition: Canuza Bey must be a Greek by birth and education, he decided (he was, in fact, a Turk), for he was "able
knowledgeably to discuss . . . the antiquities of the province,

and especially the great temple of Cyzicus."[11] While snooping around Bursa's port, Cyriacus had spotted numerous ancient marble blocks built into modern structures. He asked the governor about their origin and was told that they had been brought from the ruins of the nearby Roman city of Cyzicus. Cyriacus pleaded with Canuza Bey to forbid further destruction of such monuments—out of reverence for antiquity and for the sake of the good reputation of the sultan. "Canuza Bey had the learning to appreciate this argument and readily promised to do what Cyriacus advised."[12] Cyriacus placed little trust in Turkish care for the classical past, but for now his conversation about antiquities with Canuza Bey and fervent advocacy on their behalf apparently defused the governor's suspicions about the merchant's motives in nosing around the province. Cyriacus was able to proceed unhindered to gather information on both the Turks and the ancients, his espionage leading him to one of his most important archaeological finds.

After his meeting with Canuza Bey, Cyriacus was burning to see Cyzicus in person. Hiring a Turkish guide, he hastened to the peninsula on the southern shore of the Sea of Marmara where the ancient town stood. The sight that greeted him was bittersweet: the place was deserted, but strewn with majestic ruins. Cyriacus followed a stretch of city walls and walked under their marble gates. He admired "a large statue of earth-shaking Neptune," marveled at a portion of aqueduct, and crisscrossed the picturesque amphitheater intersected by a stream probably used by the ancients to fill the arena with water for mock naval combats and to clean it between performances. Immensely excited and stirred by these remains,

Cyriacus recalled Ovid's verses, penned as the poet traveled in this region: "On this side Cyzicus, clinging to the shore of the Propontis: Cyzicus, noble creation of the people of Thrace."[13]

Cyzicus had, indeed, been splendid in its heyday, when it prospered thanks to its two harbors, which attracted almost all Propontic shipping; its coinage was one of the most widely used. The Roman geographer Strabo recorded in the first century AD that Cyzicus rivaled "the foremost of the cities in Asia in size, in beauty, and in its excellent administration of affairs both in peace and in war."[14] Unfortunately, the area was highly seismic and repeatedly rattled and damaged by powerful tremors. In 123 AD a major earthquake so devastated the city that when the emperor Hadrian visited it the following year, he was moved to pity and resolved to sponsor a reconstruction campaign. He made an especially large donation for a new temple to Jupiter. With generous imperial backing, the building went up remarkably fast, given its vast dimensions, and was completed by 139 AD. Hadrian's bust, placed in the center of the pediment, gazed benevolently at the grateful citizens of Cyzicus, who extolled the emperor as the thirteenth Olympian god.

The gigantic size and splendid sculptural decorations of the new temple made it one of the wonders of the ancient world. But over the centuries further earthquakes, as well as pillaging by various people in the area, reduced it to a ruin. Countless blocks had been carted off to build structures in Mudania and Bursa, and Emperor Justinian apparently plundered the site when constructing Hagia Sophia in Constantinople. Still, Cyriacus found awe-inspiring the towering remains of the superb temple of Jupiter with its lofty marble walls which still show the marks of the golden thread described by Pliny in his *Natural History*: "The temple at Cyzicus also survives, where the architect inserted a golden thread in all the joints of the polished stone, etc." Still remaining are various statues of gods on the highly ornamented facade of the temple and the very wide bases of long rows of columns; and although the majority of the original columns have fallen to the ground, thirty-three of them with their architrave are still standing.[15]

Cyriacus must have spent a whole day or more examining the shrine in every detail. He consulted ancient books—Pliny and Strabo—which he apparently carried in his bag, but relied chiefly on direct scrutiny of the blocks. He drew the monumental doorway adorned with carved foliage, and transcribed the Greek inscription above it: "From the level earth, with the wealth of the whole of Asia, and with countless hands, the god-like Aristainetos erected me." In another drawing he captured columns entwined with carved vines and between them a colossal visage of a gorgon, the averter of evil. He also sketched the mythological characters and scenes on the sculpted freeze above the columns, and various blocks scattered on the ground. Cyriacus's documentation of the temple was driven by both admiration and worry—reinforced by seeing so many of its blocks reused in Turkish buildings in Bursa—that it would not last much longer.[16] His sense of alarm about the future of this and other ancient treasures across the classical landscape would come to feed his enmity toward the Turks.

✦✦✦

Having completed his reconnoitering in the Ottoman lands, Cyriacus set out to tackle the second part of his mission: cajoling the Byzantines to join forces with the Latins against the Turks. It should have been a natural alliance, since the Byzantines had repeatedly lobbied various European rulers for help in saving their shrinking empire from complete Ottoman takeover. Yet two enormous obstacles stood in the way of their mutual agreement: religion and history.

For centuries the Roman Catholics and the Greek Orthodox had been divided by church politics and conflicting interpretations of dogma. Their biggest point of disagreement was the procession of the Holy Spirit. The Latins believed that it emanated from the Son as well as the Father, the Greeks that it proceeded from God the Father alone. Each side considered the other's views heretical. Their divergence on the nature of the pains of purgatory, the use of leavened versus unleavened bread in the Eucharist, and the precise moment when the Eucharistic wafer turns into the body of Christ drove them further apart. These religious differences were exacerbated by the Latin sack and devastation of Constantinople in 1204 and the subsequent colonization of Greek territories. As much as they desperately needed Western help against the Ottomans, especially in view of the recent conquest of formerly Greek lands, the Byzantines were not keen to see a fifth Crusade on their doorstep.

Cyriacus, with his customary audacity, endeavored to overcome the long history of conflict and distrust between the

Greeks and the Latins and to convince the Byzantine emperor, John VIII Palaeologus, to come to a rapprochement with the West. The first step would be for John and his religious leaders to come to Italy, to bridge the divide between the Greek Orthodox and the Roman Catholic churches. Then, united in spirit, the Greeks and the Latins would join forces in expelling the Ottomans from the Greek lands.

Cyriacus had some political skills from serving on Ancona's civic government, acting as lieutenant to the *podestà* during his sojourn on Cyprus, and enchanting King Janus while there. But the task he faced now was of a different magnitude. Undaunted by his inexperience and emboldened by his zeal, Cyriacus, probably with papal backing, donned the mantle of a diplomat and sought an audience with John VIII Palaeologus.

In his diary, Cyriacus discreetly noted only that he wanted to collect "all intelligence he could concerning a union with the Greeks and the whole Eastern Church."[17] But a contemporary Italian humanist and bishop of Padua, Iacopo Zeno, left rapturous praise of Cyriacus's intercession with the Byzantine emperor:

> What could be more useful, more noble and glorious to the Christian universe than that excellent single union of the Greeks and reintegration of universal faith with a just and sincere truth? To this, truly, you have brought great effort and diligence, and the achievement of this sacred and divine union seems to emanate for the greatest part from you. Having neglected all of your private affairs, you have set out for Greece to address the emperor with your

most persuasive speeches and have prevailed with most vehement persuasions.[18]

John VIII was Cyriacus's near contemporary, born a year after him, in 1392, in the Byzantine capital. He had received a humanistic education in the learned Constantinopolitan milieu, quoted Homer, consorted daily with Aristotle and Plato (in the words of an anonymous panegyrist), and was praised for his learning by Italian scholars.[19] Cyriacus could discuss with the Byzantine ruler their mutual love of antiquity and arouse his sympathy for the cause of preserving Greek and Roman heritage from the Ottomans. Like Cyriacus, John was also an idealist. His father, Manuel II, had remarked,

My son, the Emperor, seems to himself to be a suitable emperor—but not for the present day. For he has large views and ideas and such as the times demanded in the heyday of the prosperity of his ancestors. But nowadays, as things are going with us, our empire needs, not an emperor, but an administrator. I am afraid that the decline of this house may come from his poems and arguments . . .[20]

John was quite willing to listen and talk to Cyriacus. Unlike Manuel II, who kept the prospect of the union dangling before the West but never agreed to it so as not to subjugate the Greeks to the Latins again, John was keen for a rapprochement that might save what remained of his empire. Manuel had admonished John on his deathbed, "Propose a council; open negotiations, but protract them interminably . . . The pride of the Latins and the obstinacy of the Greeks will never agree. By wishing to achieve the union you will only strengthen the schism."[21] But John reasoned that he had no choice but to negotiate with the pope, or else lose his throne to the Turks. As he talked to Cyriacus in the imperial palace, seeing his surroundings through the eyes of his well-traveled visitor might have made him even more painfully aware of the dire need of the Byzantines for help. In the words of Pero Tafur, "The Emperor's palace must have been very magnificent but now it is in such a state that both it and the city show well the evils which the people have suffered and still endure."[22]

Yet, willing as John may have been to hold discussions with the Latins, there were plenty of powerful players in Constantinople who vehemently opposed dealing with the West.[23] The doctrinal difference made many Greeks view the Latins as schismatics, so for them union was out of the question. Some were willing to consider it, but only if talks were to take place in Constantinople. Patriarch Joseph, the head of the Greek church, argued that in the West the Greeks would be at the mercy of the Latins, all the more so because they did not have enough money to travel to Italy and would depend on the pope for subsistence. Cyriacus likely promised John, on Eugenius's behalf, to pay the Byzantine delegation's travel and living expenses if they were to come West.

Seven years would pass before the Byzantines would finally agree to attend a church council in Italy, and numerous ambassadors would shuttle back and forth across the Mediterranean in hopes of striking a deal. But it was Cyriacus who seems to have set the process in motion. And when the Byzantines would at last arrive in Italy, Cyriacus would be by the emperor's side, having won his trust and friendship on that visit to Constantinople.

❧

For now, in the autumn of 1431, having done all he could in the Ottoman lands and at the Byzantine court, Cyriacus was ready to sail home to present his findings to the pope. Casting around for a ship to take him to Italy, he found that his kinsman Pasqualino, with whom he had first come to Constantinople and who made regular trade voyages between Ancona and the Byzantine capital, would be heading back in a month. Too impatient to sit still and wait for departure, Cyriacus crossed the sea to Lesbos, another island ruled by the Genoese, to investigate its antiquities and probably to determine the attitude of its ruler toward the Crusade: would he side with the Europeans or the Turks? The lord of Lesbos, Dorino I, had married his daughters into Greek imperial families—one to the son of the emperor of Trebizond on the Black Sea, where the Genoese had major trade interests, another to the Byzantine emperor's brother Constantine. Yet, living just across a narrow straight from the Turks, Dorino also maintained amicable relations with the Ottoman sultan and paid him an annual tribute in return for peace. Touring the island with his nephew, Giorgio Gattilusio, Cyriacus must have made careful inquiries about the political leanings of the family. But that did not distract him from the ancient remains.

Lesbos had been in antiquity a major center of trade and communication, famed for its high standard of education and the relative freedom enjoyed by its women, the most renowned of them being the poet Sappho. Other notable intellectuals associated with the island included the native Terpander, the father of Greek music; Aristotle and Epicurus, who came to teach there; and Aristotle's pupil Theophrastus, a great popularizer of science, the author of over two hundred books, and an outspoken defender of animals—he opposed the eating of meat because, he said, it killed creatures who could feel and reason just as did humans. Theophrastus reputedly died at age 107, lamenting that life was too short and that he was just beginning to gain insight. Alas, few monuments survived from those glorious days. Cyriacus saw only remnants of a theater said to have been so beautiful as to inspire the first theater of Rome, a marble arch, a portion of aqueduct, and some columns, statues, and Greek and Latin inscriptions, which he lovingly recorded in his notebook.

Cyriacus departed from Lesbos with Gattilusio's letters of introduction to Turkish authorities, crossed the narrow strait to the Asiatic shore, and headed for Pergamon. Hiring a Turkish guide, he climbed up the steep road toward what used to be the most splendid metropolis of Asia Minor, perched on a mount rising 1,100 feet out of the plain of the Kaikos River. After gazing at a spectacular view of surrounding valleys and hills, Cyriacus turned to the vestiges of the ancient city. He was the first person to visit the site for the sake of its monuments in a millennium.

Pergamon had begun its rise to glory when, following the death of Alexander the Great, his general Lysimachos took possession of this natural citadel. Busy with wars, Lysimachos entrusted the stronghold and his treasury to his officer Philetairos. When Lysimachos fell in battle in 281 BC, Philetairos appropriated both the fortress and the money and initiated the construction of a handsome city. His heirs, the Attalids, continued what he had begun and turned Pergamon into the new cultural and scientific center of the Greek world. One of its major industries—the large-scale production of *pergamena*, the writing material made from treated animal skins (later called parchment)—allowed the Attalids to develop a library rivaling that of Alexandria.

The Attalids devised a theatrical layout for their city, spreading it on a series of terraces on the slope of the mount. While the residential neighborhoods clustered on the plain, public structures ascended upward from the plateau to the summit in a programmatic way. At the bottom stood the Agora, where commercial affairs were transacted. Above it rose several gymnasia, where boys learned reading, writing, mathematics, literature, music, and physical prowess, and listened to lectures by leading philosophers and orators. At the top of the hill perched the edifices dedicated to the gods and high culture: the great altar of Zeus adorned with high-relief carvings of serene Olympians defeating writhing giants, the temple of Athena with an adjacent library, and the theater from which one beheld a striking panorama of the plain below. The royal palace sprawled at the apex.[24]

The last Attalid king bequeathed Pergamon to the Romans, who added a second theater, an amphitheater for gladiatorial games, a stadium for chariot races, and a temple to the god of healing, Asklepios—all on the plain below the rather crowded mount. In the course of the Middle Ages the city passed through the hands of the Arabs, the Byzantines, the

Latin crusaders, and the Turks, and the once opulent buildings gradually crumbled to ruins. Yet even these remained striking. Cyriacus was entranced by the scale of the monuments: "vast temples, two great amphitheaters, a number of colossal marble statues of gods and famous men."[25]

After Pergamon Cyriacus headed back to Chios to meet up with Pasqualino and sail home. While waiting for him to arrive, he basked for a few days in Andreolo's company, recounted to his friend his archaeological discoveries, read the Greek manuscripts which he had sent from Thessaloniki, and packed his goods for the voyage, presumably including ancient coins, gems, and statues bought on his travels with an eye to making a profit from them at home. Cyriacus's slave Niccolino arrived from Gallipoli to help with the preparations and brought along the remainder of the wares and books purchased in Adrianople and intended for resale in Italy.

Greek codices were especially prized by Italians because they were so rare in Europe. Their reintroduction and translation into Latin expanded the horizons of available knowledge. Among the books which Cyriacus imported to Italy was Strabo's *Geography*—the most detailed, wide-ranging, and meaningful account of the known world then in existence. Strabo described the terrain and waters of different regions, their particular animals and plants, the history of the local inhabitants and the marvels of their cities. He argued that such data was valuable not only for its own sake, but for educating politicians and military commanders. Before Cyriacus found the *Geography* in Constantinople, it was unavailable in Italy. He sold the volume to Guarino da Verona, who translated it into Latin and made it accessible to Europeans for the first time. Guarino then assigned it to his aristocratic students—future rulers of the Gonzaga, Este, and Montefeltro families—so that they might learn from it how to govern wisely.[26]

A few days later Pasqualino's ship sailed into harbor. Cyriacus was about to load his possessions when the Genoese authorities forbade them to leave. Reports had come in that a large Venetian fleet was heading toward Chios, intent on taking the island. No one was permitted to sail west, lest they be intercepted by the Venetians and interrogated on the state of affairs in the Genoese colony.

It was another flare-up in the ongoing enmity between the two maritime states. Venice had just won a naval battle against Genoa off Portofino, on the Ligurian coast, and decided to sail east to finally seize Chios, which it had long coveted. The Venetian commanders were instructed by their government "either *de plano* and by agreement and treaty, or by force, or by any other means you find suitable, ensure and take all possible measures to secure the reduction of the land, castle, and island of Chios to the sway and unrestricted subjugation of our lord [the doge]."[27] The leaders of the expeditions were also ordered to dispatch an envoy to Sultan Murad with assurances that the Venetian rulers of Chios would continue to pay him tribute just as the Genoese had done.

As soon as the Genoese heard of the impending Venetian attack, they contacted Murad and asked him to give them men and food for the defense of Chios. They also readied what supplies and forces they had on hand. Meanwhile, Pasqualino's ship languished in the harbor. Cyriacus, impatient to reach Rome and to get the Crusade under way, begged Andreolo to plead with his government to give them leave. He had vital intelligence for the pope and could not wait for the Venetian arrival and siege. Andreolo took Cyriacus's case to the island's authorities. After several days of negotiations, the Anconitans were permitted to depart.

Pasqualino, his passengers, and crew must have sailed anxiously toward Italy, apprehensive about running into the Venetian fleet. In the harbor of Corfu, they did. They were traveling with papers issued by the Genoese, risking capture by the Venetians, who could well have taken them prisoner as collaborators of the enemy. Cyriacus and Pasqualino presented themselves before the Venetian commander of the expedition, Andrea Mocenigo. He peered at their documents, asked several questions, and cleared them to proceed.

Tivoli as depicted by Piranesi in Giovanni Battista Piranesi,
Vedute di Roma, *Rome: G. Piranesi, 1761–1793, vol. 12, pl. 2.*
(Research Library, The Getty Research Institute, Los Angeles, CA)

*He was magnanimous, but without moderation; his actions
were guided by his desires rather than by his powers.*
—Aeneas Sylvius Piccolomini on Pope Eugenius IV[1]

Poised and Thwarted

CYRIACUS SPENT ONLY a few days in Ancona, settling his
business affairs and visiting with his family, before has-
tening to Rome. He traveled there in early 1432 in the entourage of Astorgio, the bishop of Ancona—a faster, safer, and
more comfortable journey than if he had gone alone, and an
opportunity to begin enlisting support for his cause in Italy.

He found Rome little changed since his last visit. It
remained a crumbling, dirty, medieval town in which the
destruction of the past continued unabated.[2] Roman officials
went on selling the right to remove stones from ancient buildings to lime-burners and marble merchants, who immured
priceless blocks in new structures or turned them into cannonballs. The popes themselves authorized the despoliation for
the sake of their projects. Pope Martin V granted permission
to Antonio Picardi and Nicolao Bellini to procure blocks from
Roman ruins for the repaving of the Lateran, and Eugenius IV
authorized scavenging for colored marbles from ancient structures for the new altar he was building at St. Peter's.[3] Cyriacus

*Cannonballs made out of ancient marble blocks in the courtyard
of Castel Sant'Angelo, Rome. (Kenneth Lapatin)*

would have agreed with Manuel Chrysoloras, who described
eloquently what was being lost. "Like our own city [Constanti-
nople]," Chrysoloras had written in 1411,

> Rome uses itself as a mine and quarry, and it both nour-
> ishes and consumes itself . . . Nonetheless, even these
> ruins and heaps of stones show what great things once
> existed, and how enormous and beautiful were the origi-
> nal constructions . . . These remains of statues, columns,
> tombs, and buildings reveal not only the wealth, large
> labor force, and craftsmanship of the Romans as well as
> their grandeur and dignity . . . , and their ambition, love
> of beauty, luxury and extravagance, but also their piety,

greatness of soul, love of honor, and intelligence . . . They speak of Rome's victories, her general well-being, dominion, dignity, and deeds of war . . . Thus one can see clearly what kinds of arms the Ancients had, what kind of clothes they wore, what the devices of their rulers were, how they formed lines of battle, fought, laid siege, and built encampments . . . Herodotus, and some other historians, are thought to have made useful contributions to our knowledge of such things. But these reliefs show how things were in past times and what the differences were between the peoples. Thus they make our knowledge of history precise or, rather, they grant us eyewitness knowledge of everything that has happened just as if it were present.[4]

Cyriacus had hoped that Eugenius IV would sympathize with his own, similar arguments about why it was crucial to preserve the testimony of ancient monuments both in Italy and in the territories threatened by the Turks. After all, the new pope had initiated a series of steps to preserve Rome's heritage and to improve its condition: he renovated the Lateran Palace and Castel Sant'Angelo, refurbished the city walls, bridges, and churches, and paved many streets. He also ordered the removal of wooden shanties and other accretions around the Pantheon.

Constructed in the 20s BC by Augustus's lieutenant and son-in-law Agrippa, and rebuilt by Emperor Hadrian around 125 AD, the Pantheon survived despoliation because it had been converted into a church, dedicated to the Virgin of the Martyrs. But the piazza before it, and its porch, became inundated with unsightly stalls hawking tripe and olives, wine and games of chance. The priests of the church profited from this market and were happy to keep it there; the municipal magistrates in charge of the city's streets sought to clear away the blight and appealed to the pope for support.[5] Eugenius's secretary, the humanist Flavio Biondo, praised the pontiff's efforts:

> By your intervention, O Pope Eugenius, and at your expense, the Pantheon's stupendous vault, torn in antiquity by earthquakes and threatened with ruin, was restored . . . That splendid church, clearly superior to all others, had had the lofty columns that support it hidden, for many centuries, by the nasty little shops that surrounded it. These have now been completely cleaned off, and their bases and capitals, laid bare, reveal the beauty of this wonderful building.[6]

Eugenius also threatened with severe penalties those caught extracting masonry from the Colosseum and other ancient structures. But his decrees were far from consistent. In October 1431 a marble merchant named Filippo di Giovanni di Pisa was granted a license to excavate and deliver to the apostolic palace blocks from the Forum of Caesar; nor was he the only one permitted such quarrying.

As soon as Cyriacus arrived in Rome, he requested an audience with Eugenius and was instructed to appear at the appointed time in the nave of St. Peter's. It was not the most dignified setting. The basilica, constructed by Constantine around 324, was more than a thousand years old, dilapidated, and collapsing. Pero Tafur wrote that "The church of St. Peter is a notable church, the entrance is very magnificent, and one ascends to it by very high steps. The roof is richly worked in mosaic. Inside, the church is large, but very poor and in bad condition and dirty, and in many places in ruins."[7] Still, Cyriacus was glad to be there.

The pope welcomed his old acquaintance like a son. Cyriacus reciprocated by presenting him with a rare gift: a pair of beautiful Indian porcelain ewers decorated with gold, which he must have bought in Damascus or Bursa. Alas, the offering was probably wasted on Eugenius. Unlike so many occupants of his office, he did not care for luxuries. "Spare, grave, and reverend in appearance, . . . the air of devotion which hung around him was such that few who looked on him could retain their tears," wrote the pope's biographer, Vespasiano.[8] Born into a rich family, Gabriele Condulmaro had given away all his inheritance to the poor when still a young man and entered a monastery. As a pontiff, he drank no wine, only water with sugar and a touch of cinnamon. He ate very moderately, and spent much of his money on alms, "being always in debt, because he saved nothing." He did not hoard treasures, and likely gave away Cyriacus's vases before long. Still, one could not come to the pope empty-handed. And if the vases could not sway Eugenius to heed Cyriacus's words, the Anconitan had a more persuasive gift for him—the intelligence he had gathered in the East.

Having dispensed with the initial greetings and pleasantries, Cyriacus "clearly and fully put forward his views, both verbally and in a written memoranda, concerning the fostering of union with the Greeks, an effective expedition against the Turks, and the payment due to Memnon for his part in this important work."[9] Cyriacus must have related to Eugenius everything he had learned about Murad II's character and forces, John VIII's favorable disposition toward the union, and the opposition of Byzantine religious leaders. He may have described the dilapidated state of Constantinople and the imperial palace, and the poverty of the Byzantines, who could not come to Italy for negotiations without a subsidy. At the end of his presentation Cyriacus asked Eugenius to send him on another diplomatic mission to the Levant—so that he could further prepare for the Crusade and continue his antiquarian studies.

Eugenius listened carefully to Cyriacus's report, asked questions, and promised to address these matters—in due course. "In due course" was not the answer Cyriacus had hoped to hear. It sounded like an indefinitely long delay.

When he was still a monk, Gabriele Condulmaro had received a prophesy from a hermit who appeared at his monastery one day: "You will be made Cardinal and afterwards Pope, and during your pontificate you will know much trouble."[10] Shortly after ascending to the papal throne, Eugenius became embroiled in a triple conflict. The Council of Basel sought to depose him, as did the Roman people, and the Duke of Milan invaded his domains. Little wonder Eugenius was not rushing into a war against the distant Ottomans.

Eugenius's nemesis, the Council of Basel, grew out of the earlier Council of Constance, which had ended the Great Schism within the Catholic Church. The schism had so severely compromised papal dignity that a general council of top ecclesiastical officials emerged as a more venerable authority, better able to deal with problems bedeviling the church. At the end of the Council of Constance, its participants agreed that another council should meet in five years to address whatever issues would then require resolution, a further one must take place seven years later, and after that a council ought to meet every ten years. Complying with this decision, Pope Martin V convoked the Council of Basel shortly before his death in 1431. On its agenda was the establishment of peace between warring European nations, the reunion of the Western and Eastern Churches, and the settlement of the hostilities in Bohemia with the proto–Protestant Hussites, who threatened the whole ecclesiastical establishment.

What preoccupied the Council of Basel even more than these political and religious troubles, though, was its fight over supremacy with the papacy. The Council of Constance had proclaimed that a general church council held ultimate authority directly from Christ, and that all Christians, including the pope, were subject to it. Eugenius IV retorted that this applied only during exceptional situations, such as the existence of rival popes, or a pope's sudden lapse into heresy; otherwise the highest power over the church rested with the papacy. Eugenius tried to dissolve the Council of Basel shortly after his election, but it refused to budge and for the next two decades went on to feud with him and attempt to depose him.[11] In the course of this conflict, the council would try to persuade the Byzantines to come to Basel for church union talks, to be held under its, rather than Eugenius's, auspices.[12] The competing conciliar and papal delegations in Constantinople (dispatched following Cyriacus's initial efforts to negotiate with the Byzantines) would nearly come to blows and have to be restrained by imperial intervention as they struggled to elbow each other out of the way before John VIII—or so reported the Greek historian Syropoulos in 1438–9. The rival parties would also clash on this issue in Basel, creating such a racket that, in the word of Aeneas Silvius Piccolomini, the future Pope Pius II, "You would have found the drunkards of a tavern better behaved."[13]

Yet the Council of Basel was only part of Eugenius's troubles. He also faced the invasion of the Papal States by the *condottiere* Niccolò Fortebraccio, commanding the troops of Filippo Maria Visconti, Duke of Milan—in retaliation for the pope's siding with Florence and Venice against Milan in the ongoing war between Milan and Venice over the control of northern Italy. Nor did Eugenius enjoy respite in Rome, where he was opposed by the powerful Colonna clan. Pope Martin V, who was a Colonna, had distributed numerous posts, castles, and lands to his kinsmen during his tenure. Eugenius tried to curb the Colonna family's power. Naturally they fought back, and the people of Rome sided with their aristocratic neighbors and patrons, so a civil war threatened the pope scarcely a month after his coronation. Eventually he would be forced out of the city into a ten-year exile.[14]

Given all these troubles, the besieged Holy Father was, understandably, not keen to take on yet another war, though he favored the idea of the Crusade in general.

Cyriacus must have been frustrated to discover that the impediments to the Crusade appeared to be greater at home than in the East, and that the pope seemed harder to move than the Byzantine emperor. But there was no hurrying or pressing the Vicar of Christ. So, curbing his impatience and trying to occupy his time productively while Eugenius deliberated, Cyriacus decided to explore antiquities in the vicinity of Rome which he had not seen on his previous trip. He was not the first person to spend a long wait for a papal answer in this way. Manuel Chrysoloras, who had returned to Italy in 1411 to ask the pope for help for the beleaguered Constantinople, had likewise busied himself with ancient monuments while awaiting an answer. As he wrote in a letter home,

> Can you believe of me that I am wandering about this city of Rome, swiveling my eyes this way and that like some boorish gallant, clambering up palace walls, even up to their windows, on the chance of seeing something of the beauties inside? I never used to do this sort of thing when I was young, as you know, and had a poor opinion of those who did. Yet here I am, getting on in years, and I scarcely know how I have been brought to this point. I suppose I am reading you a riddle. Hear, then, its answer.
>
> I do this in the hope of finding in these places beauty not in living bodies but in stones, marbles and images . . .[15]

Cyriacus went to seek ancient beauty in Tivoli and Ostia.

He seems to have been invited on a trip to Tivoli by a friend of Eugenius's, the powerful Cardinal Giordano Orsini. Giordano came from one of the most ancient and distinguished families in Rome—rivals to the Colonna—many of whose members made brilliant careers in the church. He had served as archbishop of Naples, became a cardinal in 1405, went as a papal legate to France and England in 1418 to try to establish peace between those two warring countries, and to Bohemia, Hungary, and Germany in 1426 to combat the Hussite heresy. Now Giordano was applying his energy and political savvy to upholding papal rights before the Council of Basel.

Besides being a gifted diplomat, Giordano was also a man of high culture. He had assembled a library of some 250 manuscripts, chiefly ancient authors, and gathered around him leading humanists—Leonardo Bruni, Poggio Bracciolini, Lorenzo Valla, and others—who met regularly at his palace, and, donning antique robes, discoursed on lofty topics such as what constituted proper human conduct within pagan and Christian frameworks.[16] Cyriacus must have been enormously flattered by Giordano's interest in him. His archaeological discoveries in the East seemed to be opening doors to elite circles to which he could hardly have aspired with his modest education and amateurish command of ancient tongues. Yet Cyriacus possessed something Giordano and his erudite entourage lacked—firsthand knowledge of the monuments of Greece and Asia Minor and access to ancient books and artifacts to be found there.

Leaving Rome by Porta Tiburtina (near the modern Termini train station), Cyriacus and Giordano followed Via Tiburtina eastward for some seventeen miles across the undulating Roman countryside, spotting here and there "many evidences of the ancient world," such as the Roman bridge of Lucanus and the towerlike tomb of Marcus Plautius. Tivoli itself appeared before them as a beguiling sight. Spreading on the lower slopes of the Sabine Hills at the end of the valley of the Aniene, the chief tributary of the Tiber, it nestled in the bend of the river and overlooked Campania. Small wonder that prosperous ancient Romans, men such as the emperor Augustus and the poet Catullus, built their villas here. But the most extraordinary of these countryside estates was created in the second century AD by the emperor Hadrian.

The grounds of Hadrian's Villa sprawled over some three hundred acres—twice the size of Pompeii. Across the rolling terrain framed by surrounding hills, Hadrian had erected some sixty structures adorned with statues, paintings, mosaics, and stucco reliefs. There was an extensive imperial residence, baths and theaters, scenic fountains and pools, a stadium, a library, a Doric temple, several banquet halls, belvederes, and buildings inspired by monuments he had admired during his many travels.[17]

Tall, powerfully built, with brilliant gray eyes, a long straight nose, and a beard modeled on the Greek heroes and philosophers, Hadrian cut an impressive figure. According to the Roman historian Dio Cassius, he was a pleasant man who possessed a certain charm and many interests: from early on he devoted himself to Greek studies, earning the nickname Graeculus ("little Greek"); he played lyre and flute, and sang; composed poetry and prose; knew architecture, mathematics, and military science; and loved to debate with philosophers. In peace as in war he preferred to be hands-on, to the point of being meddlesome. Traveling around various Roman provinces, Hadrian inspected garrisons and forts, examined weapons, engines, and ramparts, inquired into the private affairs of soldiers and officers and corrected their behavior. He expected them to follow his lead: even as an emperor, he walked or rode everywhere rather than being ferried about in chariots, and "covered his head neither in hot weather nor in cold, but alike amid German snows and under scorching Egyptian sun he went about with his head bare," wrote Dio Cassius. By his example and force of personality Hadrian trained such a disciplined military throughout the whole empire that it "explains why he lived for the most part at peace with foreign nations; for as they saw his state of preparation and were themselves not only free from aggression but received money besides, they made no uprising."[18] Hadrian "aided the allied and subject cities most munificently," Dio Cassius continued. "He had seen many of them,—more, in fact, than any other emperor— and he assisted practically all of them, giving to some a water supply, to others harbors, food, public works, money and various honors."[19] Cyriacus had seen the effects of Hadrian's generosity at Cyzicus and in Rome, where, in addition to erecting his colossal mausoleum, renamed in the Middle Ages Castel Sant'Angelo, Hadrian completely rebuilt the Pantheon after it had burned down twice.

Cyriacus would have found much in common with the intensely curious emperor. Hadrian keenly studied both natural features and man-made creations. "So fond was he of travel," wrote an anonymous biographer, "that he wished to inform himself in person about all that he had read concerning all parts of the world."[20] Having spent a great deal of time in Greece and Asia Minor, Hadrian, like Cyriacus, became captivated by the region's past. On the grounds of his villa he re-created the Vale of Tempe, a picturesque gorge in northern Thessaly carved by the Pineios River and framed by high cliffs—celebrated by the Greek poets as the favorite haunt of Apollo and the Muses. A lover of Greek learning, he also reproduced a number of the famous educational institutions of Athens, including the Lyceum and the Academy.

Cyriacus and Giordano must have felt at once elated and thwarted as they explored Hadrian's personal paradise. Time and generations of stone-hunters had turned the villa into a tattered web of stone, brick, and vegetation. As early as the 320s, Constantine had carted off blocks and sculptures from the estate to beautify his new capital in Byzantium. In the Middle Ages the site was regularly plundered for masonry and lime. The despoliation intensified in the Renaissance, as humanists and princes came looking for statues, columns, and inscriptions. Cyriacus and Giordano were pioneers in visiting Tivoli to hunt, not for souvenirs or building materials, but for knowledge of the past. Alas, all Cyriacus could see of Hadrian's kindred delight in discovering and bringing home the magic of foreign lands were picturesque ruins, evocatively described by Pope Pius II in 1461:

> About three miles from Tivoli the Emperor Hadrian built a magnificent Villa like a big town. Lofty vaults of great temples still stand and the half-ruined structures of halls and chambers are to be seen. There are also remains of peristyles and huge columned porticoes and swimming pools and baths . . . Time has marred everything. The walls once covered with embroidered tapestries and hangings threaded with gold are now clothed with ivy. Briars

and brambles have sprung up where purple-robed tribunes sat, and queens' chambers are the lairs of serpents.[21]

In the seventeenth century the architect Francesco Contini noted that "the majority of the ruins were so covered by earth and debris that their foundations could not be made out; indeed, most of the ruins were overgrown by dense and thorny thickets."[22] Still, what peeked out of the wild flora was impressive: massive brick walls rose high above the visitors' heads; broken vaults invoked the elegance of Hadrian's halls and bathing complexes; faded and half-peeled frescoes and exposed bits of mosaic floors suggested the visual richness of the villa's interiors; crumbled fountains and grottoes seemed to echo faintly with tinkling water.

Returning to Rome, Cyriacus inquired and still received no answer from the pope, who had a tendency to be both vacillating and obstinate. So he set out on another excursion—this time without Giordano—to Ostia, the once thriving commercial port of ancient Rome.

Whatever he may have expected, the town he arrived at was a desolate place. Even its medieval buildings were falling into pieces. As Pius II described it shortly thereafter,

The older and more extensive city walls long ago fell in ruins and the circuit was narrowed to enclose only the cathedral church and a few dwelling houses, some of which were built directly on the aqueduct itself . . . The church, which must have been of some distinction, has been destroyed by age or violence. Only the upper part with the high altar still stands . . . The other buildings in Ostia lie in ruins. The Episcopal palace was roofed over and partially repaired by Eugenius's chamberlain, Lodovico, but there is no other habitable building except a sort of public tavern and a high, round tower built by Martin V to guard the place, that the harbor dues might not be evaded, and to serve as a watchtower to prevent an enemy making a surprise landing . . . Such today is Ostia whose fame was great in antiquity. Only a few fishermen from Dalmatia and the guards of the tower live there.[23]

Yet Cyriacus was happy to explore even the most disintegrated ruins, and spent a day or more poking around the old Roman site. He was among the first to do so in the Renaissance.

Ostia began as a small fort guarding the coastline and entrance to the Tiber (*ostium* means "mouth"—in this case, the mouth of the river). As Rome grew in size and population and came to rely more and more on products from abroad, especially grain, Ostia developed into its harbor, receiving and shipping all of its overseas imports and exports. During the war with Carthage, it also became a naval base. The city reached its peak of prosperity in the first half of the second century AD, when Roman elites built coastal villas in the area and Ostia's population swelled to some 50,000 people. Imposing buildings, long porticoes lining major avenues, colored marbles adorning the seventeen bathing complexes all proclaimed Ostia's wealth.

Even its public latrines were large, comfortable, warm, and well decorated, serving not only hygienic but also social needs. As the poet Martial joked in one of his epigrams,

> *Why does Vacerra spend his hours*
> *In all the privies, and day-long sit?*
> *He wants a supper, not a shit.*[24]

Cyriacus could see only a faint trace of this affluence in the ruined porticoes where ancient Ostians used to hide from the midday sun, fragments of statues that commemorated emperors and notable citizens, crumbled walls of temples where locals prayed for the continued wealth of their families and town, and civic structures where they assembled for public debates and legal proceedings. He gazed at the vestiges of Ostia's residential blocks, erected in response to the population growth, and probably tried to imagine the lives of the people inside. These *insulae* originally rose up to five stories high and had shops on the ground floor and apartments of various sizes above. Some were small and modest, others quite luxurious, with painted walls, mosaic floors, large reception and dining rooms, and private toilets. Life in such semi-communal settings, even in the better apartments, was not always restful, as Seneca vividly recounted in one of his *Epistles*. A certain Pedo Albinovanus, occupying an apartment above Sextus Papinius, was tormented by his neighbor's nighttime routine. "About nine o'clock at night I hear the sound of whips," complained Pedo. "I ask what is going on, and they tell me that Papinius is going over his accounts" (and punishing his slaves for the errors he noticed in their day's work).

About twelve there is a strenuous shouting; I ask what the matter is, and they say he is exercising his voice. About two a.m. I ask the significance of the sound of the wheels; they tell me that he is off for a drive. And at dawn there is a tremendous flurry—calling of slaves and butlers, and pandemonium among the cooks. I ask the meaning of this also, and they tell me that he has called for his cordial and his appetizer, after leaving the bath.[25]

The noise and conflicting schedules of neighbors was, apparently, a millennium-old problem, and one Cyriacus was familiar with from his experiences on both land and sea.[26]

Ostia started to decline under Constantine the Great, who favored the settlement around Portus—a large artificial harbor two miles to the north, which Cyriacus also explored. It was begun by Claudius and completed by Trajan to accommodate merchant vessels too large for Ostia's port.[27] In the Middle Ages and the Renaissance, Ostia turned into a quarry for people up and down the coast. The Pisans raided it for stone for their cathedral, so did the inhabitants of Amalfi and Orvieto; the Florentines built Ostian blocks into their baptistery, and from the fifteenth century onward the town was systematically exploited for new construction in Rome and looted by connoisseurs of ancient artifacts. When Poggio Bracciolini came to look around with Cosimo de' Medici in 1427, he was disappointed at not finding inscriptions in the Capitolium.

Cyriacus, having grown up in a port town, one likewise created by the Romans, could probably visualize what Ostia once looked and felt like better than many other antiquarians. He was especially impressed by the great shipyard at Portus built by Trajan, the man who had also made Ancona into a thriving maritime city.

❦

Back in Rome, there was still no reply from the pope. Talks with the Byzantines were dragging on unproductively, and Eugenius's struggle with the Council of Basel continued to claim his attention. Time was ticking away, both for the monuments and for Cyriacus. He was forty-one years old now, and given the average life expectancy of about forty years, how much longer did he have? Seeing his impatience, Eugenius decided to dispatch the Anconitan on a diplomatic assignment that would serve them both.[28]

King Sigismund of Hungary had recently arrived on the peninsula to be crowned Holy Roman Emperor. Theoretically, he shared the highest authority with the pope, being the supreme temporal ruler of Christendom, while the pontiff was its spiritual head. In reality, the emperor's power was fairly limited, for although he superseded other rulers in status, he reigned only over parts of Germany and eastern Europe. To come into full possession of his lofty office, he had to be crowned by the pope—which is why Sigismund was in Italy, biding his time in Siena while his ambassadors negotiated with Eugenius. At issue was not just the logistics of the upcoming ceremony, but a more delicate matter. Sigismund was closely involved with the Council of Basel, and Eugenius wanted him to back papal prerogatives before that assembly. The emperor needed to find a way to uphold the council's work without compromising his coronation.[29]

Sigismund was both a thinker and a warrior. He spoke several languages, admired erudition, and loved to debate ideas, though he could be quite strong-headed. On one occasion, during the Council of Constance, a cardinal dared to correct his Latin, to which the king replied, "I am the king of the Romans, and am superior to rules of grammar," which earned him the nickname Super-Grammaticus. He doubtless found Cyriacus's stories of his archaeological investigations around the Mediterranean fascinating. And having personally led troops into battle against the Ottomans, he must have listened with interest to Cyriacus's reports on the enemy.

In 1396 Sigismund had fought the Turks at the battle of Nicopolis, on the lower Danube—to disastrous results. Sultan Bayezid routed the European army, captured scores of prisoners, and executed so many of them—sparing only those under twenty, who could be sold into slavery, and the rich ones, who could be handsomely ransomed—that "blood spilled from morning until vespers."[30] Sigismund escaped and shifted his attention to another major disruption of European peace— the Great Schism. He called for the Council of Constance and played a crucial role in the election of a single pope. Now, at the Council of Basel, he pressed for church reforms and the suppression of the Hussites, who wreaked havoc in his lands. But he still dreamed of a Crusade and hoped that by resolving the political and religious conflicts dividing Christians, he could pave the way for a new effort against the infidel.

Cyriacus wasted no time in courting this powerful ally to his cause. He presented Sigismund with "many cogent arguments as to the deeds to be done only by an emperor of his sovereign authority, dignity, and worth, particularly with regard to a crusade to repel the barbarians."[31] To incite Sigismund to action, he offered him a gold coin of the emperor Trajan, who had expanded the borders of the Roman Empire to their greatest extent. Cyriacus, a proponent of universal monarchy—an idea he first embraced while learning Latin through Virgil, knew that the coin was a triply meaningful gift. Not only was it a valuable ancient artifact well suited to its learned recipient, but it provided a flattering comparison between Trajan and Sigismund, and presented the man about to receive his own imperial crown with a Roman exemplar to imitate. The gesture also echoed a similar offering made to Sigismund's father by the illustrious Petrarch: in 1354, when Charles IV was on his way to be crowned emperor in Rome, the great poet had presented him with gold and silver coins of Augustus.

An ancient artifact was an astute gift in any case. Antiquity, whether in literary or material form, was becoming not only a prestigious intellectual pastime but a valuable political commodity, as individuals and states competed to claim superior virtues by linking themselves to glorious predecessors. Cyriacus clearly made a favorable impression on Sigismund with his gift, his arguments, and his congenial personality, for "the generous prince . . . magnanimously admitted Ciriaco into the circle of his imperial court."[32]

Cyriacus remained in Sigismund's suite until the coronation and beyond. He must have witnessed the king's solemn entry into Rome on May 21, 1433, greeted by a multitude of people who jammed the streets to gawk at the distinguished visitor and his splendid reception. It was, indeed, a marvelous sight. The procession opened with a party of Roman citizens and ambassadors of foreign rulers, including the Byzantines (a small delegation which must have come to Italy as part of negotiations over the union of the church), who caught everyone's eyes with their long robes, tall hats, and uncut hair and beards. A crowd of trumpet players and flutists marched behind them, filling the air with festive sounds. Then came boys representing the thirteen districts of Rome, their colorful clothes and silk flags adding color to the spectacle. After them proceeded the magistrates of the city, dressed in golden robes fashioned after those of the ancients. A long line of people on foot followed, some carrying olive branches, others Roman-style torches, such as were borne before the emperors on ancient reliefs. Cyriacus recorded in his diary that he had influenced the pope in making arrangements for the official reception of the emperor, so he may well have suggested these ancient elements, which he had seen on Roman triumphal arches and columns. Sigismund himself rode on a white horse, under a gold canopy carried by noblemen on gilded poles. His expression kind and his beard white and thick, he looked at once affable and majestic, projecting an aura of benevolent authority. Arriving at St. Peter's, he was received by Eugenius who awaited him in front of the church. Loud cheers and applause filled the air as the two men exchanged greetings and entered the basilica to hear the solemn Mass.[33]

Cyriacus likely participated as one of the king's honorary courtiers in the coronation itself, which took place ten days later. He would have seen Sigismund enter St. Peter's, solemnly approach the high altar, and be anointed with the sacred oil by the Bishop of Ostia. The king was then ceremonially kissed by Eugenius, who placed on his head a white miter topped by a golden crown and handed him a golden orb, scepter, and a naked sword, symbolizing that he was now a soldier of Christ, ready to take up arms to defend the church and the Christian faith—as the newly minted emperor was already keen to do. After the ceremony, the pope and the emperor mounted their horses and rode together toward the Bridge of Hadrian. At Castel Sant'Angelo, Eugenius turned homeward, while Sigismund continued on to the Basilica of the Lateran amid the applause of the rejoicing populace.[34]

Sigismund stayed in Rome through the summer and Cyriacus personally toured him around the ancient sights, using this as another opportunity to lobby the emperor. Pointing out the "mighty ruins everywhere thrown to the ground," Cyriacus begged him to act for the sake of antiquities:

> troubled by the terrible destruction and inspired by the divine presence of the Latins, he [Cyriacus] stirred the emperor's heart with these words: "I was sure you would be deeply shocked by the way the marble of these huge and elegant buildings throughout the city, these fine statues and columns, which the ancients erected so nobly at such cost, and with such craftsmanship and architectural skill, and these important historical inscriptions, are continually being burned up into lime by the present inhabitants of the city in so lazy, barbarous, and indecent a fashion, that there will very soon be nothing left of them for posterity to see. What a crime! . . . For these are the shining witnesses the ancients left behind them and they possess particular power to fire the minds of noble men to the greatest deeds and to the pursuit of undying glory."[35]

Moved by these sights and by Cyriacus's impassioned pleading, Sigismund applauded his concern to preserve such vestiges everywhere. But when Cyriacus begged him to press Eugenius for a quicker rapprochement with the Byzantines and a proclamation of the Crusade, the emperor proved as discouraging as the pope. "The emperor replied that he and the pope were thoroughly agreed on their plan but felt that their first task was to get the dangerous council of Basel dissolved."[36]

So Cyriacus was still in the same place he had been for a year and a half: seemingly poised on the threshold of a Crusade and thwarted by those whom he had considered to be his greatest allies. He had been working on and off in Ancona during that time, but yearning to leave behind his mercantile career and engage in diplomacy on behalf of the pope. Now he set out on an extended journey around Italy to enlist support for his cause elsewhere, to offer his inventory of artifacts to collectors, and to look for more antiquities. Notebook in hand and stylus at the ready, he hunted for carved and inscribed blocks—standing alone, built into city walls, tucked away in churches—in Pisa and Parma, Milan and Verona, Bologna, Genoa, and Mantua (the birthplace of Virgil). But his most important destination was Florence, the home of Cosimo de' Medici whose help he hoped to obtain, and the hub of humanism and the revival of antiquity. It would provide a real gauge of what he had achieved so far.

*Brunelleschi's dome for Florence cathedral, from Adolfo Venturi,
ed.,* Architetti dal XV al XVII secolo. Filippo Brunelleschi,
Rome: Biblioteca d'arte illustrata, 1923.

I used both to marvel and to regret that so many excellent and divine arts and sciences, which we know from their works and from historical accounts were possessed in great abundance by the talented men of antiquity, have now disappeared and are almost entirely lost . . . But after I came back here [to Florence] . . . I recognized in many, but above all in you, Filippo [Brunelleschi], and in our great friend the sculptor Donatello and in others, Nencio [Ghiberti], Luca [della Robbia] and Masaccio, a genius for every laudable enterprise in no way inferior to the ancients.

—Leon Battista Alberti, *On Painting*[1]

The Measure of a Man

E AGER AS HE WAS to meet the men who were unearthing ancient texts from centuries of obscurity and bringing ancient arts back to life, Cyriacus must have wondered how he would be received in the city famous for its learning. For Florence was not only rich in antiquarian expertise, but notorious for snobbish and fractious scholars and artists ready to take down their rivals. When Manuel Chrysoloras arrived there to teach Greek in 1397, he signed a five-year contract, but he left after only three years, reputedly driven out by the jealousy of Niccolò Niccoli, one of the city's most prominent humanists.

Three scholars who succeeded Chrysoloras in his post, having been inspired to learn Greek by him, likewise discovered the Florentine milieu to be less than humane.

Guarino da Verona, an artisan's son whose mother insisted that he get a Latin education, had met Chrysoloras in Venice just as the Byzantine scholar was heading home and followed him to Constantinople to study under his tutelage. Having mastered Greek and assembled a library of Greek manuscripts, Guarino came back to Italy in 1408 and taught in Florence from 1411 to 1414. He possessed a mastery of Greek and Latin, a wonderful memory, indefatigable industry, and a pleasant disposition. But his Florentine colleagues made his life miserable:

> There was no day in Florence when I wasn't tormented by insults, arguments, and petty quarrels. There exists in this circle such wicked madness, such avarice for glory . . . that in order to get it people have no regard for the reputations of others. No one gives praise except with blunted and slighting phrases . . . they resent those who receive praise, and carp at those who give praise. There is animosity among themselves and hatred for outsiders. Rather than friendships, there are political alliances.[2]

Such was also the experience of Guarino's friend Giovanni Aurispa. Born in 1369 in Noto, Sicily, Aurispa likewise had journeyed to Constantinople to study ancient Greek and to search for old books. Returning to Italy in 1423, he was hired as a professor of Greek by the University of Bologna, before moving to assume the same job in Florence. It did not take him long to experience the nastiness of local humanists. Writing to Guarino, Aurispa complained:

> I thought that when I'd left the vicious jockeying for status among the Greeks and their royalty [in Constantinople] I'd be safe and no one would attack me, if I kept to myself; but quite the opposite is true. For I used to find peace and quiet sometimes even at the palaces of royalty there . . . but here feuding and intriguing go on everywhere; I can find no peace of mind at all. The whole place is full of hostility and petty jealousies; here all the literati, all the elite are engaged in backbiting, and there is paranoia everywhere.[3]

Aurispa was glad to obtain a post as a secretary to Eugenius IV and to retain it under the next pope, Nicholas V, a great patron of classical learning. The pontiffs seemed easier to get along with than the Florentine humanists.

Francesco Filelfo fared even worse. Born in 1398 in Tolentino, in the Marches, he was a dear friend of Cyriacus and something of his mentor. Filelfo had been a prodigy. Having mastered Latin grammar, rhetoric, and literature at the University of Padua, he showed such brilliance that as a mere seventeen-year-old he was asked to teach rhetoric and moral philosophy at Vicenza—a remarkable achievement for someone so young. In 1417, not yet twenty years old, he was invited to lecture on these subjects in Venice, the success of his teaching there earning him the republic's honorary citizenship. Two years later, appointed secretary to the Venetian consul-general in Constantinople, Filelfo sailed to Byzantium, where he divided his time between performing diplomatic missions for John VIII Palaeologus (including going to Buda to discuss the crusade with King Sigismund) and learning ancient Greek with John Chrysoloras, nephew of Manuel. Filelfo actually lived in his teacher's household and married his fourteen-year-old daughter, a great match since Theodora was also a blood relation of the emperor.[4] In no time the marriage stirred up gossip and grousing among the competitive Italian humanists, jealous of Filelfo's brilliant career at such a scandalously young age. Ambrogio Traversari, a friend of Poggio Bracciolini and Niccolò Niccoli, wrote to the latter:

> Recently I received a letter from Guarino in which he inveighs against fortune with vehemence because that upstart [Filelfo] has got the daughter of the famous John Chrysoloras: although he is a man of considerable talent, he was certainly unequal to that match. Guarino complains in disgust that the wife of Chrysoloras has a venal virtue, and had possessed a lover before she acquired a son-in-law.[5]

This was the beginning of scabrous rumors about Filelfo that his colleagues would circulate with gusto, the habit of personal attacks on their rivals being rife among them.

The one man whose goodwill Filelfo could trust was Cyriacus. It is not clear where and when they met, but by the late 1420s they were fond friends, linked by a shared passion for the ancient world. In a letter to Cyriacus penned in October 1427, Filelfo wrote,

> In light of your special affection, I would be an ingrate if I did not love you ardently. I love you, Cyriacus, not only

because of your affection for me, but also and especially because of the careful attention and zeal which you show in the discovery of those things which, on account of their great age or negligence of our fathers have been lost to us.

Do continue to apply yourself, as you do, to such a noble and laudable task, of causing rebirth of antiquity or saving it from death! Isn't it true that there is much pleasure and benefit in those eulogies and inscriptions which you, with such ardor and labor bring to Italy from nearly all parts of the universe? And thanks to them you not only make yourself loved by those living, but earn the eternal blessing of the dead.[6]

Cyriacus wrote to Filelfo about his finds, which the humanist gratefully acknowledged—as he did in the summer of 1428, thanking Cyriacus for inscriptions copied in Egypt—and came to visit him whenever his travels permitted.

In 1429 Filelfo took up the Chair of Greek at the University of Florence, a position previously occupied by Chrysoloras, Guarino, and Aurispa, and secured for him by Cosimo de' Medici and the leading humanists of the city, such as Niccolò Niccoli and Leonardo Bruni. Everyone was enchanted with the dynamic thirty-one-year-old teacher, and Filelfo wrote to a friend that four hundred people packed the lecture hall daily to hear him speak about Cicero and Livy, Thucydides and Xenophon. But within a year Filelfo got into a fierce feud with Niccoli. According to Traversari, Filelfo got "terribly disgruntled because Niccolò did not applaud his every word."[7] Whatever Niccoli actually said to or about Filelfo, the young scholar lashed back by ridiculing Niccoli in public and calling him a literary ignoramus, which, given Niccoli's deep learning and extreme touchiness, did not go over well. Niccoli's friends—Cosimo de' Medici, Ambrogio Traversari, and Poggio Bracciolini—rallied behind him, and soon Filelfo was at war with them all. Traversari wrote to a friend with glee that Filelfo was struggling to make ends meet and had to grind out translations from Greek to Latin to survive. Filelfo was, apparently, fond of good living and seemingly spent everything he earned. He was paid quite decently, but did not have the landed wealth or the support of affluent patrons. Bracciolini, meanwhile, composed venomous invectives accusing Filelfo of stealing from his benefactors, living like a filthy beggar, and engaging in every manner of sexual vice, from rape to sodomy, from being a procurer to a voyeur, of pursuing incest at his wife's parents' house and a ménage à trois at home, and becoming a teacher only in order to recruit boys for his stable of male prostitutes. Filelfo did end up having three wives, as two of them died, and he did father twenty-four children, indulge in mistresses, and quip that he had three testicles. Still, Bracciolini's accusations reflected little truth and a great deal of the indecorous side of Italian (and especially Florentine) humanists, quick to deploy their eloquence, wit, and perfect Latin as barbed weapons against their opponents.

Filelfo's conflict with the Florentines reached a critical point just around the time of Cyriacus's visit. In dire need of a friend, Filelfo must have been as delighted to see him now as he would be in July of 1440, when he would write, "you announce that you will visit me shortly. I cannot express what great joy your letter has caused me!" As the beleaguered humanist showed his friend around the city, he must have regaled him with a litany of the abuses he had suffered in this supposedly civilized place. Only recently, he had narrowly escaped death. He was walking to the university when a Medici hireling jumped on him, slashed his face, and almost murdered him. Filelfo had compounded his troubles by not only falling out with Cosimo de' Medici's humanist friends, but by siding with his political rivals to boot.

This was the snake pit which Cyriacus entered in the late summer of 1433.

❧

What a surprise and relief it must have been to be greeted with friendliness—for the most part. The great pioneer of the revival of ancient texts, Poggio Bracciolini, did not take kindly to the Anconitan, calling him "mad, arrogant, and annoying as a cicada, a verbose and inexhaustible talker, more importune than a fly, an ass on two feet."[8] Bracciolini, according to his biographer, Vespasiano, "was given to strong invective, and all stood in dread of him . . . he was very free of speech . . . and was prompt to take up his pen in vituperation of certain men of letters"—as he did against Filelfo.[9] He may have lashed out against Cyriacus because he was Filelfo's friend. He could well have been worn out by Cyriacus's energy and voluble enthusiasm; he was certainly appalled by his language skills—"Greek mostly mixed with Latin, incorrect verbs, poor usage, clumsy constructions, no sense," he grumbled.[10] The two men also clashed ideologically. Cyriacus held Greek culture to be superior to Roman, whereas Bracciolini praised the merits of the latter and focused all his studies on it (he did not know Greek very well). And while Cyriacus admired Julius Caesar and the Roman Empire, Bracciolini championed Scipio and the Roman Republic.

Renaissance Italy consisted of both republican city-states and monarchical principalities, often in competition and at war with one another. Humanists serving different rulers defended their employers' political philosophies and practices. But the conversation spilled beyond the courts and town halls, and regular citizens weighed in on the subject. Inspired not only by Caesar himself but also by Dante and Virgil, Cyriacus embraced the imperial model, as he wrote to Leonardo Bruni in a letter titled "Caesarea Laus" ("Caesarian Praise"):

> [That monarchy] which, when founded by our C. Caesar himself through the highest virtue of his mind, was so pleasing to the highest Jove himself, that, when the son of Caesar the divine Augustus reigned, and when [the Temple of] Janus had been closed by him, the fierce arms put away and the whole world pacified, when the Golden Age had come—that he, descending from the highest fortress of the heavens to the earth, in a miraculous and unprecedented order, deigned to unite himself with the human race.[11]

Cyriacus's arguments were, as usual, highly poetic. And how poetry was to be read and interpreted was another topic of intense argument between humanists. Bracciolini was critical of using poetic allegory to attain truth, while Cyriacus clearly reveled in it and employed it in his own writing at every opportunity. So Cyriacus and Bracciolini, though they shared a passion for the past, were in many ways philosophical antagonists.[12]

Most other humanists, artists, and even Cosimo de' Medici, however, treated Cyriacus as an honored guest and vied to show him around Florence. They also yearned to hear first-hand about his discoveries in the Greek lands. Cyriacus had been assiduous in publicizing his finds in letters to his correspondents in Italy, and his accounts circulated among the cognoscenti, who hungrily absorbed his descriptions and drawings of classical monuments. Most of them did not mind that Cyriacus was not a trained humanist but a merchant dabbling in archaeology. In fact, they may have valued him more because he was a businessman.

Cosimo de' Medici was one, too, and he was a great patron of learning; and Niccolò Niccoli had been in that line of work until, "feeling he had been born for higher and nobler goals," he turned to the full-time study of Latin.[13] International merchants such as Cyriacus were conduits of invaluable information about faraway lands and their cultures, be it China in the case of Marco Polo, or Alexandria, Adrianople, and Damascus in the case of Cyriacus and his colleagues—places Italian humanists would never see for themselves. Venetian patricians viewed a period of trading abroad as an important training for a successful career in civic politics because it expanded a young man's horizons and taught him diplomacy through the experience of interacting and concluding deals with a wide range of people. And Cyriacus offered still more: combining his mercantile and archaeological vocations, he brought the antiquities of Greece and Asia Minor to Italy not only in word but in the flesh, as it were. Many of the famous men he was meeting were his current or future customers, eager to procure from him ancient coins, sculptures, and books.

❧

Among those who enthusiastically welcomed the Anconitan to Florence was Filippo Brunelleschi, who invited Cyriacus on a personal tour of the cathedral dome that he was erecting at the time. Crossing the building site, which looked like an ant-heap—with men carting sacks of sand and lime, bricklayers mixing mortar, stonecutters shaping blocks, blacksmiths forging and repairing tools amidst clouds of smoke, and workmen crawling all over the scaffolding—Cyriacus followed Brunelleschi up more than four hundred steps, first inside one of the piers supporting the cupola, then around its base, and further up from there, to see the construction up close.[14]

Even before Brunelleschi started building his dome, the cathedral was the city's chief landmark. Intended to hold the entire Florentine population (it is the fourth largest church in the world, after St. Peter's in Rome, St. Paul's in London, and the cathedral of Milan), it was begun in 1296 and envisioned as "the most beautiful and honorable church in Tuscany." By the 1360s it was built up to the rise of the cupola, but how to crown the 140-foot-wide opening left for it nobody knew—until Brunelleschi, more than half a century later, came up with his visionary plan.

Showing Cyriacus the completed portions of the dome, Brunelleschi might have pointed out how it resembled and differed from the ancient Pantheon, which he had examined in minutest detail during his sojourn in Rome two decades earlier. During that stay, oblivious to food, clothing, and other comforts, the young architect had lived immersed in the world of antiquities, scrutinizing all the ruins he could find for clues to Roman building techniques. He dreamed of restoring the ancient style of architecture, and among other things, "he had noted down and drawn all the ancient vaults, and was for ever studying them," wrote the Renaissance art historian Giorgio Vasari.[15] Brunelleschi wished he could replicate the majestic half-sphere of the Pantheon in Florence's cathedral. But the existing opening for the dome was octagonal in shape and could only take a ribbed vault, typical of Gothic architecture. Such structures usually relied on external buttresses to support their outward thrust. Brunelleschi wanted to avoid such an ungainly and backward solution. So he invented a cupola that merged ancient and contemporary elements in complex and elegant ways. He may have explained to Cyriacus his vision, though without sharing any of its specifics, for he was famously reticent about revealing the details of his plans to anyone, lest they be stolen by competitors.[16]

Brunelleschi's rival Lorenzo Ghiberti was also keen to meet Cyriacus, show him his workshop, located opposite the convent of Santa Maria Novella, and impress him with his collection of antique sculptures, medals of his friends that he made in emulation of ancient coins, and current projects. Since gaining a commission for a set of bronze doors to the Baptistery in 1401, Ghiberti had become the preeminent sculptor in Florence, boasting that there were few things in the city worthy of note that he had not either made or inspired. He never suffered from excessive modesty. But he did create many influential works and trained the next generation of artists, including Donatello, Masolino, Pallaiuolo, and Uccello.

Ghiberti, like Brunelleschi, was swept up in the revival of ancient arts. His bronze statues of St. John the Baptist and St. Matthew, which Cyriacus would have seen on the facade of Orsanmichele, Florence's public granary and oratory, were the first monumental bronzes to be cast since antiquity. Ghiberti's lost-wax technique was that used by the ancients, an intricate craft he mastered to such a degree that Vasari, writing a history of Renaissance arts, declared Ghiberti's second Baptistery doors—the ones he was working on at the time of Cyriacus's visit—to be "the most beautiful work which has ever been seen in the world, whether ancient or modern."[17] Ghiberti, too, had gone to study the ruins of Rome and was especially transfixed by sarcophagi carved with reliefs. These inspired him as he now worked on Old Testament door panels—some still in the drawing stage, others modeled in wax, and a couple already cast in bronze, though still needing hammering, carving, incising, and polishing (the doors would occupy him from 1425 until 1452). Ghiberti set the biblical stories in complex architectural and landscape spaces, with successive episodes appearing in different planes of relief. Looking at the action receding into illusionistic distance, Cyriacus must have marveled at how Ghiberti's figures seemed to be reincarnations of the people he had seen on ancient columns, sarcophagi, and tombstones.

Cyriacus also visited Donatello, who had worked with Ghiberti on the first set of Baptistery doors and traveled to Rome with Brunelleschi. Donatello had journeyed to the Eternal

City several times "seeking to imitate as much as possible the works of the ancients."[18] He had been there just recently, during the coronation of Emperor Sigismund, and contributed to the preparations for the ceremony and the surrounding festivities.[19] Donatello was as ardent about antiquity as Brunelleschi, Ghiberti, and Cyriacus. He had imbibed the Roman style of sculpture so fully that the Medici entrusted him with the restoration of their ancient marbles, and Vasari credited him with inspiring Cosimo to collect antiquities in the first place. Donatello not only assembled his own collection of antiquities from which he could learn further but also advised Cosimo de' Medici, Poggio Bracciolini, and others on worthwhile pieces to buy: in one letter to Niccoli, Bracciolini mentioned that he was considering a sculpture for purchase and that "Donatellus saw it and praised it highly."[20]

A sculptor of extraordinary technical and emotional range, Donatello drew on classical sources and styles for works as diverse as his sensual bronze David with a smooth adolescent body and a large modish hat, standing nonchalantly on the head of the defeated Goliath, and the gruesome wooden Mary Magdalene, gaunt and disfigured after thirty years of penitence in the desert. He pioneered shallow, yet illusionistically deep relief in both marble and bronze, and would later create a monumental equestrian bronze portrait of the *condottiere* Erasmo da Narni, nicknamed Gattamelata ("honeyed cat"), based on the ancient Roman statue of Marcus Aurelius and embellished with reliefs derived from Cyriacus's Greek drawings.

❦

The leading intellectuals—Leonardo Bruni, then chancellor of Florence, and Carlo Marsuppini, who would succeed Bruni in that post—also received Cyriacus as an esteemed visitor and toured him around the city's notable landmarks, which duly impressed their guest:

> its extensive solid stone walls, its regal gates, its broad streets, and its large churches . . . the remarkable marble baptistery . . . anciently dedicated to Mars and now to St. John the Baptist, the outside of which is adorned by three very beautifully sculpted bronze doors depicting sacred histories, . . . the lofty, towered palaces of the city-magistrates, the public and private porticoes, the great houses of leading citizens, the fine buildings all over the city, the four wide stone bridges—Rubaconte, Vecchio, Trinità, and Carraia—spanning the Arno, and finally the large iron cages of lions, symbols of popular liberty.[21]

An outsider and not a rival to Florence's touchy artistic and literary elite, the cheerful, easygoing Cyriacus got along better with each of them than they did with one another. His diplomatic skills honed in trading abroad and paying court to King Janus of Cyprus, Pope Eugenius IV, and Emperor Sigismund, he was adept at winning over all kinds of people. And he was able to supply the humanists with materials they could not otherwise obtain. Leonardo Bruni, a taciturn and solemn man who proceeded through the streets of Florence slowly and majestically, clad in a long scarlet robe, had written a monumental *History of Florence* and translated a number of Greek texts into Latin. In the following years he would exchange letters with Cyriacus and gladly received from him copies of inscriptions from Delphi and Athens. Carlo Marsuppini—the pale, hypochondriac homebody who succeeded Filelfo in the Chair of Greek at the University of Florence and translated Book I of the *Iliad* into Latin—showed Cyriacus his collection of antique gems and composed a poem in his praise. Cyriacus would later send Marsuppini a drawing of an ancient relief depicting Mercury. Even the prickly and critical Niccolò Niccoli gave Cyriacus a hearty welcome.

Niccoli—obese but handsome of face, with a lively and jovial personality, though tinged with gravity and self-importance—was one of the pillars of the Florentine humanist circle. A great scholar and aesthete, he loved and praised everything ancient, wore plum-colored garments in imitation of the purple robes of Roman patricians, and ate only from the finest antique vessels. Allergic to everything unrefined, he "could not bear the noise of a braying donkey, a saw, or a mousetrap moving around," wrote his contemporary Giannozzo Manetti.[22] Niccoli could be affable, gracious, and witty—the heart of a party: "his funny stories and mordant raillery (for he naturally overflowed with comic jests) would make all his listeners laugh continuously."[23] Together with his learning, this endeared him to Poggio Bracciolini, Carlo Marsuppini, and Cosimo de' Medici—all his steadfast friends. But if one went against the humanist's grain, he quickly turned "tender and sensitive . . . [as if] made of glass," in Poggio's words. And he irked his colleagues with his pedantry and pretentiousness. Guarino da Verona scoffed that "neglecting the other aspects of books as quite superfluous he expends his interest and acumen on the points (or dots) in the manuscript . . . As to the paper, that is the surface, his expertise is not to be dismissed and he displays his eloquence in praising or disapproving of it. What a vacuous way to spend so many years if the final fruit is a discussion of the shape of letters, the color of paper, and the varieties of ink." Leonardo Bruni mocked Niccoli strutting through the streets of Florence, expecting admiration from all: "Look at me and know how profoundly wise I am. I am the pillar of letters, I am the shrine of knowledge, I am the standard of doctrine and wisdom. If those about him should fail to notice he will complain about the ignorance of the age."[24] Niccoli, in his defense, insisted that to restore Latin texts to their original versions one had to be precise about the smallest details, including dots and lines. And no one knew such minutiae better that he.

Tremendously erudite, Niccoli had such a grasp of Latin literature, that "he alone seemed to possess a full and correct knowledge of that subject . . . his memory of the old histories was so tenacious that whenever he wanted he could recite every single deed of great men with perfect precision and in such a way that it seemed, almost, that he had witnessed them personally."[25] A "glutton for books," he assembled a library of some eight hundred volumes, which he generously shared with scholars during his lifetime and upon his death bequeathed to the city so that it would be "a kind of public library which would be open to all scholars in perpetuity."[26] (Cosimo paid for many of these books and took partial credit for establishing the library.) Niccoli's house was always crowded with visitors and aspiring young humanists come to read his books, discourse on scholarly topics, and show him their writings. Niccoli "excelled all others in judging whether an author or an orator was polished or puerile," and supplicants often heard that their creations were worthless—he had "a kind of frank and free-wheeling license in censuring others," noted Manetti.[27] Yet Niccoli's perfectionism silenced him more than it did others. "Seldom or never did he undertake to speak or write in Latin," wrote Manetti, "the reason being, in my opinion, that he approved of nothing unless it were full and perfect, and so feared that his own writings, like those of others, would fail to satisfy him completely."[28]

Like Cyriacus, Niccoli had an "extraordinary curiosity about and love for all things ancient" and bought from every source he could find gems, coins, bronzes, and marbles.[29] Poggio wrote that "he had a greater number of these things, and more choice ones, than practically anyone else . . . [In his house] could be seen statues and pictures, likenesses of men of old, and coins dating back to that earlier age when bronze first began to be struck and coined money began to be stamped."[30] Cyriacus especially admired his "remarkable gem by Pyrgoteles, carved of *nicolo* [a bluish onyx], representing a lupercalian priest, and his bronze statue of a wing-shod Mercury."[31] As with his books, Niccoli made his artifacts available to fellow scholars, and guests to the city "all deemed that if they had not visited Nicolao [*sic*], they had not been to Florence at all."[32]

Niccoli was as impatient to see Cyriacus as the Anconitan was to pay his respects to the famous sage. Cyriacus recalled his time with Niccoli "with special pleasure," and commented that Niccoli "relished discussing all the antiquities [Cyriacus] had discovered over the world, in the great eastern cities of Asia and Europe, and in the islands of Ionia and the Aegean. Niccolo particularly enjoyed Ciriaco's report on the wonderful temple at Cyzicus."[33] While Niccoli drew most of his knowledge from books, Cyriacus had seen with his own eyes the cities and monuments built by the Greeks and the Romans and could evoke for Niccoli the appearance and feel of Hadrian's majestic temple at Cyzicus, the great citadel of Pergamon, the island of the poet Sappho, and other legendary sites. He was a kind of Mercury, a messenger from Niccoli's beloved past.

For Cyriacus, the enthusiastic reception by Niccoli and other renowned Florentine humanists provided a deeply satisfying validation of his efforts by the people who recognized and in their own ways promoted the importance of ancient civilization. While they restored ancient texts to their original perfection letter by letter, he was bringing back to light the remains of the ancients block by block. Their eagerness to learn from him meant that he was making a real impact through his archaeological discoveries. What was more, he was considered an authority on the antiquities of Greece. Elated by his achievements, he would boast to one of his correspondents, a learned prelate named Johannes Ricinatus, "It is obvious, most worthy father, that we are able by our art not only to raise from the depth monuments which have been destroyed, but also to bring the names of cities back into the light."[34] Archaeology had elevated Cyriacus intellectually and socially; he received another affirmation of this when Cosimo de' Medici, the man who held power behind the scenes in Florence and wielded great influence with rulers of other Italian states, invited him to his home.

Just two years older than Cyriacus, Cosimo looked like an old man—his face wrinkled, cheeks sagging, lips pursed, eyes underlined with bags. He carried a great deal on his stooped shoulders: a major international bank, Florentine political machinery, diplomatic negotiations with heads of other states, all the while suffering the pains of gout which plagued the Medici men and often confined him to bed or to a special chair in which he was carried around by servants. These cares, as well as a naturally grave temperament that shunned frivolity, gave Cosimo a rueful and watchful look. But he received Cyriacus with benevolence. For unlike Eugenius IV, who, sadly for Cyriacus, was mainly preoccupied with piety and monastic reform and did not really care for ancient arts and letters, Cosimo keenly participated in their revival.

Born into a family of businessmen, like Cyriacus, Cosimo had become, thanks to his keen intelligence, not only a financier of princes and popes and a crafty politician who commanded authority at home and abroad, but a philanthropist and an amateur humanist with an impressive command of Latin and a fine taste in art. His biographer Vespasiano commented that Cosimo "had a knowledge of Latin which would scarcely have been looked for in one occupying the station of a leading citizen engrossed with affairs."[35] Cosimo relished the society of humanists—Poggio Bracciolini, Niccolò Niccoli, Carlo Marsuppini, and Leonardo Bruni—and fostered the new arts based on classical models. He commissioned Ghiberti to mount his ancient gems, nurtured Donatello's career, asked Brunelleschi to design his family palazzo (though in the end he chose a more modest structure by Michelozzo for fear that the grandeur of Brunelleschi's building would arouse the envy and displeasure of his fellow citizens). Of course Cosimo's association with leading intellectuals and artists augmented his own prestige, but he was genuinely fond of arts and learning, and assembled his own collection of antiquities and a library of classical authors—in addition to helping Niccoli pay for his.

Graciously welcoming Cyriacus into his palazzo on Via Larga, Cosimo showed the Anconitan his antique vases carved from semiprecious stones, engraved gems, and coins stamped with faces of Roman emperors. He, too, must have asked about Cyriacus's journeys in the East, and may have offered to sponsor some of Cyriacus's archeological expeditions. Cyriacus was delighted to gain such a valuable ally: rich, powerful, interested in preserving ancient culture, and able to bend the ear of the pope. Cosimo was the pope's banker and supporter, and would shelter Eugenius IV in Florence when, the following year, the Romans drove him out of their city. To cultivate Cosimo's goodwill, Cyriacus presented him with a unique gift—a drawing of a giraffe he had sketched in Egypt, an animal last seen in Europe when Julius Caesar paraded one in his triumphal procession in through Rome in 44 BC.

*Cyriacus's drawing of the Parthenon, from Giuliano da Sangallo,
Il libro di Giuliano da Sangallo Codice vaticanobarberiniano
latino 4424 riprodotto in fototipia, ed. Cristiano Huelsen,
Lipsia: O. Harrassowitz, 1910.*

*So this is Greece! For her I have crossed this vast expanse
of sea, abandoned Italy, my parents and my friends; all
for this land! And why could I not make this journey in
my own study . . . ? Could I not have read the ancient and
modern travelers, and learned painlessly about all Greece
holds . . . ? Yes, . . . I could have done; but then I wanted
to make it in order to feel . . . What does it matter that
Sparta, Athens and Corinth are gone for ever? The soil where
they stood still holds in its breast the sublime ideas that it
inspired in ancient times . . . And the silence! It will allow
me to be moved and to breathe freely in this majestic theater
where so many glorious deeds were done.*

——Saverio Scrofani, *Viaggio in Grecia, 1799*[1]

Into the Greek Past

I F FLORENCE WAS an indication of what Cyriacus had
attained through his explorations around the Mediterranean, his next journey would expose both his achievements
and failings at the heart of the classical world. He would set
out to investigate and document places that no one had sought
in a millennium, and at the same time contribute to shutting
the door to them for the next two hundred years.

After a two-year hiatus, which Cyriacus spent mostly in Ancona continuing his mercantile affairs, the pope was finally ready to move toward a Crusade. He sent Cyriacus on an intelligence-gathering trip around mainland Greece. Traveling no longer as a merchant but as a papal agent, Cyriacus was to visit and ascertain the political positions of various rulers jostling for power in the patchwork of small kingdoms established by the Franks after the Fourth Crusade.

Mainland Greece was of minor political significance to Europe, and for the current war it was largely a secondary player, offering ports for the Christian fleet and a bulwark against further Ottoman expansion. Unlike the Aegean islands, such as Cyprus, Chios, or Crete, the Greek mainland produced relatively few valuable commodities for international trade— some honey, wine, medium-weight silk exported to Constantinople—and so did not draw many merchants, which is why Cyriacus had never gone there before. Western Europeans in general viewed this part of the world as the home of pagans in the past and of heretical Eastern Orthodox at present. And the Greeks did not welcome foreigners with open arms, having been subjugated by them for centuries. The few Westerners who passed through the region complained about its primitive conditions, bandits lurking on every road, no inns for travelers, and hardly any horses to be had for hire. Cyriacus's contemporary Bertrandon de la Broquière advised that one had to bring along everything one might need, or go without.

Certainly no one went to Greece for its ancient ruins. A couple of decades before Cyriacus, Christophoro Buondelmonti, a Florentine priest five years Cyriacus's junior, did undertake an extensive journey around Greece to study the language and the land. He had been inspired by Manuel Chrysoloras's teachings in Florence and by the manuscript of Ptolemy's *Geography* that the Byzantine scholar had brought with him.[2] But Buondelmonti was drawn to the islands rather than the mainland, and was interested mainly in topography, which he attempted to correlate with historical and mythological information gleaned from ancient writers and native informants. He recorded his findings in two books: *Description of Crete* (1417), dedicated to Niccolò Niccoli and possibly written to satisfy the humanist's curiosity (Buondelmonti also bought books for Niccoli during his peregrinations), and *Book of Islands* (1420), dedicated to Cardinal Giordano Orsini, with whom Cyriacus had visited Hadrian's Villa at Tivoli. This book, with its account of seventy-two islands in the Ionian and Aegean seas, became a bestseller, and Cyriacus owned a copy. Here and there in his writings Buondelmonti mentioned some ancient monuments and commented appreciatively on statues and coins he chanced upon in the course of his travels, but he remained focused on landscape and geography.

Cyriacus headed to mainland Greece hoping to recover the physical remains of its ancient history and to experience firsthand places that had become purely mythical to his fellow antiquarians at home. He was keen to visit two sites in particular: Delphi, the most important ancient Greek sanctuary, and Athens, the preeminent locus of classical culture and art.[3]

The voyage did not begin well. Cyriacus left Ancona in November 1435 and quickly ran into foul weather. Late autumn storms forced his ship to seek shelter on the island of Meilita, in the Adriatic, opposite Apulia; then to loop back to Zara in Dalmatia, across from Ancona. Cyriacus took this detour and delay with his customary buoyancy—as a chance to inspect the walls of Zara for ancient inscriptions and to make excursions to nearby sites. Two weeks later the weather calmed enough for him to resume the journey and sail down the Dalmatian coast toward Corfu, though contrary winds kept stalling his progress. He had hoped to stop at Corfu for Christmas celebrations, but as he got near, news reached his ship that plague was raging on the island, so there would be no docking there. Instead, on December 26 he disembarked at Butrinto, ancient Buthrotum (in what is now southern Albania), made a quick tour of the surviving triple circuit of walls enclosing the acropolis, the theater on its southern slope, and a few other ruins, and headed down toward Arta, the capital of Epirus.

That region of northwest Greece was ruled by Carlo II Tocco, who had inherited the lands in place of his cousin Memnon, Cyriacus's friend and surreptitious ally. Though a Neapolitan by blood, by his political situation Carlo II was the subject of the sultan, and Cyriacus was probably directed by the pope to determine whether, in the event of a Crusade, he would side with the Europeans or the Ottomans. Ever the canny salesman, Cyriacus applied himself to gaining Carlo's trust and goodwill.

He spent January of 1436 in Arta attending court events and examining the town's ancient walls, gates, sculptural fragments, and inscriptions. In the company of Carlo's secretary he made excursions to other sites nearby, including Nikopolis, founded by Octavian on the spot where he camped on the eve of the battle of Actium in 31 BC. Against the thick green carpet of overgrowth, the weathered grayish ruins of the Roman theater, baths, and aqueduct stood out picturesquely, but mutely, giving little hint of the momentous event that gave birth to the town. But for Cyriacus, being able to walk on the very ground from which Octavian had launched his victory over Antony and Cleopatra and ascended to the leadership of the Roman world must have felt like a dream.

❧

Far from any kingdom, trade, or pilgrimage route, ignored and all but abandoned by the Greeks and foreigners, lay another site, once considered to be the most holy place in the ancient world. For hundreds of years kings, generals, and more modest supplicants flocked there from all parts of the Mediterranean to seek divine guidance. In the inner sanctum of the temple of Apollo at Delphi the god's priestess, called Pythia, intoxicated by the fumes seeping out of the ground, gave cryptic answers to their questions, leading some to wise actions, others to disastrous missteps. Oracles were a significant part of Greek religion. States contemplating military expeditions or the foundation of new colonies consulted Apollo, the god of prophesy, on whether their undertakings were wise. Individuals asked if they should proceed with a proposed marriage, or if they would produce a son. Apollo's oracle at Delphi was deemed to be the most reliable, though its answers were not always clear. In the most famous instance of a misunderstood message, King Croesus of Lydia, planning a campaign against Persia, asked the Pythia what he should do. If you attack, you will destroy a great empire, replied the oracle. Croesus took these words as encouragement, only to suffer a crushing defeat and realize, too late, that the empire he obliterated was his own.

In addition to revering Apollo's oracle, the ancients extolled Delphi as the most beautiful spot in Greece, poised as it was between the craggy slopes of Mount Parnassus and the fertile Pleistos Valley stretching toward the Gulf of Corinth. The ancient geographer Strabo described it as "a rocky place, theater-like, having the oracle and the city on its summit . . . Situated in front of the city, toward the south, is Cirphis, a precipitous mountain, which leaves in the intervening space a ravine through which flows the Pleistus River."[4] The site was made more handsome still by splendid buildings and rich dedications proffered by worshippers from all over the ancient world. Cyriacus must have decided to visit Delphi after reading ancient sources, such as Plutarch, who had served as a priest in Apollo's temple in the first and second centuries AD and wrote of "the god completely surrounded by choice offerings and tithes . . . and his temple crowded with spoils and booty from the Greeks [dedicated in gratitude for victories]."[5] Strabo commented that the shrine "was held in exceedingly great honor. Clear proof of this are the treasure-houses, built by both the people and the potentates, in which they deposited not only money which they had dedicated to the god, but also works of the best artists." He continued,

> although the greatest share of honor was paid to this temple because of its oracle, since of all oracles in the world it had the repute of being the most truthful, yet the position of the place added something. For it is almost in the center

of Greece taken as a whole . . . and it was also believed to be in the center of the inhabited world, and people called it the navel of the earth.[6]

Cyriacus arrived in Delphi on March 21, 1436, after crossing the Gulf of Corinth and disembarking at the port of Kirrah, which, he noted with pleasure, the locals called "Ancona." Approaching Delphi from the west, he rounded a sharp ridge of the mountain, and suddenly there it was—an austere and majestic place nestled in the angle formed by two sheer rocks, the Phaedridae, with a mountain-rimmed valley spreading below. The setting was spectacular, but as he drew nearer, no ruined temple or treasury buildings came into view. All Cyriacus could see was the poor little village of Kastri—a cluster of wretched dwellings cobbled together from ancient blocks scavenged on the site and timber cut from the surrounding woods. It soon became clear to him that over the centuries wars, earthquakes, and avalanches had all but obliterated Delphi, burying its ruins beneath rocks and earth. But he was here and determined to find what remained of the once celebrated sanctuary.

For six days Cyriacus walked all over the area, peering at odd blocks sticking out of the ground, running his hands over inscriptions that whispered fragmentary words from eroded stones, trying to puzzle out the few surviving remains. At the lower edge of the site he came upon a large semicircular niche which he interpreted as the temple of Apollo. In fact, it had been a monument of the kings of Argos, and used to contain ten bronze statues of the Argive rulers, who traced their lineage to Herakles. Seeing this structure—the only decently preserved one in sight, situated at the beginning of the sanctuary, and seemingly similar in shape to the Pantheon in Rome—Cyriacus made the logical deduction that it must have been the main shrine. There was no one to tell him otherwise; the villagers had no interest in or clue to the history of the spot they occupied.

Proceeding onward in his solitary exploration, Cyriacus climbed uphill, toward the forbidding rocks towering over Delphi. Soon he stumbled upon a theater built into the slope, its fan of stone seats remarkably well preserved, but the proscenium building in ruins. The theater looked out on a breathtaking panorama of the Pleistos Valley, lush with olive groves and silhouetted by hills, with the glimmering sea far in the distance. But Cyriacus was more enchanted by the stones at his feet. He probably knew from classical authors that the ancients honored gods not only with sacrifices and precious offerings but also with theatrical and athletic competitions, held every four years at major sanctuaries. In preparation for the Pythian games staged at Delphi, messengers went forth to all parts of Greece and beyond, inviting contestants and spectators to come and take part in the processions, sporting displays, and lyrical and dramatic performances. Strabo wrote that "as for the contests at Delphi, there was one in early times between cithara players, who sang a paean in honor of the god . . . [later] the Amphictyons [who administered the sanctuary] instituted equestrian and gymnastic contests in which the prize was a [laurel] crown, and called them Pythian Games."[7]

The walls of the theater were covered with inscriptions, most of them recording the manumission of slaves. Sanctuaries were a perfect place for this ceremony, since the gods could witness and sanctify it; and sanctuary buildings served as a kind of public archive, their walls incised with notices for all to see. Cyriacus examined and copied a number of these inscriptions. Soon after his visit the theater was buried by a rockslide, and would not be seen again until archaeologists began to excavate the site systematically in the late nineteenth century.[8]

From the theater Cyriacus climbed further up a winding path framed by pine trees until he was rewarded with another bit of old Delphi: the stadium where athletic competitions—foot races in armor and in the nude, wrestling and boxing—were held during the Pythian Games. The stadium had once welcomed some 6,500 spectators. As he walked its length and gazed at the empty rows of weathered benches, Cyriacus must have imagined the excitement of watching the contests here: the cheering of international crowds, the exertion of athletes, their bodies glistening with oil and sweat, the parade of laurel-crowned victors at the conclusion of the games. Now the track was overgrown with grass, moss covered the seats, and shrubs stood guard on the edges of the deserted arena.

Urged on by ancient ghosts, Cyriacus crisscrossed Delphi again and again, spotting tombs on its outskirts, observing fragments of sculpture and architecture, recording inscriptions in which the voices of kings and emperors mingled with those of local officials promulgating laws and decrees, supplicants to Apollo enumerated their offerings to the god and sang hymns in his praise, notables boasted of honors received, and slaves celebrated liberation. As Cyriacus scribbled his notes and sketched in his worn diary, an occasional shepherd or a villager foraging for wood must have looked on in bafflement, never having seen anyone behave in this way. This strange and cheerful foreigner would not be followed here by another enthusiast of the past until 1675.

❧

Having seen Delphi, Cyriacus was burning to behold Athens, the cultural epicenter of ancient Greece. Not wanting to miss anything else of historic importance, he stopped at Thebes— famous as the birthplace of the god Dionysos, the prophet Tiresias, and the poet Pindar, as the site of King Oedipus's tragedy, and as an ally of Sparta when it defeated Athens in the Peloponnesian War. He detoured to the island of Euboea, running parallel to the mainland, to visit Chalchis, renowned for its bronze manufacture, and Eretria, one of the chief maritime states of ancient Greece. The first traveler to rediscover this town, Cyriacus recorded in his diary: "In Euboea is located Eretria, a great city on the coast, about fifteen miles from the Euripos; . . . ancient walls are found there all around, built with great stones; at the summit of the citadel there is a theater."[9] He sketched a plan of the walls, the theater, and the fortifications of the acropolis. After him, Eretria would not see another archaeologist for four hundred years. He also explored Eleusis, the site of an ancient mystery cult; Corinth, with its half-ruined temple picturesquely silhouetted against the monolithic rock on which the city's acropolis once stood; and Sikyon, celebrated for producing some of the greatest artists, including Polykleitos, Lysippos, and Pamphilos, the master of Apelles. And he made the trek to Sparta, which no one troubled to see because its history was largely forgotten and, far from the sea, it was hard to reach.

Cyriacus's drawing of a funerary relief found near the village of Kairiai in the Peloponnese, from R. Sabbadini, "Ciriaco d'Ancona e la sua descrizione autografa del peloponneso trasmessa da Leonardo Botta," in Miscellanea Ceriani: Raccolta di scritti originali per onorare la memoria di M.r Antonio Maria Ceriani, prefetto della Biblioteca Ambrosiana, *Milan: Ulrico Hoepli, 1910.*

But Athens was his ultimate goal. He was forty-five years old and it had taken him fifteen years—since he first committed himself to antiquity—to arrive at this heart of the classical world. From reading Plutarch's *Life of Pericles*, Cyriacus may have hoped to see

Cyriacus's drawing of two inscribed monuments at Laconia in the Peloponnese, from R. Sabbadini, "Ciriaco d'Ancona e la sua descrizione autografa del peloponneso trasmessa da Leonardo Botta," in Miscellanea Ceriani: Raccolta di scritti originali per onorare la memoria di M.r Antonio Maria Ceriani, prefetto della Biblioteca Ambrosiana, *Milan: Ulrico Hoepli, 1910.*

that which gave most pleasure and ornament to the city of Athens, and the greatest admiration and even astonishment to all strangers, and that which now is Greece's only evidence that the power she boasts of and her ancient wealth are no romance or idle story, . . . the public and sacred buildings [erected by Pericles] . . .

For every particular piece of his work was immediately, even at that time, for its beauty and elegance, antique; and yet in its vigor and freshness looks to this date as if it were just executed. There is a sort of bloom of newness upon these works of his, preserving them from the touch of time, as if they had some perennial spirit and undying vitality mingled in the composition of them.[10]

However much of this timeless beauty Cyriacus may have expected to still be there, he probably had heard that the splendid metropolis once admired, envied, and feared by its allies and enemies had been greatly diminished over the centuries. Michael Choniates, who in the early thirteenth century came from vibrant Constantinople to Athens to serve as its archbishop, bemoaned the backwardness of the place. He found it to be the boondocks at the edge of the civilized world, its inhabitants uncouth peasants, speaking barbarously and living in material and spiritual poverty.[11] The city had improved little since Choniates's day. Unlike Delphi, it was relatively easy to reach, but gave most people little reason to bother.

At once excited and frustrated by what he encountered as he approached and entered the town, Cyriacus recorded in his diary:

On April 7th [1436] I came to Athens, the celebrated city of Attica, where I saw, first of all, large walls everywhere in a state of collapse owing to their age. Both inside the city and out in the fields there were marble buildings beyond all belief—houses, sacred shrines—as well as various works of art remarkable for their marvelous execution and enormous columns, but all in heaps of shattered ruins everywhere.[12]

Athens itself, he saw, was now no more than a gathering of humble houses cobbled together from ancient blocks and clustered at the foot of the Acropolis. The famous citadel, which Strabo described as "the sacred precinct of Athena, comprising both the old temple of Athena Polias, in which is the lamp that is never quenched, and the Parthenon built by Ictinus, in which is the work in ivory by Phidias, the Athena," stood imprisoned by medieval crenellated walls and guarded by belligerent rectangular towers.[13] The rest of the landscape was a sparsely populated hilly countryside.

As was his custom upon arriving in a new place, Cyriacus went to pay his respects to the local overlord—at that moment Nerio II Acciaiuoli, Duke of Athens and Thebes. On the pope's behalf, Cyriacus needed to determine Nerio's political views; on his own, to obtain permission to examine antiquities around the city, and especially within the citadel, where the duke lived. As Cyriacus climbed up the steep path toward Nerio's palace, the forbidding bastion loomed over his head, its walls assembled from marble blocks scavenged from ancient buildings. Scanning the stones for interesting details, Cyriacus glimpsed an inscription. Squinting and angling his head to decipher the letters on the battered stone, blackened by fire and inserted upside-down into the wall, he made out that it honored a generous donor who had helped build the late-antique gate to the Acropolis. Cyriacus paused to copy it into his notebook, then walked on until he found a single narrow doorway into the fort—a testament to the embattled state of Athens, constantly threatened by pirate raids, the competing claims of rival European powers, and the Ottomans.

Nerio's palace was built into the Propylaea, the monumental ancient entryway to the Acropolis on which Pericles spent almost as much money as on the Parthenon, erecting

Model of the Acropolis of Athens in the fifteenth century,
Acropolis Study Center, Athens. (Kenneth Lapatin)

a structure of great elegance and majesty. It was hard to see now, hidden as it was by the fortification wall. The Franks had also closed off the spaces between the columns and raised a boxy second story above. Displaying selective myopia, Cyriacus ignored the current aspect of the building and wrote in his diary: "what I noticed with special pleasure when I had carefully looked over the handsome work which was this distinguished palace, was its extraordinary portico."[14] Cyriacus's intense focus on classical remains was not only his accomplishment, but was also a flaw. He neglected to appreciate that the medieval makeover of this and other ancient buildings had served to safeguard as much as to corrupt them. Had the Propylaea and its neighbors been left in their ancient purity, as Cyriacus described them imaginatively, they would have fallen into decay and been dismantled for building blocks or burnt for lime. In his passionate dedication to the Greek past, Cyriacus failed to recognize that the transformation of ancient buildings into palaces and churches (and later, under the Turks, into mosques and harems), and their integration into the ongoing life of the city assured their survival far better than would a military Crusade to save them.

Having obtained permission to explore the city and the citadel, Cyriacus hastened to feast his eyes on the preeminent achievement of the Periclean building program. What awaited him as he emerged from the maze of medieval structures crowding the Acropolis was as much of a hybrid as the Propylaea. In February 1395, Niccolò da Martoni, a notary from Capua, had passed through Athens on his way back from the Holy Land—not by choice, but because his ship docked there to avoid pirates that lurked in the waters near the city and pounced on both its inhabitants and visitors. Climbing up to the fortress, Niccolò was impressed by

the great church inside the fort, which is named after Mary. The church is built of great blocks of marble, which are all joined together with lead, and the church is as big as the church in Capua. Around the outside of the church are 60 large columns. Each one of these is higher than the ladder used for the wine harvest, and so thick it would take five men with outstretched arms to encircle them . . . It is impossible for a human mind to imagine how such a great building can have been constructed.[15]

Aside from the building's remarkable dimensions, Niccolò was awed by the baldachin around the altar supported by four jasper columns, the portrait of the Virgin painted by St. Luke himself and encrusted with gems, a copy of the Gospels written in gold letters on parchment by St. Helena, the mother of Constantine, and the cross incised into one of the interior columns by Dionysios the Areopagite, the first bishop of Athens, at the moment when an earthquake struck the earth as Jesus expired on the cross.[16]

A church was what everyone now saw atop the Acropolis, for sometime in the sixth century AD the Parthenon had been Christianized and rededicated as Our Lady of Athens. To accommodate it to this new use, the medieval inhabitants of Athens made various alterations. Since churches opened to the west, while classical temples faced east, the Christians blocked the Parthenon's ancient portal with an apse and set up an altar at that end of the building. To add more light to the interior, they cut windows through the sculpted frieze. The gold and ivory image of Athena inside the shrine was gone by that time, but the exterior sculpture remained and offended the Christians with its paganism. So they took down the birth of Athena group from the east pediment and defaced the metopes along three sides. The contest between Athena and Poseidon on the west pediment was spared because medieval Athenians interpreted it as some kind of biblical story. Meanwhile, they painted the walls inside the church with scenes of the Last Judgment, the Passion, saints and bishops, and lined the ceiling of the apse with a mosaic showing the Virgin and Child.[17]

Cyriacus turned a blind eye to the Parthenon's Christian transformations. Imbued with the mental image of the ancient city and its architecture he must have formed by reading Plutarch and Strabo, he wrote in his diary:

> I was most pleased to observe that on the top of the citadel there is a huge, wondrous temple of the goddess Pallas, the noble work of Phidias. It is tall, with fifty-eight columns of marble seven feet in diameter, is decorated everywhere with handsome statues—on both facades, on the topmost band of the walls, and outside on the architraves, whereon a battle of centaurs is seen, marvelous products of the sculptor's art.[18]

He was the first traveler since antiquity to seek out the Parthenon as such, to give an accurate account of it, and to record its architectural and sculptural features in both words and pictures.[19]

❧

Cyriacus stayed in Athens for sixteen days, seeking out and documenting ancient vestiges all over the city.[20] His investigations would preserve vital information about monuments that would disappear for good or be severely compromised in the following centuries, partly as a result of the war he was advocating.

There was, of course, a great deal lost already. The Greek Agora, formerly the bustling civic center of Athens located to the northwest of the Acropolis, was now abandoned terrain with a random scatter of battered stones. Its only surviving structure was a classical temple that, like the Parthenon, had been saved by being converted into a church. Now dedicated to St. George, in antiquity it had been a shrine to the less agile, but more skillful Hephaistos, the lame metalsmith and artificer of Olympus, and the area around it used to house metal workshops. Cyriacus again overlooked the Christian aspect of the building and admired "a splendid temple of Mars in the open country of Athens still standing intact with its twenty-four columns."[21] A temple of Ares (a Greek version of Mars) used to stand nearby, but it did not survive; Cyriacus must have read about it in some ancient source and conflated the two shrines, or deduced the name of the god from the battle scenes on the temple's frieze.

East of the Agora, he came upon another nearly complete gem: "the octagonal temple of Aeolus. On it are eight winged figures of the winds, with their attributes, at the top of each angled wall—marvelous pieces of sculpture. And each figure has his name written above in large, Attic-style lettering, as we observed from close at hand."[22] This remarkable building, popularly known as the Tower of the Winds, was actually not a temple, but an *horologion*, a timepiece designed in the mid-second century BC by the astronomer Andronikos of Kyrrhos. Its top had once been surmounted by a bronze weathervane shaped like Triton holding a rod which indicated the direction of the wind. The sides of the building were incised with sundials that reflected the ancient Greek practice of dividing each day into twelve periods of sunlight, with shorter hours in the winter and longer ones in the summer—the origins of our twenty-four-hour day (the Greek system was a refinement of the ancient Egyptian twenty-four-hour day with ten hours of light, two of twilight, and twelve of darkness). The sculpted representations of the winds above the sundials each had an attribute appropriate to the weather that could be expected from that quarter: the northerly winds, dressed in boots and heavy cloaks, carried basins of rain or hailstones; the southerly ones, their feet bare and light mantles fluttering behind their shoulders, carried flowers or the stern of a ship—a promise of fair sailing. Inside the tower was a water clock composed of two tanks of water: time was measured by letting water from the upper tank flow into the lower one. An axle suspended over the water had a chain wrapped around it, with a float affixed to one end and a counterweight to the other. As the water in the bottom tank rose, it lifted the float, turning the axle and moving a rotating disk attached to it by a series of gears. The disk was marked with hours, days, and phases of the moon. The ancient Athenians reckoned time by this central clock.[23] Early Christians converted the tower into a baptistery, and, after Cyriacus's day, the Turks would use it as a gathering place of dervishes. And so this jewel of architecture survived largely intact.

To the southwest of the Acropolis, on a hill sacred to the Muses, Cyriacus spotted a marble monument gleaming in the spring sunshine. Climbing the slope, he came face-to-face with the splendid mausoleum of a Syrian prince, C. Julius Antiochus Philopappos, who had lived in Athens in the second century AD and greatly benefited the city. The structure's curved facade was two stories high, with three niches enclosing sculpted portraits of Philopappos and his royal antecedents above, and a frieze carved in high relief showing Philopappos riding a chariot in a procession below. Five inscriptions boasted of his accomplishments. (Behind this facade was a rectangular burial chamber containing the man's sarcophagus, but it had been dismantled by the Acciaiuoli dukes and its blocks used to construct the Christian bell tower next to the Parthenon.) Cyriacus lovingly sketched the memorial and copied its inscriptions. By the time the next European visitor saw Philopappos's monument two centuries later, its right side would be entirely gone. We know of its original appearance only thanks to Cyriacus's drawings.

There were other structures Cyriacus saw better preserved than would his followers in the seventeenth century. He must have felt especially delighted to encounter traces of the emperor Hadrian, having marveled at his villa at Tivoli and his mausoleum and the Pantheon in Rome. A devotee of Greek culture, Hadrian had bestowed several grand structures on the city: a library that was really a cultural center containing an extensive collection of scrolls, works of art, lecture halls, and a garden; an aqueduct that brought in water from springs on the slopes of Mount Párnes; an elegant gateway that marked a transition between the old town and Hadrian's new expansion; and a gigantic temple to Olympian Zeus. Cyriacus took pains to record or sketch the remains of all of them.

The Olympieion, the most astonishing of these monuments, was actually a product of three ambitious men. It was begun by Peisistratos, the first tyrant of Athens, in the sixth century BC, but abandoned after his death. In the second century BC King Antiochos IV of Syria, known for his megalomania, resolved to resume construction on a temple to a god with whom he felt distinct affinity. To do justice to Zeus and

Sangallo's drawing of the Philopappos monument in Athens after Cyriacus. From Giuliano da Sangallo, Il libro di Giuliano da Sangallo Codice vaticanobarberiniano latino 4424 riprodotto in fototipia, *ed. Cristiano Huelsen, Lipsia: O. Harrassowitz, 1910.*

to himself, Antiochos envisioned a building some 360 feet long by 140 feet wide (about the size of an American football field) with a forest of 104 Corinthian columns. He died before his dream could be realized, and it was Hadrian who finally finished the shrine in 122–3 AD. Hadrian's achievement outshone its divine dedicatee, and medieval Athenians thought of the temple—largely toppled by time and earthquakes—as "Hadrian's Palace." It stood just outside the gate to Hadrian's expansion to the city and seemed imposing enough to have been an imperial dwelling. Cyriacus, who, unlike most travelers, took local lore about ancient monuments with a grain of salt, believed this designation probably because he had seen the size and grandeur of Hadrian's Villa at Tivoli and could imagine that, if that was the emperor's countryside retreat, his Athenian palace might well have been this spectacular. In his diary he recorded his wonder at "the home of the emperor Hadrian, with enormous marble columns, most of which have fallen down. However, there are still standing twenty-one columns, with their architraves intact and forming straight lines. Their diameter is seven feet; their capitals fourteen feet in diameter, and their height is sixty feet."[24] When the temple was still intact, it had been filled with statues of Hadrian erected in the emperor's honor by cities from all over the Roman Empire. These had vanished by the fifteenth century, but their bases remained, and Cyriacus, exploring every bit of the structure inside and out, copied inscriptions on eight of them. Today they are all lost.

Cyriacus's investigations and descriptions of Athenian monuments were unique. No visitor since antiquity had journeyed to the city for the sake of its classical heritage, and no

VEDUTA DEL CAST. D'ACROPOLIS DALLA PARTE DI TRAMONTANA.

Explosion of the Parthenon as a result of Venetian bombardment, engraving in Francesco Fenelli, Atene attica: descritta da suoi principii fino all'acquisto fatto dall'armi venete nel 1687, *Venice: Appresso Antonio Bortolo, 1707. (Research Library, The Getty Research Institute, Los Angeles, CA)*

one offered such precise observations of what survived. Yet by pursuing the course of war in the name of securing the past, Cyriacus helped precipitate a clash between Europeans and Turks that would not only make Greece largely inaccessible to other archaeologists for the next two centuries, but claim its most spectacular victim: the Parthenon itself.

Within twenty years of Cyriacus's visit to Athens the Turks gained control of the city. Though Cyriacus was not directly responsible for this, his incessant pressing for a military rather than a diplomatic solution to the growing conflict between the Ottomans and the Greeks and Europeans contributed to the escalation of hostilities between them. Perhaps it was inevitable in any case, but Cyriacus and his contemporaries do not seem to have considered a more constructive alternative. For the next two hundred years, the Turks and the Venetians waged an intermittent but ongoing war—not only in Greece, but across the Mediterranean—making the region largely inpenetrable to European explorers. In 1687–8 the Venetians succeeded in occupying the lower part of Athens and attempted to expel the Turks from the Acropolis, where an Ottoman governor had replaced the Florentine one. As the Venetians tried to dislodge the enemy, the commanding general, Francesco Morosini, learned that the Ottomans had placed their ammunition, as well as women and children, inside the Parthenon. On September 28, 1687, he ordered the shelling of the building. Impact scars on the marble indicate that some seven hundred cannonballs struck the shrine. Eventually a missile pierced the interior, igniting the gunpowder. The resulting explosion, which shook the whole city and killed three hundred people inside and outside the temple, blasted out the Parthenon's roof, walls, and numerous columns. In a few minutes the magnificent structure that had survived nearly intact for over two millennia was reduced to a ruin. When Morosini arrived on the Acropolis to review the results, he saw that the west pediment remained mostly unharmed and decided to take its central figures back to Venice. As they were being lowered, the machinery employed for the task broke and the sculptures crashed to the ground, smashing into bits.

Cyriacus, having worried so long about the danger to antiquities in Greece, had never stopped to consider that the Crusade toward which he was striving might lead to far greater harm—inflicted by his own countrymen—than centuries of indifference and neglect.

208

EVGENIVS IV.
rius Venet. creatus
Sedit an.15.men.ii.
Februarij an.1447.

Gabriel Condulme.
die 3.Martij 1431.
dies 21.Obijt die 23.
Vac.Sed.dies 10.

Portrait of Eugenius IV in Cronologia summorum
romanorum pontificum, *Rome, 1805. (Research Library,*
The Getty Research Institute, Los Angeles, CA)

*That which separates the Greeks from you is not so much
a difference of dogma as the hatred of the Greeks for the
Latins provoked by the wrongs they have suffered. It will be
necessary to confer some great boon on them to change their
feeling . . .*

—Barlaam of Calabria to Pope Benedict XII[1]

Meeting of the Minds

CYRIACUS RETURNED HOME from Greece just in time
for an event he had long been striving for—a gathering
peaceful in principle, but militant in its ultimate aim. In February 1438 a vast Byzantine delegation comprised of Emperor
John VIII Palaeologus, Patriarch Joseph II of Constantinople,
twenty bishops, numerous prelates and monks, a contingent
of learned laymen, and various courtiers—some seven hundred in all—landed in Italy. They came to negotiate with the
pope and the Catholic clergy about the reunion of the Eastern
and Western Churches as a prelude to a Crusade against the
Turks.

The physical journey of the Greeks toward the West had been
as arduous as the advance negotiations and as disheartening
as the forthcoming discussions would prove to be. Their ships
were repeatedly ambushed by storms that either drove them

forward uncontrollably, or carried them back to their starting points. Calm spells stranded them for days. The emperor's galley was nearly captured by Catalan pirates, who gave chase to his vessel and had to be fought off. Broken booms, frayed stays, a collision that damaged the oarage of one ship, an illness which required the emperor to convalesce on an uninhabited island, and other accidents hampered the voyage and presaged the difficulties ahead. Even seemingly good days brought little respite. Sailing aboard merchant vessels crammed with slaves and other merchandise, the Greeks were crowded, nauseous, and homesick. One member of the delegation recorded that "the Patriarch and the other aged prelates, and sometimes the Emperor too, neither ate nor drank nor slept, except in port. So if there had not been numerous islands with harbors controlled by the Venetians or the Greeks, assuredly they would not have been able to reach Venice."[2] The exhausted travelers were relieved to arrive on February 8, 1438, and hopeful that their suffering had not been in vain. The following months would sorely test their resolve to reach a union with their Western rivals in faith, and their dream to save their home from heathen foes in the East.

For the moment, though, the doge of Venice and the republic's leading citizens welcomed the Greeks with great pomp and toured them around the city, though the splendor of the reception was dampened by mist and showers. The Greeks were overwhelmed by the beauty all around them, especially compared to the dilapidated state of Constantinople: "a glorious and marvelous Venice, verily marvelous, marvelous in the extreme and rich and varied and golden and highly finished and variegated and worthy of limitless praise," gushed

Syropoulos, one of the Byzantine prelates who left a detailed account of the delegation. The sight of the treasury of San Marco, crammed with objects pilfered from Constantinople in 1204, cooled their enthusiasm somewhat and filled the Greeks with sorrow and renewed misgivings about the upcoming talks.[3] How fairly could they expect to be treated by those who had caused them so much grief?

Distrust between the Greeks and the Latins ran like a deep ravine—as Cyriacus knew from his conversations with the emperor and other Byzantines. Since the official break between the Eastern and Western Churches in 1054, there had been some thirty attempts to reunite them.[4] All had led to nothing. Now, with Murad's conquest of Thessaloniki, Gabriele Condulmaro's accession to the papal throne, and Cyriacus's tireless efforts, the two sides seemed more committed to negotiations than ever.[5] Everyone had a vested interest in the union: Eugenius IV stood to augment his power and to prevail over the Council of Basel, which remained determined to undermine and depose him; John VIII Palaeologus would receive Western aid for his rapidly diminishing empire; and Cyriacus hoped to preserve antiquities from the Turkish menace. He had lobbied for the union since 1431 and doubtless rejoiced to see the Greeks finally come to Italy. His optimism would be challenged before long.

After a month in Venice, the Byzantines set out for Ferrara, chosen to host them because it was a pleasant and well-fortified city, neutral in the constant conflicts between various Italian states, easily accessible from Venice by a system of waterways, and blessed with a fertile countryside that could feed the huge influx of visitors. The emperor reached it on March 4 in driving rain. The patriarch arrived four days later, his advent nearly derailing the whole enterprise. Informed that he would have to salute the pope in the traditional Western manner, by genuflecting and kissing his foot, the octogenarian Joseph II flatly refused to abase himself and the Orthodox Church in this manner. "Whence has the Pope this right? Which synod gave it to him?" he fumed. "Show me from what source derives this privilege and where it is written? The Pope claims that he is the successor of St. Peter. But if he is the successor of Peter, then we too are the successors of the rest of the Apostles. Did they kiss the foot of St. Peter?"[6] Eugenius's representatives tried to persuade him that it was an ancient custom for all to kiss the pope's foot. The patriarch snapped back, "This is an innovation and I will not follow it," and threatened to return to Venice. For a day messengers went back and forth between the two camps. In the end the patriarch won the skirmish, but not without painful concessions: he did not have to kiss the pope's foot, but was obliged to set aside his ceremonial head-dress and staff as he approached Eugenius, and be received not in a formal public ceremony but in a discreet private audience, where few Westerners would see the omission of proper subordination to the pontiff. This unhappy beginning was a preview of the wrangling that would punctuate the meeting and jeopardize it at every step, as the Latins strove to assert their superiority and the Greeks their equality.

Another major confrontation took place over the seating arrangements planned by the pope for the summit, to be held in the cathedral of Ferrara. Eugenius declared that since he was an arbiter of the proceedings, his throne should be placed in the middle of the church, with the Greeks to his left and the

Latins to his right. John VIII took this as an infringement of his imperial rights: in Byzantine practice it was the prerogative of the emperor as vicar of God to preside over ecumenical councils. After much haggling, the papal throne was placed on the side of the Latins, but elevated above all others including that of the emperor. The Greeks were right to worry about the evenhandedness of their hosts.

The Council of Ferrara solemnly opened on April 9, 1438. But the emperor demanded that doctrinal discussions be postponed by four months, to allow Western princes time to come to Ferrara or to send their representatives with offers of military aid for Constantinople. To while away the time, John VIII plunged into his favorite pastime. "Having discovered a convent some six miles from Ferrara," wrote Syropoulos with consternation, "he set himself up there with a few archons, some soldiers, and janissaries, leaving the greater number in town. He spent all his time hunting without bothering in the slightest with ecclesiastical affairs."[7] John VIII also exasperated the Marquis of Ferrara, who begged him "to restrain his enthusiasm for the chase owing to the damage he was causing to the property of the countryfolk and to the decimation of the game that the marquis had imported for his own pleasure."[8] The emperor ignored his pleas and, trailed by his favorite dog, galloped through the forests and meadows.

Meanwhile, his entourage chafed at being stuck idly in Ferrara and agonized about the safety of their homeland. News had arrived from Venice that the sultan was about to attack Constantinople with a fleet of 150 ships and an army of 150,000 soldiers. The Greeks despaired about the fate of their wives and children, churches and possessions, and tried to raise a fund for the immediate defense of their city—without success. Impecunious, they depended on the pope for their maintenance, and Eugenius was running out of funds. He had not planned on supporting so many people for months on end and grew increasingly wary as his treasury drained away while the council made no progress whatsoever.

In the middle of the summer, as the temperature and the impatience rose, the two sides decided to hold a conversation on the subject of purgatory, one of the issues that cleft them apart. The Latins believed that sinners were punished by fire while in purgatory; the Greeks denied that such a trial took place or was even possible for bodiless and immaterial souls. They also argued over the degree to which souls in that transitory state could see God. Did the Greeks compare their current predicament to that of the damned, as their arguments failed to lead to any agreement with the Latins? Their anxieties about home were augmented by fears of dying in Ferrara, as plague arrived in the city and began to decimate the population, including members of the Russian Orthodox delegation. Cyriacus, serving in Ancona's government that summer and fall, missed these months of stagnation and malaise, but he must have heard and felt dispirited that all the work and hope he had put into the council were being squandered.

By October, eight months after the Greeks came to Italy, it became clear that no Western princes would appear at Ferrara, so the council's formal deliberations finally got under way. The main topic of discussion was the greatest problem separating the two churches: the *Filioque* clause in the Latin Creed. The original creed described the Holy Spirit as proceeding from the Father. In the eleventh century Rome added the phrase

Filioque, "and [from] the son." The Greeks saw this amendment as illegal and the resulting doctrine as erroneous. The Latins could not possibly admit that they were heretics and insisted on its validity. For two months they argued heatedly about the legitimacy of the addition. By December they stood farther from union than they had been when the Greeks arrived.

A few comic and ridiculous moments punctuated the overall gloom. At the beginning of the council, John VIII insisted on being able to reach his throne in the cathedral on horseback, so a wall had to be broken to allow adequate passage. Until the hole was made, sessions were suspended. In the emperor's defense, it was usual practice in Byzantium for him to appear in public on horseback. But to hack through a church for the sake of this prerogative must have seemed absurd to the Latins. On another occasion, the Burgundian envoys of Duke Philip the Good brought a letter from their lord to the pope and addressed him in their speeches, paying little heed to John VIII. The emperor, incensed, demanded redress of the insult. So a special session was convened in which the ambassadors presented him with a similar, but fictitious letter.[9] During one of the theological debates, the Greek scholar Georges Amiroutzes stood with a companion in a far corner of the cathedral, out of sight of the high clergy, but facing Marcus Eugenicus, the most vocal opponent of union, and surreptitiously jeered and made funny faces at him to distract him from his defense of Orthodoxy (the Greeks being by no means united on this subject, on the best methods of negotiating with the Latins, or on the feasibility of the union in the first place).[10]

Alas, such instances of unintentional humor were rare, and the Greeks especially grew ever more miserable. Unable to find common ground with the Latins, and unwilling to compromise their dignity, they worried that they would be stuck in Italy forever, while their country perished. Their spirits were not improved by their financial despair: the pope had run out of money and was five months behind in his payments for their sustenance. The Greeks, particularly those of lower rank, suffered privation and had to sell their possessions for food. Meanwhile, plague continued to claim lives, and Ferrara was now also threatened by the mercenary troops of the Duke of Milan, an enemy of the pope.

To ease these woes, Eugenius decided to move the council to Florence, where the Medici offered to underwrite its expenses, and where no threat to health and life poisoned the air. Cyriacus, having completed his term of office in Ancona, hurried to Florence. The accord he had been striving for was proving elusive, as the dogmatism of the Greeks and the Latins drove them further apart in person than it had at a distance. But an unexpected positive development was emerging amidst the disunion, and Cyriacus was eager to participate.

The arrival of the Byzantines proved to be an enormous boon for Italian humanists, giving them an unprecedented opportunity to meet their Greek counterparts and to discuss ancient literature and philosophy with men who preserved an unbroken link with classical civilization. The erudition of the Greeks awed the Latins.[11] Georges Gemistus Pletho, an ardent octogenarian neo-pagan, knew more about Plato than anyone and gave public lectures on the subject to the enraptured Florentines. (Inspired by him, Cosimo de' Medici would later found a Platonic Academy.) Gemistus Pletho was also happy to converse with the Italians informally, and to pass judgment on their abilities, including their lack of sound learning and qualification to appreciate Plato and Aristotle. The thirty-five-year-old Basilios Bessarion, metropolitan of Nicaea, meanwhile, discoursed equally brilliantly on ancient culture and church doctrine. A passionate bookworm, he was keen to bring Greek literature to Italy. Having assembled the greatest Greek library of his day, complemented by many Latin volumes, and anxious to preserve this cultural treasury from the Ottomans, he bequeathed it to Venice, where it came to form the heart of the Biblioteca Marciana, a preeminent Renaissance public library. John Argyropoulos, a renowned translator of Aristotle and the leading expert on ancient mechanics, was a gifted teacher whose pupils would include Lorenzo de' Medici and Leonardo da Vinci.

In addition to the vast knowledge stored in their bearded heads, the Byzantines brought along an array of books to be cited and consulted during the council. These made the Italians salivate. Ambrogio Traversari wrote to a friend that he had seen the emperor's beautiful Plato, Plutarch, Aristotle, Diodorus, and Dionysius of Halicarnassus, and was hoping to see much more.[12] He confided that when Bessarion told him that he had packed only a few books, "but had left a big pile at Modon [in the Peloponnese]," including two large volumes of Strabo, "How ill I took it that he had not brought the volumes along! But I had to conceal the fact. I am led to hope, nevertheless, that they are to be brought."[13] Many of the Greek texts were unavailable in Italy. Now Traversari and his friends had a chance to study the precious works. The Greeks were happy to copy their manuscripts for the Florentines, and cheaply, glad to earn a bit of money to supplement their scanty funds.[14]

The Italian and Greek humanists came to the council to lend their expertise as textual scholars and learned secretaries. But it was their informal exchange with each other that produced the most encouraging and enduring results. Cardinal Cesarini, one of the key figures in the congress, threw dinner parties to mull over philosophical questions with Bessarion, Gemistus Pletho, and Georges Amiroutzes, whose expertise comprised theology, philosophy, natural sciences, medicine, rhetoric, and poetry.[15] Such conversations, far more congenial and constructive than the endless haggling of the theologians, would yield lasting fruit. While the union of churches would remain an elusive and moribund dream, its intellectual offshoots would nurture the whole of Europe. By bringing their books and knowledge to Italy and igniting the curiosity of Western colleagues, the Byzantines furthered the study of not only Greek literature but other disciplines: astronomy and geography, medicine and mechanics. Ironically, the fall of Constantinople a few years later would further enrich the West. As Greek intellectuals fled their vanquished home, they carried along as many ancient tomes as they could, giving another powerful boost to the Renaissance. Cyriacus's belief that war could preserve ancient civilization would thus be proven right, but for entirely wrong reasons.[16]

For now, he must have relished his time among the Italian and Greek scholars. He knew many of them already— Gemistus Pletho from Mistra, near Sparta, which he had visited during his trip through mainland Greece because John VIII's brother Constantine XI held court there; the Italian humanists from his previous sojourns in Florence and Rome. It was a treat for him to converse with fellow devotees of the past, and valuable for them to include in their discussions the man who possessed unique knowledge of the material remains of antiquity. Cyriacus was also invited to join John VIII's entourage. Having gained the emperor's trust by his unstinting efforts to convene the council and organize the Crusade, Cyriacus was now made the emperor's courtier, attending him in Florence and beyond.

∽ঌৎ

The progress of the council itself was far less satisfying. The Byzantines arrived in Florence in January 1439, during the Carnival, and were greeted by gaily dressed citizens jamming the streets, balconies, and rooftops along the processional route—until the skies suddenly opened and torrential rain scattered them, leaving the soggy imperial procession to dash indecorously toward their allotted palazzo. It took the Greeks and the Latins nearly two months to resume their deliberations. Picking up again the unresolved matter of *Filioque*, they shifted their arguments from its legality to its status as doctrine. In no time the talks became mired in bickering over who had the more accurate version of key church texts. This distanced the two sides further and made the Greeks even more glum. The Latins, they complained, seemed to be able to go on arguing forever. For every word uttered by the Greeks they responded with a dozen. When the pope urged the Byzantines to accept the Latin arguments or to refute them in another public session, the exasperated Greeks replied:

> We are having no more public discussions, because disputations produce nothing except irritation. If we say anything, you are never at a loss for an answer and that at great length. Hearing the endless things you say—who can go on listening and answering for ever? So take counsel to see if there is some other way leading towards union and tell us of it. If there is no such way, we have said as much as we can.[17]

In truth, the Greeks were concerned less with defending the Orthodox doctrine than with preserving their dignity. The experience of being dominated and humiliated by the Franks after the Fourth Crusade stoked their fears that if they accepted *Filioque*, they would again become subjects. "I will not give up our dogma and become Latinized," exclaimed one Greek bishop. Others declared that they would prefer the turban of the sultan to the tiara of the pope. They had a point: the Turks had generally followed Islamic precepts of tolerance toward Christianity and permitted the conquered Greeks to practice their religion as they wished. Nor did the Byzantines trust Western promises of aid. The Orthodox polemicist Joseph Bryennios asserted, "Let no one be deceived by delusive hopes that the Italian allied troops will come to save us. If they pretend to rise to defend us, they will take arms only to destroy our city, our race, and our name."[18] Indeed, Petrarch had remarked already a century earlier that "The Turks are enemies, but the Greeks are schismatics and worse than enemies."[19] Little wonder that neither side was willing to give way. And so the acrimonious and fruitless debates dragged on.

As the chasm between the Latins and the Greeks widened, Cyriacus watched with exasperation. Unable to participate in theological debates, for which he had no training, he pursued the cause of the Crusade by writing letters to various Italian rulers and exhorting them to conclude their domestic wars so as to direct their attention and resources to the fight against the Turks.

～

In late May 1439 the pope, pressed by his financial troubles, the Council of Basel, and the specter of failure, decided to compel the council to a resolution. Addressing the assembled Latins and Greeks with emotion in his voice, he recalled the joy with which he had welcomed the Byzantine delegation after it had braved a perilous journey for the sake of union. He then recounted his growing disappointment as fifteen months passed without any result, and his despair at disagreements that continued to this day. "What am I to say?" he intoned.

> I see division everywhere before my eyes and I wonder what use to you division will be. Still if it shall be, how are the western princes going to look on it? And what grief will you [the Greeks] yourselves have; indeed how are you going to return home? Union however once achieved, both the western princes and all of us will greatly rejoice and will provide generous help for you. And our aid will be a

source of great alleviation to the Christians dwelling in the East and to those in the power of the infidel. I exhort you then, brethren, following the precept of Our Lord Jesus Christ, let there not be division in the Church of God, but be urgent, be vigilant, let us give glory to God together.[20]

Eugenius's words touched his listeners, worn out and dispirited by endless and useless debates. They set to work with renewed determination and by June 8 found a way to reconcile their differences. The doctrine of the two churches was the same in substance, they decided, even if phrased differently: the Latin *Filioque*, "from the Son," was in essence equal to the Greek "through the Son." The Greeks, with a few exceptions, accepted this compromise, some out of conviction, others under imperial and patriarchal pressure, still others from sheer exhaustion and desire to be done. The whole assembly breathed a sigh of relief at finally reaching an accord. The Latins and Greeks were even moved to embrace—a gesture of geniality remarkable for all the preceding acrimony. As soon as the *Filioque* problem was solved, John VIII asked the pope for a specific military aid package, with its terms set down in writing and the banks of Venice, Genoa, and Florence ordered to disburse the funds. The pope agreed. Things began to look promising. Then, two days later, the patriarch Joseph II died suddenly after supper.

Though old and ailing, he had been an anchor of the Greek community. An affable man of grave manner, simple spirituality, and abundant common sense, he had worked hard to maintain peace among the Byzantines, as factions within the delegation argued about their divergent interpretations of dogma and the feasibility of compromising with the Latins. Joseph, neither militantly unionist nor anti-unionist, had retained everyone's confidence and affection. Now the Greeks were bereft of his wise guidance, just as the union was within sight.

There was no other course but to push forward and hammer out the remaining points of contention. Through the remainder of June the two sides came to a mutual understanding on the subjects of purgatory, the use of leavened versus unleavened bread in the Eucharist, and papal superiority. On this last, thorny issue, the Latins affirmed the authority of the pope as universal head of the Eastern and Western Churches, but added that "all the rights and privileges of the patriarchs of the East are excepted." Whatever that meant in practice, they could finally put an end to the seemingly interminable council.

It must have been hard for the Greeks and the Latins to believe that, at long last, they had overcome their differences— or managed to agree, however grudgingly, to set them aside. The abyss that had kept the two churches apart for nearly four centuries could now close. What an achievement it was, and what a shock. On July 6, 1439, the two sides gathered together in the cathedral of Florence under the magnificent dome recently completed by Brunelleschi. It was Monday, but all the shops and businesses closed and the populace crammed into the church and the adjacent squares to witness the historic event. The cathedral had been prepared with thrones for the ecclesiastical and secular dignitaries and tribunes for participants of lesser rank. The Byzantine emperor entered the church clad in the full splendor of his brocaded damask silk gown and jeweled pointed hat. Though small and stooped, John VIII looked majestic in his attire and exotic with his forked beard—as if he had stepped out of a painting of the Adoration of the Magi. The pope entered shortly thereafter and proceeded to serve Mass, with the Epistles and the Gospels read in both Latin and Greek. At the conclusion of the service, Cardinal Cesarini mounted the pulpit placed near the papal chair and read in Latin the official proclamation of the union between the Eastern and Western Churches. He was followed by Bessarion in Greek. Cyriacus must have basked in this moment. He had labored for it for seven years. Finally the Latins and the Greeks could proceed to the real purpose of their accord: a joint war on the Turks.

While Cyriacus must have felt triumphant, as did Eugenius IV, the Greeks were less jubilant. They had made more concessions than they had wished to, and many of them would repudiate the accord as soon as they returned home. True union would never materialize, and the Crusade would only precipitate its unraveling and the end of Byzantium.

❧

For the moment, the enterprise still had a veneer of success, and Cyriacus savored it alongside the emperor. John VIII, relieved at the end of the ordeal, wanted to clear his head with a bit of sightseeing before embarking on the homeward journey. He invited Cyriacus to accompany him. The imperial party rode to Pistoia to have a look at its many pretty churches, and to Prato, famous for manufacturing fine textiles and for the Girdle of Our Lady in its cathedral. En route back to Florence, fatigued by the July heat, John VIII decided to stop at Peretola, a small town some three and a half miles northwest. He sent ahead Angelo Acciaiuoli (first cousin of Nerio II, Duke of Athens), appointed by the Signoria to escort the Byzantines. Acciaiuoli chanced to run into Giovanni de' Pigli, a local citizen who offered his house to the distinguished guests and recorded the imperial visit in his diary.[21] Pigli named only three people specifically in this event of his lifetime: the emperor, Acciaiuoli, and Cyriacus.

John VIII, Pigli wrote, arrived with a suite of forty or fifty knights, plus his barons, lords, and gentlemen. Mistaking imperial dignity for infirmity, Pigli thought that "because he had lost the use of his legs, he came right up to our hall on horseback, without anyone's seeing him dismount, except his own gentlemen and attendants." Cyriacus was used to such sights, but Pigli drew his own conclusion. After a nap and a meal, the emperor stayed indoors as the sun beat down on the town, and played backgammon with one of his barons. Pigli gawked in wonder at his exotic guest: "Messer Angelo and Ciriaco of Ancona, a man most learned in Greek and Latin, and I stood there all day in the hall, the emperor always playing backgammon and joking with his people." John VIII was savoring a brief moment of rest and relaxation between the tribulations of the council and the looming task of salvaging the remnants of his empire.

❧

The union agreed upon—or so it seemed in Italy that summer—Cyriacus wrote a letter to Eugenius imploring him immediately to begin preparing a general expedition against the Turks. But though Eugenius had promised material aid to John VIII, and was now truly committed to the anti-Ottoman offensive (which would further enhance his prestige and disarm the Council of Basel), he had no means to underwrite it himself. He could provide money and a fleet, but he needed Western rulers to furnish the troops. Yet the European princes were too wrapped up in their own affairs to concern themselves with Byzantium: England and France were just emerging from their endless war, the German emperor and electors were still embroiled in a contest for power, Austria and Hungary were divided on the succession to the Hungarian crown. Eugenius sent embassies and exhortations across Europe, but they yielded no results.

Meanwhile, the Turks had steadily extended their reach. In 1438 Murad had launched attacks on Transylvania and Hungary (urged upon this bellicose course by his vizier, according to the Greek historian Doukas). To the terror of the local inhabitants, the sultan swept down on them not only with his swarms of warriors, but also with a thousand camels bearing the army's equipment. Having destroyed several cities and pillaged the countryside, he enslaved 80,000 prisoners. The following year, while the council deliberated in Florence, Murad led an expedition into Serbia, captured Smederevo, the capital of the Balkan despotate, and reduced to servitude all but the province of Novo Brdo, the center of the gold- and silver-mining district. In April 1440 the Turks laid siege to Belgrade, hoping to use it as a gateway to Hungary. During the assault, Murad sent raiders into southern Hungary. They returned with so much booty that "they sold slave-girls for the price of boots." Belgrade held out, and after six months Murad raised the siege.[22] But the danger lifted only temporarily.

Cyriacus, no longer John VIII's courtier after the Byzantine delegation sailed home, and loath merely to return to trade, tried to find a way to continue his political involvement and antiquarian research. On October 18, 1441, he wrote to Eugenius asking to be sent as a papal emissary to Egypt and Ethiopia, to help bring the Copts and the Jacobites into union with the Latin church, while conducting archaeological investigations in those areas. He was driven, Cyriacus explained to the pope, "by the ardent desire to visit the world in order to search for ancient monuments spread in all the regions of the universe, which have been for a long time the principal goal of my study, in order to be able to record in writing that which from day to day falls into ruin due to the ravage of time and negligence of man and yet which is worthy of memory."[23] Eugenius denied this request. But after Elizabeth of Hungary died in 1442 and her crown was assumed by the ambitious eighteen-year-old Ladislas III, king of Poland, the Crusade finally acquired the additional support it needed. On January 1, 1443, Eugenius proclaimed it officially. Within a few months he sent Cyriacus as his agent to Greece and Asia Minor, to pave the way for the Christian fleet. This voyage would turn out to be Cyriacus's—and the West's—last chance to gain access to Eastern antiquities before the Ottoman gates slammed shut.

*Cyriacus's drawing of the "Aristotle" bust at Samothrace, in
Bartolomeus Fontius, Bodleian Library Ms. Lat. misc. d. 85,
f. 141r, Bodleian Library, Oxford University.*

Men willingly believe what they wish.
　　　—Julius Caesar, *Commentaries on the Gallic War*[1]

The Last Crusade

C YRIACUS RETURNED TO the East, his mission to enlist and maintain the cooperation of all those who might be useful to the naval arm of the expedition, to keep them abreast of its progress, and to report back to the pope. With his extensive knowledge of Greece, Byzantium, the Ottoman lands, and their key political players, he was ideal for this job. For him it must have been a dream assignment: feeding his love of adventure, giving him an active role in the cause for which he had agitated for a decade, and granting him access to ancient sites he had not been able to visit as a businessman.[2]

He had come a long way: from a wide-eyed young merchant eager for knowledge, to an authority on the ancient world admired by humanists and artists, to a diplomat welcomed by rulers at home and abroad—all as a result of having fallen in love with ancient monuments and becoming their passionate champion in the face of neglect and destruction. But over time his zeal seems to have eroded the open-mindedness that had led him to study the past in the first place. He had been pushing for a Crusade for so long, and against so many obstacles, that his mission hardened from an intellectual rescue operation to an all-out war. From an idealist, Cyriacus turned into an ideologue. The Ottomans had treated him generously over long years of trading—and even spying—but now he spouted militant rhetoric and cast them as barbarians, drawing on ancient history to justify his stance. As he wrote to Giuliano Cesarini, the papal legate in charge of the Crusade, on December 3, 1443,

> I am equally compelled to observe, praise, and extol greatly the fact that the excellent king of Hungary, Ladislas, will obey you in the most holy enterprise; indeed, for my part, I believe it would be unjust to suppose that this loyal and most devoted king has not applied his great spirit to the successful execution of this most worthy campaign against the Turks, since tradition tells us that, long ago at Rome, in the time of Caesars, the fateful books of Sibyl revealed that the Parthians could be subjected only by a king. For it is well known and altogether clear that the Turks and Achaemenids take their origins from the Parthians.[3]

Cyriacus had always been given to hyperbole and poetic interpretation of current events, but now he drew on ancient literature and mythology for less benign reasons. Neglecting, as those blinded by passion do, the lessons of history, he seemingly forgot the effects he had observed in Constantinople of the previous Crusade in 1204. And so he failed to foresee his own plans' potential for disaster. His last journey around the Mediterranean would prove to be his most paradoxical:

he would try to save with one hand what he unwittingly con-
demned with the other.

∾§∾

Cyriacus arrived in Greece in January 1444 and paid visits
to Thomas and Constantine Palaeologus, brothers of John
VIII ruling Patras and Corinth. He reported to the Byzantine emperor that Constantine had captured Thebes and was
planning to repair the fortification wall across the Isthmus
of Corinth—which Herodotus says was first built in 480 BC
to protect against the invading Persians—and press beyond it
with a large army so as to create a front against the Turks in
central Greece. In March 1444 Cyriacus reached Athens, Constantine's advances having made it strategically important for
the Crusade, though, naturally, he also yearned to lay his eyes
again on the city's ancient remains.

This was something of a homecoming. "We went back to
see the octagonal marble temple of Aeolus," he wrote to his
friend Andreolo, referring to the Tower of the Winds. He also
scrutinized with greater care the Propylaea on the Acropolis:

> When I had rather carefully inspected the very imposing
> workmanship of [the Duke of Athens'] exceptional palace, I
> saw that its admirable porch consists of four finished mar-
> ble columns and, above, ten marble beams in a row.
>
> But after we had come into the main hall itself, we saw
> that six huge columns, arranged in two rows, three feet
> wide in diameter, supported a marble, coffered ceiling and
> twenty-four beams, entirely of polished marble, arranged

Sangallo's drawing of the Parthenon, copied and adapted from Cyriacus. From Giuliano da Sangallo, Il libro di Giuliano da Sangallo Codice vaticanobarberiniano latino 4424 riprodotto in fototipia, ed. Cristiano Huelsen, Lipsia: O. Harrassowitz, 1910.

in three rows. Each beam is twenty-four feet long and three feet wide, in my estimation. The stately marble walls themselves consist of finished stone equally large, entrance to which is by a single, remarkably big door.[4]

Cyriacus must have made a sketch of the Propylaea and, as was his habit, sent it and his verbal description to his friends in Italy, because in the 1480s the architect Giuliano da Sangallo, who had copied into his album of designs a number of Cyriacus's drawings of ancient buildings of Athens and Constantinople, would use the majestic ancient gateway to the Acropolis as a model for the grand entrance to Lorenzo de' Medici's villa at Poggia a Caiano.[5]

"But my special preference," Cyriacus continued in his report to Andreolo, "was to revisit on that very same bright citadel that greatly celebrated temple of the divine Pallas [the Parthenon] and to examine it more carefully from every angle." Cyriacus was the first modern European to explicitly identify the builder of "this extraordinary, marvelous temple . . . the admirable work of Phidias, as we know from the testimony of Aristotle's instructions to king Alexander as well as from our own Pliny and a host of other notable authors." He was also the first to carefully record the particulars of the structure: "58 columns: 12 at each of its two fronts, two rows of six in the middle and, outside the walls, seventeen along each side . . . The columns support the entablatures nine and one-half feet long and four feet high, on which one sees the battle in Thessaly between centaurs and Lapiths, sculpted with amazing skill." And he made the first drawing of "this absolutely splendid building."[6] His description and images of the Parthenon were the first to reach Europe since antiquity, and they captivated Renaissance artists. Donatello, casting a monumental equestrian bronze statue of the military commander Erasmo da Narno (a.k.a. Gattamelata) in the late 1440s, included on the rider's saddle horsemen with billowing drapery derived from the Parthenon frieze.[7] Sangallo copied Cyriacus's sketch of the temple into his notebook to serve as an inspiration. Humanists, too, were fascinated by Cyriacus's reports and replicated them in their own manuscripts. But the Parthenon would not become a widespread model for European public buildings until the nineteenth century, after the liberation of Greece from the Turks.

Cyriacus next sailed to Asia Minor, to confer with John VIII Palaeologus regarding the Crusade. He disembarked at New Phocaea, the Genoese alum production center, and treated himself to a brief visit to several ancient sites on the western coast of Turkey: Miletus, Chryse, and Sardis. The latter struck him as particularly evocative:

> The first thing we noticed when we arrived at the city of Sardis was the Pactolus river flowing downhill in front of the city's walls; a tiny stream, but more famous than all others for its monetary worth as it carries the gold-bearing sand from which, it is said, Croesus [the king of Lydia, whose capital was Sardis] once acquired enormous wealth, relying on a technique for causing gold to coagulate. We

carried off a small sample of this sand . . . It seems to glitter with numerous tiny particles of gold.[8]

Returning to New Phocaea, Cyriacus was about to catch a boat to Constantinople when an unexpected encounter altered his plans.

Francesco Draperio, a Genoese merchant of enormous wealth and influence, lived permanently in Pera—the suburb of Constantinople located across the Golden Horn from the city and inhabited by Genoese traders—but traveled on business all over the Mediterranean, leasing and operating alum mines at New Phocaea and Lesbos, carrying on extensive commerce in silk, soap, and slaves, and enjoying the favor of the Ottoman sultan. Having just visited his mines, Draperio was heading to Adrianople. Cyriacus asked to join him in order to find out where Murad stood on the eve of the Christian campaign.

Thus, May 1444 found Cyriacus back in the Ottoman capital. In Draperio's company he was able to gain a far closer access to Murad than on his previous sojourn, attending an audience with the sultan rather than simply watching him from afar. As he wrote to Andreolo: "The royal door opened to an enormous hall full of vast brilliance and pomp, and, around the room, a great throng of magnificently exotic courtiers of the king, seated on carpets strewn in the usual manner, with his leading men and distinguished princes, and beside him, his son Celebi, in the splendid manner of exotic royalty."[9] More crucially, Cyriacus overheard vital and troubling intelligence.

"When I was packed up and ready to leave Adrianople and

to depart for Byzantium," he wrote to Andreolo and to Eugenius IV,

> I learned that delegates from Hungary to the great king
> himself would arrive here shortly, so I decided to wait
> around. Not many days later, we observed that four emis-
> saries had arrived here, accompanied by sixty knights. One
> is Stojka Gisdanic, representing Ladislas, the famed king
> of Poland and Hungary; the second is Vitislao, represent-
> ing that superb master of the horse, John Hunyadi; in addi-
> tion, there are two representing George [Brankovic], despot
> of the silver-producing province of Serbian Moesis . . .[10]

His suspicion aroused, Cyriacus undertook to discover the delegation's mission.

Probably thanks to Draperio's contacts, he succeeded in
obtaining and copying two classified documents. One was
a letter to Murad from Ladislas recommending his ambassador to the sultan: "He is a man faithful to us in deed and
enterprise, fully instructed and adequately informed to negotiate on our behalf with all our authority and the fullness of
our power." The second was the sultan's reply to the purpose
of the embassy: to conclude a peace between the Ottomans
and Poland, Hungary, and Serbia—a tremendous and wholly
unexpected blow to Cyriacus and the Crusade. Murad's letter
to Ladislas stated his agreement to the terms brought by the
Polish ambassador:

> We relate to your lordship that the aforesaid envoy, Stojka,
> spoke to us first of all concerning the lord despot, Georges

[Brankovic], to the effect that I should give back his sons
and his territories and that Georges himself should be
bound entirely to our service . . . This I granted to your
Excellency in view of our brotherhood.

He also stipulated that I should be pleased to make peace
with Lord Vlad [Drakul], the voivode of Walachia . . . [in
return for] the usual tribute . . . Out of love for your Excellency we are content with this . . .

The understanding behind these concessions is that
your Excellency and I will observe a mutual good peace,
fraternity and friendship . . . without any guile or deceit for
ten years.[11]

The accord suited all the parties involved. Murad desired peace
on his western front so that he could quell the revolt of his
Karaman subjects in the east (their uprising had been planned
in collaboration with the Europeans as a double offensive
against him). Brankovic hoped to receive back all the Serbian
lands that Murad had seized from him, as well as his sons,
held hostage in Adrianople, in exchange for vassalage. Poland
would obtain relief from waging a draining war with an army
insufficient to defeat the Turks.

Cyriacus had everything to lose by this development. He
was shocked and distressed by his allies' betrayal, and frustrated at having to hold his tongue. He dispatched a polite and
restrained letter to Hunyadi:

one must assume that all this was initiated, set in motion
and carried through on the best advice, since it emanates
from princes of great foresight and wisdom and experience

in grand enterprises. Therefore, we hope that the result of all this will turn out to be ever better and more successful for you and for the holy and religious Christian campaign, which must be kept alive.[12]

Once he made his way to Constantinople, he whipped up a flurry of activity to set the Crusade back on course. Penning another letter to Hunyadi, with a similar version to Cesarini, Cyriacus declared: "Most Christian prince, I wrote the enclosed from Adrianople. Its tone with respect to the barbarians was as moderate as possible, to avoid a cruel and savage death. For I would like to have said more about the situation there and about the peace." The Turks, he went on to assure Hunyadi, were terrified of the European attack, "frightened with mighty fear . . . they spend every day repairing their walls, fortifying their towers with ramparts of wood, and preparing their army for retreat, rather than battle." Meanwhile, Murad, faced with a threat on his eastern frontier, left his twelve-year-old son in Adrianople and hastened to repel that attack. Therefore, Cyriacus urged, the time was ripe not for peace, but for war.

If you undertake to observe this unsound and utterly detestable peace, as soon as Murad has closed with Karaman . . . he will cross back over the Hellespont with his heart and forces augmented in Asia, and . . . will make for Moesia [Bulgaria and Serbia] and Hungary with all his military power . . . But if he learns that you have taken what we now clearly perceive to be the more reasonable course, and one that he now fears, i.e. that of repudiating utterly the disadvantageous peace, and are moving your unconquered forces into Thrace itself . . . and observes that the Helles-pont will be occupied by your fleet, he may choose the less shameful course of remaining in Asia rather than risk being cut off in Europe. Act, therefore, excellent princes, and declare a war worthy of the Christian religion and may you be willing never to shrink from bringing to its desired conclusion a most holy and glorious campaign.[13]

This militant, harsh Cyriacus sounds very different from the good-natured merchant joyfully hunting for ancient ruins. His obsessive desire to save them seems to have been trans-formed into a willingness to obliterate a culture that he saw as threatening the one he cherished. Visiting Cyzicus again confirmed his sense of the Turkish menace:

But alas! How unsightly a structure we returned to, com-pared to the one we inspected fourteen years ago! For then we saw thirty-one columns standing erect, whereas now I find that twenty-nine columns remain, some shorn of their architraves. And the famous walls, almost all of which were intact, now in great part lie ruined and dashed to the ground, evidently by the barbarians . . . when I had seen the city everywhere in ruins and had recognized that, day by day, it had been utterly ruined by the barbarians, I grieved.[14]

Whether the temple had fallen into further ruin as a result of Ottoman despoliation for building materials, or additional earthquakes, Cyriacus was quick to lay blame. To preserve, at least in writing, what still remained, he measured all the important dimensions, mapped out the plan of the structure, and calculated that sixty-two columns, standing fourteen feet apart, originally encircled the temple.[15] His account of the shrine is the only record of this glorious building, for in the following centuries it would be entirely denuded, so that today all that remains is its crumbled and overgrown substructure.

Back in Constantinople, Cyriacus found an anxious letter from Andreolo. Times were unquiet, and the Anconitan was imperiling his life by snooping around the Ottoman lands. His worried friends were prone to believe dire rumors. Cyriacus tried to allay their fears:

> I was displeased that you and very many other friends of yours were grieved by some rumor or other, based on a mischievous source, of my demise; and I was surprised that you gave easy credence to this false report, since you know your Cyriacus and all his guardian gods and goddesses, powerful over land and sea, and how I prepare for such a voyage with the emphatic approval of the gods.[16]

Brushing aside whatever anxieties he may have felt himself, he carried on his diplomatic work.

In late August 1444, to his delight and that of the Byzantines, the greater part of the crusading fleet reached the Dardanelles and blocked the straits to prevent Murad from crossing to Europe once he returned from his eastern campaign. Cyriacus wrote to Cesarini:

Be assured that this fleet has the Hellespont and the Bosporus under such close observation, that, effectively, no Turk can pass from one side to the other.

Not long after that an even greater happiness was added to our joy—mine and our most steadfast emperor John's. For a few days ago, on the 7th of September, when I was with him in his court, . . . we saw enthusiastic and cheerful dispatches . . . from the king [Ladislas] and from the invincible Prince John Hunyadi . . . We, for our part, first read them to His Majesty after translating them into Greek, and I could not explain easily in writing with how great a joy and gladness we saw these letters filled him, as well as his entire court and the city and the colony of Pera across the way.[17]

Ladislas's letter reported his renewed commitment to the Crusade. Cesarini had absolved him of his oath of peace with Murad by declaring that since the treaty had not been approved by the pope, it was invalid. Hunyadi, meanwhile, wrote that the Christian army was heading toward the Danube. Cyriacus sent copies of these dispatches to King Alfonso of Aragon and to other princes, pressing them to join the Crusade now, when, at long last, it was truly under way. At the same time he informed Cesarini that John VIII and his brothers promised to add to the papal fleet ships from Lemnos, Imbros, and other Aegean islands under their control. The war effort was picking up speed.

Sultan Murad, unwittingly, made the moment even more auspicious for the Christians. Having gained submission from

Karaman without much of a struggle, he decided not to return to Adrianople. Instead, he abdicated in favor of his twelve-year-old son, Mehmed. "I have given my all—my crown, my throne—to my son. You should recognize my son as Sultan," he proclaimed as he left for his retreat at Manisa, near Izmir. Whether it was grief over the death of his favorite son, Alaeddin, the previous year that spurred Murad to retire, or the destructive and fruitless campaigns he had waged against the Hungarians over the winter, he hungered for a quiet and contemplative life. The Byzantine historian Doukas asserted that the sultan had gone to war in the Balkans in the first place under the influence of his vizier, for, being "guileless, with no evil in his heart," he was not personally keen on warfare.[18] Having secured his eastern border by subduing Karaman, and safeguarded his European frontier by signing a treaty with Poland, Hungary, and Serbia, Murad assumed that he could at last enjoy the tranquil existence he desired. It was ironic that he, whom Cyriacus now called the "cruel and dangerous foe of our nurturing faith, . . . that savage prince Murad Bey," sought peace, while the Christians hungered for war. As Cyriacus declared to Cesarini, "may the impious foes be everywhere put to flight, overwhelmed, and butchered."[19]

On this last trip to the East, Cyriacus did more than ever to make antiquity available and vital to his contemporaries and successors, and at the same time contributed to making its physical vestiges inaccessible.

In October 1444 he traveled to Samothrace, ruled by the

Genoese Gattilusio family. The Genoese were anxious to maintain good relations with the Turks, since they traded extensively in their territories, and Cyriacus must have gone to discover what they might do once the war with the Ottomans reached the Aegean—a prescient concern. But the island also beckoned him with its illustrious past.

As he approached it in a small boat manned by four rowers, Samothrace's majesty came into full view: its grand and harsh coastline, awe-inspiring rocky profile, and Mount Phengari soaring some 5,000 feet into the sky. "As we glided in toward the southern side of the island," Cyriacus recorded in his diary,

> we observed from close at hand the taller, cloud-enshrined peak, from whose lofty perch, as we read in the bard Homer's divinely-inspired song, Neptune once watched the Greek fleet and wind-swept Ilium and Hector's army.
>
> The next day . . . we walked about a hundred stadia [one stade is over 600 feet] over steep, mountainous terrain to the island's modern inland town. There, I first looked up Janos Laskaris, the governor [representing] Palamede Gattilusio, who received me very kindly and did me the honor of accompanying me . . . to the ancient city itself . . . situated by the sea in the northern part of the island.
>
> There, under his personal guidance, we first looked at the ancient walls, built of large stones. Extending from a high, steep hill over a long stretch of a decline that slopes down to the sea, they survive to our day, provided in some part with towers and gates in marvelously diverse architectural styles. Moreover, to add to the island's accumula-

tion of celebrity, it was on it, according to Plutarch, that the young Philip came to know Olympias, the mother of that most noble king Alexander.[20]

His mind suffused with Homer's telling of the island's ancient history, Cyriacus saw traces of it in the ruins scattered here and there. Traversing a rocky valley, he came upon the "vast remains of the marble temple of Neptune, fragments of immense columns, architraves and statue bases and doorways decorated with garlanded boukrania and other very beautifully and artistically sculpted figures." Homer had referred to Neptune on the heights of Samothrace, watching the battle for Troy, but the structure Cyriacus identified was actually not a shrine to the sea god, but a Hieron, the main temple of a mystery cult that had made Samothrace famous in antiquity. Initiates who flocked here from all over the Mediterranean were promised special protection at sea and in times of peril, and, according to the ancient Greek historian Diodorus Siculus, became "both more pious and more just and better in every respect than they were before."

Descending from the sanctuary to the medieval castle built from its reused blocks, Cyriacus spotted in its fabric a relief depicting a row of dancing maidens. Taking them for Muses and nymphs, he sketched them in his notebook with the names of the Muses added above in Greek letters. Andrea Mantegna, a painter passionately interested in antiquity, would use this drawing as a model for his *Parnassus*, in which Mars and Venus stand arm in arm on a natural arch, watching the Muses dance.

Elsewhere on the deserted site Cyriacus encountered

a weathered bust of a bearded man with closed eyes and a skullcap. Samothrace being the place where, as the ancient biographer Plutarch reports, Alexander the Great's parents met and fell in love, Cyriacus seems to have decided that the marble must be the likeness of the conqueror's famous tutor, Aristotle. In the fifteenth century no ancient portraits of the famous philosopher were known, though classical and medieval writers described him as having a long beard, a bald head, and very small eyes. Seeing the stone face before him, Cyriacus connected the pieces of the puzzle—putting together the actual bust, the place where he found it, and the words of the ancient authors—and thrilled to his conclusion, which would be proven mistaken only centuries later. It must have felt wondrous for Cyriacus to imagine himself the first man since antiquity to gaze upon the visage of the great sage. Elated, he drew the bust in his notebook, inscribing it "Aristotle" in Greek.

The drawing, and Cyriacus's identification, would prove astonishingly influential. For four centuries Europeans would rely on his sketch to depict Aristotle in paintings, engravings, sculptures, and medals. Raphael would use it as the basis of his portrait of the philosopher in the *School of Athens* fresco in the Vatican. Leonardo da Vinci would model his own appearance on it. Only in the nineteenth century would this vision be challenged, as archaeologists unearthed an inscribed portrait of Aristotle with a completely different appearance.[21]

By then the bust that Cyriacus had drawn had disappeared. When it was rediscovered in the twentieth century, it looked somewhat different, its eyes having been "opened" by recarving in the intervening centuries. By comparing it with Cyriacus's sketch, scholars realized that the figure with its long beard and originally closed eyes probably depicted the mythological seer Tiresias, the blind prophet summoned by Odysseus in Hades to advise him on how to return home safely (advice Odysseus disregarded, to his cost). The bust likely formed part of a narrative composition showing this scene in the pediment of a temple of Samothrace's mystery cult, which had to do with death and afterlife. The figure is flat and uncarved on the back and truncated at the waist, suggesting that Tiresias, placed against the wall of the pediment, was emerging from the ground at Odysseus's call.

～⟨～

From Samothrace, Cyriacus sailed to Thasos, another island ruled by the Gattilusio clan and famous in antiquity for its marble quarries and gold mines; then on to Mount Athos, a sacred mountain peppered with Orthodox monasteries perched high in solitude. Far removed from the rest of the world, he did not hear that the Christian army had made its way toward the Black Sea, battling Turkish garrisons across Bulgaria, killing civilians caught in the crossfire, burning houses and fields; nor that Murad, enraged by the violation of the peace treaty, had rushed back from his retirement in Manisa. Reaching the Dardanelles, the sultan found the crossing blocked by enemy ships. But the Genoese proved willing to betray their fellow Christians and, under cover of darkness, ferried the Ottoman army of some 40,000 men across the strait, charging one golden ducat per head. As Murad hastened north, his army swelled to 60,000 or as many as 80,000 fighters, far outnumbering the Christian forces.

During that time Cyriacus peacefully explored the treasures of Mount Athos. At the monastery of Vatopedi he came across a very old *Iliad* and a Greek translation of Ovid. At the monastery of the Pantocrator he perused a volume of Dionysios the Areopagite "in which are written in an ancient script and in correct order all the works of the same preeminent author, and the annotations of the great commentator Maximus, from which we took pains to copy in alphabetical order the brief vocabulary list that it had at the beginning." The sacristan of the Iveron monastery showed him "numerous books of sacred and secular writings . . . and among these there was a fine volume of Plutarch, in which were written the same philosopher's *Moral Essays* in fourteen books as well as numerous other works. With great pleasure I purchased this splendid volume from him." The richest library was housed at the Grand Lavra:

It stands at the foot of the highest peak of Mt. Athos, not far from the sea, constructed at the very farthest shore of the promontory and extensively fortified by turreted walls . . .

I was most pleased to examine the very considerable library filled with a multitude of volumes of Greek writings on every kind of discipline. . . . among these I especially picked out sacred authors . . . Chrysostom, Basil, Dionysius, Gregory, Eusebius, Cyril, Athanasius, Polycarp and others; and among the secular writers, the works of Plato, Aristotle, Galen, Hippocrates, and numerous other ancient works of philosophers, but also the works of Herodotus, the noted historian.[22]

Cyriacus copied into his notebook his favorite opening lines from some of these volumes:

> Of Libanios the sophist *On Rhetoric*: "The wolves asked the sheep for the respite of peace . . ."
>
> Of Eustathios *On the Iliad*. "Of Homer's Sirens: perhaps it would be good if one should shy away from [them] from the beginning . . ."

While Cyriacus was leafing through these dusty volumes, the sultan caught up with the crusaders at Varna, in eastern Bulgaria. With the papal fleet anchored at the Dardanelles, the Christian army, outnumbered nearly four to one, found itself with no support. In the dawn hours of November 10, 1444, the Europeans and the Ottomans came face-to-face under a serene sky. They stood for three hours without engaging. Suddenly, a great storm broke over the surrounding mountains, beating down on the Christians and tearing their banners to tatters. It was not a good omen.

The battle began around nine in the morning. At first the Hungarians seemed to gain the upper hand, turning to flight the Anatolian and Rumelian contingents of Murad's army. Then King Ladislas attacked the Janissaries guarding the sultan and the battle raged through the afternoon, "heads rolling on the field like shingle," according to an Ottoman chronicle. Eventually the Turkish forces regrouped around Murad, just as the Hungarians began to weaken. At this point Ladislas, backed by five hundred of his best cavalrymen, decided to rush the sultan's infantry in a romantic gesture of bravery and in a hope of rallying his troops. In the ensuing clash, he was struck with a club by a strong-armed warrior and knocked off his horse. While he was down, one of the Janissaries decapitated the young king and carried his head triumphantly to the sultan. Murad ordered it to be impaled and displayed across the battlefield. The gruesome sight drained the Christians' courage and threw them into panic.

As night fell and the two sides withdrew from the battlefield—the Ottomans in good order, the Christians in wild disarray—they were uncertain as to who had won. But with Ladislas dead and Cesarini missing in action, the battered remnants of the Christian army beat a homeward retreat. The Ottomans triumphed, though at the cost of 30,000 men, including some of their best commanders. Surveying the battlefield, Murad reputedly said to one of his intimates, "Is it not amazing that they [the Christian dead] are all young men, not a single graybeard among them?" His companion replied, "If there had been a graybeard among them, they would not have embarked on so rash an undertaking."[23]

❦

When he learned of the disaster, Cyriacus refused to accept defeat. He was fifty-three years old in 1444, and constant travel was sapping his strength. A skin disease that had bothered him for some years refused to yield to any cure. How much time did he have left? As the Turks continued to win more battles and conquer more of Greece, he traveled on around the

Aegean, trying to keep the cause of Crusade alive despite all odds. In January 1445 he heard an encouraging rumor "that the Hungarians have gone back to their country to restore and increase their forces."[24] In August he returned to Constantinople "to revisit the Cardinal Legate [Condulmaro] in connection with the most welcome rising of the Hungarian nation against the Turks."[25]

Cyriacus did not give up. Half a year later, quite remarkably, he returned to Turkey in the company of Francesco Draperio and once again visited the sultan. Murad, grateful to the Genoese for their assistance on the eve of Varna, welcomed Draperio and his companion generously. As Cyriacus wrote to his dear friend Andreolo on Chios, the sultan

> did not betake himself to the open courtyard where he customarily received foreign and domestic delegations, but invited our Franzesco to enter a separate, private, inner chamber, where no outsider may so much as step on the threshold. The great prince himself and his satraps also showed him many other signs of extraordinary good will. I was glad to see all this, both for his sake and for yours, because I felt than this was very profitable, not only for him personally, but for your republic as well.[26]

Through Draperio, Cyriacus, ever the opportunist, asked for and received once more from the sultan "a written plenary authorization to insure my safe travel everywhere in every one of his territories. This was the principal object of my profound desire and it was for this that I chose the excellent company of Franzesco and completed a journey of such magnitude that involved our crossing the Hermus and other rivers."[27] If Murad ever suspected Cyriacus of espionage, he must have been secure enough in his victories not to be concerned. Or perhaps he found the affable and effusive Anconitan too odd—hunting for old blocks regardless of weather, hardship, and dangers—to present any threat.

Political setbacks seem not to have slowed Cyriacus's archaeological explorations—if anything, he probably felt more pressed to carry on his work. In April 1445, on Paros, he penned a vivid and unprecedented account of this marble-producing island, its ruined cities and awe-inspiring quarries:

> Who could describe these distinctive, richly adorned buildings of a once-great city fallen to the ground in every direction, an enormous confusion of ruins: the extensive remains of temples, numerous statues extraordinary for their marvelous symmetry and artistic quality?—though we observed that in great part they were diminished and fallen to the ground in ruins by the long passage of time and the lazy neglect of human beings. Who could describe these tombs, too many to recall, made of the finest marble, the architraves, the fragments of giant columns, the statue bases and grandly lettered inscriptions, and the numerous, huge triumphal monuments of our divine princes, the Caesars, ornaments in gleaming white marble?
>
> . . . On the next day . . . we came to the marble mountains fifty stadia from the city. There we saw three huge and marvelous—I would call them, not so much stone

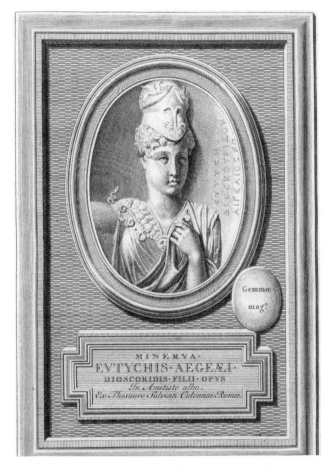

Alexander/Athena gem seen by Cyriacus on board a Venetian galley, engraving from Bernard Picart, Pierres antiques gravées, sur lesquelles les graveurs ont mis leurs noms, *Amsterdam, 1724. (Research Library, The Getty Research Institute, Los Angeles, CA)*

quarries, as an achievement of human capability, ominous and inexpressible because more worthy of wonder than all the products of human ingenuity. For after I had chosen to look inside the first, there came into view vast, widely-gaping, hand-wrought caverns . . . And when . . . we penetrated with lit torches through the vast heart of the mountain to shafts of immeasurable height . . . we learned that the caves, carved out by hand with iron tools, extended for several stadia to a precipice . . . I am surprised that Gaius Pliny passed over this tremendous human achievement when he listed the labyrinths. Indeed, such remarkable works as these seem no less worthy of mention than the foreign marvel of the pyramids at Memphis.[28]

In October 1445, as he took passage on a Venetian galley commanded by Giovanni Delfino, Cyriacus examined with rapture the captain's collection of ancient coins and gems. Turning them in his hands by the wavering candlelight, he was particularly smitten by

a splendid crystalline signet seal the size of a thumb that is engraved in deep relief with a bust of helmeted Alexander of Macedon, the marvelous workmanship of the artisan Eutyches; and adorning the polished helmet, imprinted on its front, were two rams' heads with twisted horns, unmistakable attributes of his father, Jupiter Ammon; and at the top of his headpiece, a tiara is seen to bear on either side swift-running, hare-mastering, Molossan hounds of extraordinary artistic beauty; and beneath the helmet the prince, very tiny strands of hair showing beneath his helmet on either side, dressed in a fine robe and foreign garment, its borders decorated along the top, seems to have moved his right arm, bare to the elbow, which is holding his vesture honorably at the top; and his countenance, with wondrous attitude and regal appearance, directing his gaze straight ahead, seems truly to manifest living features made from gleaming stone as well as his own heroic greatness.[29]

The gem, in fact, depicted Athena. But though he misidentified the subject, Cyriacus employed a scientific method of comparative iconography that he was inventing in the very process of his investigations and which archaeologists continue to use to this day. Cyriacus was familiar with ancient coins minted by Alexander the Great that show a very similar helmeted Athena with the inscription "Alexander" above her head. Since coins usually depict the persons named in their inscriptions, Cyriacus concluded, not unreasonably, that these represented Alexander, rather than the deity invoked as his protectress. Faced with the gem carved with a similar helmeted figure, Cyriacus made a logical deduction that since it looked very much like the figure on Alexander's coins, it too represented the conqueror. As with the marble he identified as Aristotle, Cyriacus drew his conclusions without the help of any guides to ancient iconography. Indeed, more often than not, his explorations were the sole basis for contemporary knowledge about ancient monuments. And his drawings were the first sources for classical imagery available to his colleagues and followers. As with the "Aristotle," Cyriacus's description of this gem, and probably its sketch, circulated widely around Europe and served as the defining image of Alexander for several centuries.[30]

❧

Despite his archaeological discoveries, the continued Ottoman gains and Christian losses must have made it harder and harder for Cyriacus to maintain his buoyancy. At the Turkish port of Gallipoli, through which he passed in February 1447, he witnessed a fate he had been spared, thanks to the protection of his divine guardian Mercury, to whom he always prayed for safekeeping. Mercury, or good luck, had preserved Cyriacus from being captured by the Turks either as a prisoner of war, a Christian, or a spy, and marched in the "long lines of barbarians laden with booty and men of our religion, too, and especially captives from the Greek nation, miserable in their iron chains"—and driven to the slave markets.

> From the patriotic lips of some of these wretches we learned that Murad Bey, the proud prince of the Turks, had invaded the Isthmus of the Peloponnesus with a huge force on the 13th of December [1446]. The turreted walls, which had been restored with great care a short time ago by the Spartan king Constantine, had been surmounted by armed soldiery and had been knocked down for the most part and ripped from the ground by powerful machines; the Greek army had scattered and the area had been devastated.
>
> You can imagine, [he wrote to Andreolo] that when I

heard their tearful tale, I could not but take it ill to learn that that cruel and destructive enemy of the Christian religion, who just about this time last year, we thought, had been beaten by the arms of our devout soldiers and had been put to flight and utterly expelled from the realms of Thrace and Macedonia and out of all Greece [in Cyriacus's over-optimistic imagination] . . . now, owing to the slothful neglect of our princes, and to the fact that our forces and those of the Hungarians were withdrawn and removed for a little while, has been made so exalted and daring by fortune and has been permitted by her to invade the Peloponnesus, such a noble and once powerful Grecian realm. What an enormity![31]

In October 1448 the Ottomans and the Europeans fought a brutal battle at Kosovo. Cyriacus heard about it from a Turkish source and wrote to a friend:

On the 17th of October, the first contingent of Hungarian infantry had joined battle with the Turks and, fighting throughout the day in fierce combat, had finally put to flight the ranks of oriental infantry with a great slaughter, though not without a huge loss of life on the part of the victors. On the next day, the Turk, reinforced by all his cavalry from Amasia, actually about fifteen thousand mounted auxiliaries, resumed battle against their foe with a great push. For two days they fought with great ferocity with the outcome in doubt, with an indescribable slaughter of soldiers on both sides.[32]

Cyriacus was uncertain of the final result: "We are again expecting emissaries . . . by whom we hope to be informed and to have a better understanding of the situation," he wrote anxiously. The news, when it arrived, proved catastrophic. The Turks not only won the battle, but destroyed the Europeans' will to continue the Crusade.

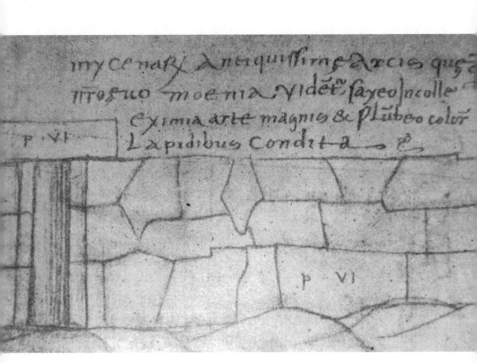

Cyriacus's drawing of a Mycenaean wall outside Argos, from
R. Sabbadini, "Ciriaco d'Ancona e la sua descrizione autografa
del peloponneso trasmessa da Leonardo Botta," in Miscellanea
Ceriani: Raccolta di scritti originali per onorare la memoria
di M.r Antonio Maria Ceriani, prefetto della Biblioteca
Ambrosiana, *Milan: Ulrico Hoepli, 1910.*

You have seen the cities of Latium, where brave deeds were done; you have seen the cities of the Greeks and the barbarians as well; you have seen sculpted gods and the martial wars they waged, and even the horse of Bellerophon; you have seen the seven wonders of the ancient world; you have seen whatever there was in the entire world.

—Leonardo Dati, epigram in honor of Cyriacus[1]

In the Balance

CYRIACUS RETURNED TO Italy in the winter of 1448–9, his assignment in the East terminated by the collapse of the Crusade, the death of Eugenius IV, and the end of papal financial support. From this point his footsteps begin to fade. In the summer of 1449 he traveled around northern Italy, stopping in Padua and composing an epigram for Donatello's statue of Gattamelata. He visited a friend in Ravenna and admired the city's ancient remains and Byzantine churches refulgent with splendid mosaics. In Ferrara, as a guest of Duke Leonello d'Este, he penned a rapturous description of a painting by the Netherlandish artist Rogier van der Weyden. And in Genoa he requested a safe-conduct to travel to Spain, but whether he went there is unknown.

The next notice concerning Cyriacus records his death in

Cremona in 1452, seemingly of plague. The dreaded disease had ravaged Italy intermittently since the mid-fourteenth century. Usually transmitted by infected fleas jumping from rats to humans, the illness first manifested itself in fever, chills, and aches all over the body, then erupted in excruciating buboes on lymph nodes in the groin, armpits, or neck. The infection coursing through the body dispatched the victim within a few painful days. But while it devoured the flesh, and before the fever sent the sufferer into a fog of delirium, he had some time to reflect on his life. Cyriacus, lying in bed, watching the bloody blotches bloom on his skin, would have had plenty to consider.

His crusading efforts, to which he had devoted so many years and hopes, had failed. Luckily for him, he would not live to learn of the sack of Constantinople by Murad's bellicose son, Mehmed II, the following year, which would also put an end to the church union that Cyriacus had labored so dedicatedly to achieve, and to European travel in Greek lands. He would not hear the laments of the humanists that the fall of Byzantium brought about the second death of Homer and Plato. Nor would he know that as Constantinople breathed its last, disgorging westward its leading intellectuals and the ancient books they carried with them as they fled, it unwittingly bestowed on Europe an influx of classical knowledge that would nourish scholars and scientists for generations.

Cyriacus would have been aware—and probably despondent—that his personal mission to safeguard ancient monuments around the Mediterranean was left unfinished, and its future looked bleak. There had been no other student

*Cyriacus's drawing of a relief at Nauplion, from R. Sabbadini,
"Ciriaco d'Ancona e la sua descrizione autografa del peloponneso
trasmessa da Leonardo Botta," in* Miscellanea Ceriani: Raccolta
di scritti originali per onorare la memoria di M.r Antonio
Maria Ceriani, prefetto della Biblioteca Ambrosiana, *Milan:
Ulrico Hoepli, 1910.*

of the past following in his footsteps during times of relative peace; there would certainly be no one now willing to venture into the eye of the Ottoman storm.

Yet all was not lost. He had done more than anyone else in his day to bring Greek and Roman cultures back to life. The most enterprising and prolific recorder of antiquities of his age, he investigated and rediscovered many sites of the ancient world and linked them with surviving texts. He set down on paper countless monuments that would subsequently vanish—not only inscriptions, but entire buildings. His drawings and measurements of Hadrian's temple at Cyzicus recorded the structure prior to its complete destruction. Similarly, in February 1446, in a letter to Andreolo, Cyriacus described the oracular shrine of Apollo at Didyma, then the best preserved ancient edifice in Asia Minor: "This remarkable temple seems to have been a structure in no way inferior to that of the famous shrine of Cyzicus, apart from statues of the gods, abundant sculptural foliage, and the gilded joins of its blocks, as I shall illustrate in my drawing of it." Cyriacus also carefully copied the long dedicatory inscription commemorating the gifts bestowed on this temple by kings Seleucus and Antiochus.[2] He was the last student of the past to see this building, which was shattered by an earthquake in 1493.

By paying careful attention to topography, Cyriacus would help modern archaeologists locate monuments he had discovered, identify and correct his findings when necessary, and contextualize stones that had been moved. During his journey through the Peloponnese, he was immensely impressed by the massive walls he saw at Katsimgri—he took them for the fortifications of legendary Mycenae. As he sketched them in his diary, he recorded their distance from Nauplion, Argos, and Merbaka, thus enabling modern scholars to pinpoint the site.

As recently as 2005, thanks to Cyriacus's precise record-keeping, an archaeologist was able to shed new light on the history of Athens. At the heart of the modern city, surrounded by unsightly modern buildings, stands a jewel of a church known as the Little Metropolis. It has long been thought to have been constructed in the Middle Ages, probably in the later twelfth century, during the tenure of the metropolitan Michael Choniates, who had decried the backward state of Athens in his day. The church is conspicuous for the profusion of ancient and medieval sculpted and inscribed blocks incorporated into its walls. The stones range in date from classical times to the twelfth century, hence its presumed dating. By looking closely at the ancient blocks and comparing them to Cyriacus's notes, Bente Kiilerich realized that one of the inscriptions the Anconitan had transcribed during his visit to Athens appears on the Little Metropolis.[3] Except that Cyriacus saw this block on the Areopagos, next to the ancient agora, which indicates that the church did not yet exist in 1436. Kiilerich surmised that it was erected after the Ottoman takeover of Athens in 1456. Prior to the arrival of the Turks, the main shrine to the Virgin was the Parthenon, which the new lords of the city converted into a mosque, and so the Athenians had to find a new home for their sacred protectress. Kiilerich proposed that the Little Metropolis was constructed as the new shrine to the patroness of the city from ancient blocks scattered around Athens and from material gathered from other churches dismantled by the Ottomans. Cyriacus's archaeological investigations thus continue to help scholars understand not only the classical past, but also the medieval and Renaissance history of the Mediterranean world.

Cyriacus was especially meticulous when transcribing inscriptions, his training as an accountant serving him well: he preserved the line divisions, indicated the letter styles, distinguished what survived from what he added as his conjectures. His drawings of buildings and sculptures were more amateurish—he had never been trained as an artist. And his interpretations were sometimes wrong, for he was a trailblazer, intuitively devising methods of study that would be perfected by his followers. But he usually provided enough information so that even as he made mistakes—as he did in the case of the bust of Tiresias from Samos, which he identified as Aristotle, or the gem depicting Athena—his successors could amend and build upon his discoveries. Cyriacus laid a foundation for cumulative scholarship, something he was interested in from the start, as he assiduously disseminated his findings to friends and colleagues. This was a mark of a true scholar, keen not to hoard data for personal advancement, but to create a dynamic knowledge base that could be used by others. And as a true scientist, he enabled his heirs to replicate his results by offering them the materials, the tools, and the process—by carefully recording data and devising methods for analyzing it—so that they could follow up on his findings and take them further.

After his death, compendia of Cyriacus's inscriptions would be used extensively by generations of epigraphers such as Giovanni Marcanova, Felice Feliciano, and Fra Giovanni Giocondo. Meanwhile, his drawings of buildings and sculptures would help artists visualize and reconstruct the past. Andrea

Cyriacus's drawing of a block inscribed with a religious edict at Cape Tainaron in the Peloponnese (where Hercules went to find the entrance to Hades in order to fulfill his last labor, to capture Cerberus). From R. Sabbadini, "Ciriaco d'Ancona e la sua descrizione autografa del peloponneso trasmessa da Leonardo Botta," in Miscellanea Ceriani: Raccolta di scritti originali per onorare la memoria di M.r Antonio Maria Ceriani, prefetto della Biblioteca Ambrosiana, *Milan: Ulrico Hoepli, 1910.*

Mantegna would incorporate Cyriacus's sketches of ancient landmarks of Constantinople into his paintings. Giovanni Bellini and Hieronymous Bosch would portray Egypt's exotic architecture, inhabitants, and animals using his accounts. Giuliano da Sangallo's copies after Cyriacus would educate and inspire future architects.[4] Cyriacus could imagine these more immediate followers, men like the artists and scholars with whom he had corresponded over the years. But he could not envision from his deathbed that his records would go on to serve archaeologists all the way into the twenty-first century, making them marvel at how this lone romantic managed to reach and scrutinize so many blocks, decipher their messages in all kinds of weather and light conditions, and accomplish so much without the help of photography, collections of comparable texts, or modern guidebooks.

As he lay dying, fighting pain and fear, Cyriacus could be certain of only one thing: that his beloved antiquities had given a richness to his life that he could not have fathomed when he first entered Piero's office as a merchant apprentice. Through his pursuit of them he had experienced the wonders of faraway lands, played—for better or worse—an important role in the events that shaped his era, received warm welcomes from the pope, the sultan, two emperors, various kings and dukes, artists and humanists. Flattering as these accomplishments were, his greatest and most constant thrill remained coming face-to-face with distant civilizations and the ghosts of their denizens, and learning about their lives, hopes, and achievements from their words and deeds immortalized in stone.

Cyriacus's passion was both his strength and weakness, spurring him single-handedly to familiarize his contemporaries and successors with the physical traces of ancient Greece and Asia Minor, and driving him to advocate a war that would threaten these vestiges with greater ruin than neglect and piecemeal scavenging had done for a millennium. In the long run, he left a legacy that would bear fruit for centuries. The first person to travel specifically in search of historic

Cyriacus's drawing of reliefs at Argos, from R. Sabbadini,
"Ciriaco d'Ancona e la sua descrizione autografa del peloponneso
trasmessa da Leonardo Botta," in Miscellanea Ceriani: Raccolta
di scritti originali per onorare la memoria di M.r Antonio
Maria Ceriani, prefetto della Biblioteca Ambrosiana, *Milan:*
Ulrico Hoepli, 1910.

monuments, to study them throughout the Greek and Roman world, to investigate them on location, and to preserve them for posterity through detailed documentation, he gave birth to the science of archaeology. At a time when other humanists focused on texts to understand the past, Cyriacus drew attention to physical remains as primary sources of information about antiquity. Tirelessly publicizing his findings by copying portions of his diaries for his friends and patrons, he ignited their desire to look closer at such monuments and to learn more about and from them. Thus, when most of Cyriacus's original autograph notebooks, acquired by the Sforza rulers of Pesaro, enthusiastic collectors of manuscripts, perished in the fire that destroyed their library in 1514, and other documents about his life burned in the conflagration at the civic archive of Ancona in 1534, many of his notes lived on in his copies and those made by his admirers and followers.

Cyriacus's fellow antiquarians treasured and perpetuated his life's work. When Leonardo Dati praised Cyriacus for having seen Italy, Greece, Asia Minor, and "even the horse of Bellerophon," he suggested that the Anconitan had tapped the well of the Muses. For Pegasus—the horse of Bellerophon—was a son of Poseidon who possessed a magic gift: wherever he struck the earth with his hoof an inspiring spring burst forth. Cyriacus's explorations, Dati implied, had generated a well of knowledge for his contemporaries and successors. Pegasus also helped his master, Bellerophon, fight against the Chimera and the Amazons, and Dati may have intended to invoke this association as well.

Antonio Beccadelli (a.k.a. Panormita), a humanist at the court of Naples, in his turn, wrote a less recondite and more straightforward eulogy: "Cyriacus, highly regarded among the poets of lofty eloquence, you who preserve all mementos of antiquity, you have traversed far-distant recesses of land and sea, you have scanned the names of ancient pyramids. Still, Ancona kept rejoicing in her son Cyriacus as much as did Mantua in her learnedly eloquent Virgil."[5] As the end of his life Cyriacus could justly take pride in having earned a comparison with the illustrious Roman with whom he first began his journey to wake the dead.

ACKNOWLEDGMENTS

The writing of this book has been a journey on which I was accompanied by friends and colleagues who have offered much generous help and support. It is my pleasure to thank Benedetta Bessi, Elena Calandra, William Caraher, Robin Cormack, Jens Daehner, Veronica Della Dora, Craig Kallendorf, Pamela Long, Robert Menna, Michael Putnam, David Shayne, and Michael Vickers for sharing their knowledge and information about various aspects of Cyriacus's adventures as well as providing valuable suggestions on how to shape his story. The staff of the Getty Research Library and Special Collections has been invariably helpful. Rob McQuilkin believed in the importance of an account of Cyriacus's life from the beginning and saw it through both rough and smooth sailing. Alane Mason, with her firm hand and discerning judgment, guided the molding of the material I brought to her into a worthy narrative. Allegra Huston with her sharp eye caught all the infelicities of text and inconsistencies of detail. Denise Scarfi ably and cheerfully took care of a myriad logistical challenges. Brooke Koven created the handsome design for the book. My parents and grandparents unwaveringly stood by me as I wrestled with various difficulties along the way. My greatest debt, however, is to my husband Ken Lapatin, who always came up with the best ideas, patiently read through countless drafts, stood by me as I grappled with all the monsters that haunt the writing of a book, and even as my own faith wavered never doubted my ability to complete it.

NOTES

Epigraph

1. Cyriac of Ancona, *Later Travels*, trans. and ed. Edward W. Bodnar (Cambridge, MA: Harvard University Press, 2003), 219.

On the Threshold of History

1. Ross, James Bruce, and Mary Martin McLaughlin, *The Portable Medieval Reader* (New York: Viking, 1955), 390.

2. Spufford, Peter, *Power and Profit: the Merchant in Medieval Europe* (New York: Thames & Hudson, 2003); Ashtor, Eiyahu, *Levant Trade in the Later Middle Ages* (Princeton: Princeton University Press, 1983).

3. We have one presumed portrait of Cyriacus, a battered relief in Ancona identified only by local tradition. The man in this plaque seems to correspond to Cyriacus's personality as it comes through in his biographical writings and in letters of his contemporaries.

4. Scalamonti, Francesco, *Vita Viri Clarissimi et Famosissimi Kyriaci Anconitani*, trans. and ed. Charles Mitchell and Edward W. Bodnar (Philadelphia: American Philosophical Society, 1996), 34.

5. Mommsen, Theodore E., "Petrarch's Conception of the 'Dark Ages,'" *Speculum* 17 (1942), 226–42; Burke, Peter, "The Sense of

Historical Perspective in Renaissance Italy," *Journal of World History* XI (1969), 615–32.

6. Cosenza, Mario Emilio, *Petrarch's Letters to Classical Authors* (Chicago: University of Chicago Press, 1910), "To Titus Livy," 100–3. Petrarch also collected Roman coins as historical evidence of what the emperors looked like.

7. Weiss, Roberto, *The Renaissance Discovery of Classical Antiquity* (Oxford: Blackwell, 1969), is a classic study on the rise of antiquarian interest in Italy.

8. Cyriacus began working on the harbor project in the fall of 1421. Although we do not know precisely the moment when the arch captured his imagination, given his budding interest in antiquities during his stay in Constantinople a couple of years earlier, it seems likely that he noticed the arch soon after starting his job at the port.

An Unlikely Hero

1. Florentine merchant Francesco Balducci Pegolotti listed 188 spices in his manual for merchants and included not only pepper, cinnamon, and nutmeg, but also almonds, oranges, and sugar. The most important spice of all, pepper, was often used in place of currency in the late fourteenth and early fifteenth centuries. Turner, Jack, *Spice: The History of Temptation* (New York: Alfred A. Knopf, 2004), offers a very readable and informative discussion of spices.

2. Ibid., 167.

3. These examples are quoted in Turner, *Spice*, 178, 185, and 192.

4. Spufford, *Power and Profit*, 310–5.

5. Landman, Neil H., et al., *Pearls: A Natural History* (New York: Harry N. Abrams, 2001); Spufford, *Power and Profit*, 316–8.

6. King, Donald, "Types of Silk Used in England 1200–1500," in Simonetta Cavaciocchi, ed., *La Seta in Europa, Sec. XIII–XX* (Florence: Le Monnier, 1993), 457–64. Meanwhile, finished cotton fabrics woven in Lombardy were exported throughout Europe and the Mediterranean. Mazzaoui, Maureen Fennell, *The Italian Cotton Industry in the Later Middle Ages, 1100–1600* (Cambridge and New

York: Cambridge University Press, 1981), 137–42. Italians exported European-made linen to Persia, Central Asia, and Egypt. They also exported paper, which they had first learned to make in the East. Spufford, *Power and Profit*, 255–7.

7. Origo, Iris, *The Merchant of Prato, Francesco di Marco Datini* (New York: Octagon Books, 1979); Thornton, Peter, *The Italian Renaissance Interior, 1400–1600* (London: Weidenfeld and Nicolson, 1991); Ajmar-Wollheim, Marta, and Flora Dennis, *At Home in Renaissance Italy* (London: V & A Publications, 2006); Preyer, Brenda, "Planning for Visitors at Florentine Palaces," *Renaissance Studies* 12 (1998), 357–74. Spufford, *Power and Profit*, 110, also notes that "The nobility wished their better houses to be lit up more often and more fully and for longer hours than other houses, and with sweet-smelling beeswax candles." Ancona was a major producer of candles, being a papal town and supplier of candles to the church.

8. There was a lively system of resale of used goods in Renaissance Italy. As Evelyn Welch writes in *Shopping in the Renaissance: Consumer Cultures in Italy 1400–1600* (New Haven and London: Yale University Press, 2005), 28–9: "A ubiquitous system of credit arrangements, both formal and informal, meant that handkerchiefs, tablecloths, aprons, scissors and kitchen pots could all be used as pledges when families needed to pay rent and taxes . . . or buy a bushel of grain. In such a system, the linens in the cupboard and plate on the sideboard provided a bulwark against famine and ill fortune, one that was as important to survival as the gardens, fields and chicken coops that were regularly cultivated by city dwellers."

9. Balducci Pegolotti, Francesco, *La pratica della mercatura*, ed. Allan Evans (Cambridge, MA: Medieval Academy of America, 1936); Spufford, *Power and Profit*, 53–4. Pegolotti worked for the Florentine Bardi firm, the largest of the four giant corporations that dominated international trade in the early fourteenth century. He described places where valuable commodities originated, such as the prime sheep-raising monasteries in England, the spice markets of Egypt and Persia, the ports on the Moroccan coast, and practical details on the silk road from Cathay. He talked about a wide range of products, from high-value, small-volume goods like silk and spices, to low-value, bulky, everyday necessities like grain, oil, and wine, and

specialty items such as cheese from Apulia and little wooden boxes from Cyprus.

10. Scalamonti, *Vita Viri Clarissimi,* 102.

11. Ibid.

12. Welch, *Shopping in the Renaissance,* 59, discusses mountebanks and charlatans in Venice and other Italian cities.

13. Newett, Margaret M., *Canon Pietro Casola's Pilgrimage to Jerusalem in the Year 1494* (Manchester: At the University Press, 1907), 128–9. In addition to the Venetians, foreigners sold a profusion of wares on the Rialto bridge, on the Piazza San Marco, and throughout the city from makeshift stalls, stands, and cloths laid on the ground (Welch, *Shopping in the Renaissance,* 125).

14. Tafur, Pero, *Travels and Adventures 1435–1439,* trans. and ed. Malcolm Letts (London: Routledge & Sons, 1926), 170.

15. Scalamonti, *Vita Viri Clarissimi,* 102.

From the Mundane to the Sublime

1. Scalamonti, *Vita Viri Clarissimi,* 114.

2. Scalamonti recounts some of Cyriacus's impressions (p. 105). Other contemporary descriptions of Alexandria come from such travelers as Tafur, *Travels and Adventures*; Fabri, Felix, *Voyage en Égypte de Félix Fabri, 1483,* trans. and ed. Jacques Masson (Cairo: Institut français d'archéologie orientale du Caire, 1975); Ghistele, Joos van, *Voyage en Égypte de Joos van Ghistele,* trans. and ed. Renée Bauwens-Préaux (Cairo: Institut français d'archéologie orientale du Caire, 1976); *The Pilgrimage of Arnold von Harff, Knight from Cologne, through Italy, Syria, Egypt, Arabia, Ethiopia, Nubia, Palestine, Turkey, France and Spain, which he accomplished in the years 1496 to 1499,* trans. and ed. Malcolm Letts (London: Hakluyt Society, 1946).

3. It is possible that Cyriacus, or his biographer, retrospectively attributed to the merchant turned archaeologist an early fascination with monuments of the past. Yet Cyriacus was clearly drawn to them far more than other travelers in the East, and his self-assumed calling grew out of early exposure to and curiosity about traces of ancient cultures.

4. It was shipped to America in 1879, while its companion was taken to London and erected on the Embankment. The story of the New York obelisk is recounted by Martina D'Alton in *The New York Obelisk, or How Cleopatra's Needle Came to New York and What Happened When It Got Here* (New York: Metropolitan Museum of Art, 1993).

5. González de Clavijo, Ruy, *Embassy to Tamerlane 1403–1406*, trans. Guy le Strange (New York and London: Harper & Brothers, 1928), 87–8.

6. Tafur, *Travels and Adventures*, 146.

7. On Constantine see, for example, Grant, Michael, *Constantine the Great: The Man and His Times* (New York: History Book Club, 1993–2000). Bassett, Sarah, *The Urban Image of Late Antique Constantinople* (Cambridge: Cambridge University Press, 2004), discusses the history of the site and its embellishments.

8. Ancient sculptures in particular saturated the new capital, giving it a sense of history and conveying Constantine's power over the Greco-Roman world.

9. Clari, Robert de, *The Conquest of Constantinople* (New York: Octagon Books, 1966), 102–3.

10. Tafur, *Travels and Adventures*, 145.

11. See, for example, Majeska, George P., ed., *Russian Travelers to Constantinople in the Fourteenth and Fifteenth Centuries* (Washington DC: Dumbarton Oaks Research Library and Collection, 1984); and Vin, J. P. A van der. *Travellers to Greece and Constantinople: Ancient Monuments and Old Traditions in Medieval Travellers' Tales* (Leiden: Nederlands Historisch-Archaeologisch Instituut te Istanbul, 1980).

12. Majeska, *Russian Travelers*, 44–7.

13. Colin, Jean, *Cyriaque d'Ancône: Le voyageur, le marchand, l'humaniste* (Paris: Maloine Éditeur, 1981), 285.

14. Scalamonti, *Vita Viri Clarissimi*, 117.

At the Crumbling Epicenter of the Past

1. Poggio Bracciolini, cited in Ross and McLaughlin, eds. *The Portable Renaissance Reader*, 381.

2. Partridge, Loren, *The Art of Renaissance Rome, 1400–1600* (New York: Prentice Hall and Harry N. Abrams, 1996), quote on p. 19.

3. Ibid. In March 1425, Martin V issued a bull re-creating the old office of Maestri delle Strade responsible for maintaining the streets, squares, and buildings in good order. But one imagines that they did not make rapid progress.

4. Hibbert, Christopher, *Rome: The Biography of a City* (Harmondsworth: Penguin, 1987), 99.

5. *The Life of Cola di Rienzo*, trans. John Wright (Toronto: Pontifical Institute of Mediaeval Studies, 1975), 40.

6. Ibid., 131.

7. Ibid., 31.

8. Ibid., 136, 146–7.

9. Ibid., 147.

10. Hibbert, *Rome*, 99–107, recounts Cola's dramatic life.

11. Ibid., 111.

12. Tafur, *Travels and Adventures*, 36, 43.

13. On the misinformation propagated by the traditional guidebooks to Rome and by the locals, see Grafton, Anthony, "The Ancient City Restored: Archaeology, Ecclesiastical History, and Egyptology," in Grafton, Anthony, ed., *Rome Reborn: The Vatican Library and Renaissance Culture* (Washington DC: Library of Congress, 1993), 87.

14. Modigliani, Anna, *Mercati, botteghe e spazi di commercio a Roma tra medioevo et età moderna* (Rome: Roma nel Rinascimento, 1998), 38–9.

15. Welch, *Shopping in the Renaissance*, 116–7.

16. Lanciani, Rodolfo Amedeo, *The Destruction of Ancient Rome* (New York: Macmillan, 1899), 30.

17. Hibbert, *Rome*, 115.

18. Lanciani, *The Destruction of Ancient Rome*.

19. Weiss, *Renaissance Discovery*, 98–9.

20. Scalamonti, *Vita Viri Clarissimi*, 117.

21. These commentaries, sadly, do not survive, having perished in 1514 in a fire at Pesaro, where Cyriacus's papers were stored. So we have to rely on the sparse information provided by his biographer as well as other contemporary accounts of early fifteenth-century Rome and the first generations of humanists who explored it.

22. Grafton, *Rome Reborn*, 93.

23. Manetti, Antonio, *Vita di Filippo di ser Brunellesco* (Florence: Rinascimento del libro, 1927), in Holt, Elizabeth G., ed., *A Documentary History of Art*, Vol. 1 (Garden City, NY: Doubleday Anchor, 1947), 177.

24. Ibid., 167–79. Donatello's trips to Rome took place in 1400, 1403–4, and 1432–3. See Janson, H. W., *The Sculpture of Donatello*, Vol. II (Princeton: Princeton University Press, 1957), 99–102, 110.

25. Scalamonti, *Vita Viri Clarissimi*, 117.

26. Ibid.

27. Bracciolini, Poggio, *Two Renaissance Book Hunters*, trans. Phyllis Goodhart Gordon (New York: Columbia University Press, 1974), 108; Zippel, Giuseppe, *Niccolò Niccoli* (Florence: Bocca, 1890), 38.

An Antiquary Born of Trade

1. Cyriac of Ancona, *Later Travels*, 161.

2. Scalamonti, *Vita Viri Clarissimi*, 121.

3. Fabri, Felix, *Wanderings of Felix Fabri*, trans. Aubrey Stewart (London: Palestine Pilgrims' Text Society, 1892–3), 124.

4. Ibid., 37–9.

5. Ibid., 28–9.

6. Ibid., 154–5.

7. The privations of life at sea are also catalogued by Pérez-Mallaína, Pablo E., *Spain's Men of the Sea: Daily Life on the Indies Fleets in the Sixteenth Century* (Baltimore and London: Johns Hopkins University Press, 2005). The quote is on p. 133.

8. Fabri, *Wanderings*, 157.

9. Ibid., 152.

10. Cited in Howard, Deborah, *Venice and the East: The Impact of the Islamic World on Venetian Architecture 1100–1500* (New Haven and London: Yale University Press, 2000), 18.

11. Bacon, Francis, *The Essays*, ed. John Pitcher (London: Penguin, 1985), 113.

12. Fabri, *Wanderings*, 121.

13. Ibid., 163.

14. Cyriac of Ancona, *Later Travels*, 231.

15. Ibid., 235–7.

16. Veronese, Guarino, *Epistolario di Guarino Veronese*. ed. R. Sabbadini, Vol. I (Venice: A spese della Società, 1915–19), 25.

17. The word "Mahona" may derive from the Greek *monas*, meaning "share, unit," or the Arabic *ma'unah*, denoting a financial contribution. The history of Chios under the Genovese has been studied by Philip P. Argenti, *The Occupation of Chios by the Genoese and Their Administration of the Island, 1346–1566* (Cambridge: Cambridge University Press, 1958), and "The Mahona of the Giustiniani: Genoese Colonialism and the Genoese Relationship with Chios," *Byzantinische Forschungen* 6 (1979), 1–35. See also Miller, William, "The Genoese in Chios," *Essays on the Latin Orient* (New York: AMS Press, 1983), 298–312.

Mastic is a resin of *Pistacia lentiscus*, a squat, gnarly evergreen bush that thrives only in southern Chios. It is collected from incisions made in the bark and solidifies into crystal teardrops. For some reason this solidifying process occurs only when the shrub is grown on Chios, and does not happen when the plant is raised anywhere else. Pliny, Dioscourides, Theophrastus, and other ancient authors extolled mastic's healing properties. Galenus of Pergamon, in his second-century AD *De Compositione Medicamentorum* (Lib. I, ch. 2), wrote that mastic from Chios was to be mixed in antidotes against baldness, mange, and snakebites. It was beneficial in treating inflammation of the stomach, intestines, and liver. And it made the best toothpaste: Roman ladies used toothpicks made from mastic trees to brighten their teeth.

Alum, a colorless crystalline substance procured from certain rocks, was indispensable to several key manufacturing processes. Textile workers used it to wash the oils out of wool and to bind dye to cloth. Tanners employed it in curing hides. Venetian glassmakers mixed it into the compound from which they spun their vases, plates, and other luxuries. Alum mines existed and were worked in various locations around the Mediterranean, but quality and price varied greatly, and the best alum came from Phocaea. The Genoese controlled the extraction and sale of this alum from 1275 to 1455, first paying for a lease of the mines to the Byzantine emperor, then to the Ottoman sultan (Fleet, Kate, *European and Islamic Trade in the Early Ottoman State: The Merchants of Genoa and Turkey* [Cambridge and New York: Cambridge University Press, 1999], 90–1). According to the Byzantine historian Doukas, every ship in the early fifteenth century sailing westward from Phocaea carried a cargo of alum (Doukas, *Decline and Fall of Byzantium to the Ottoman Turks*, trans. and ed. H. J. Magoulias [Detroit: Wayne State University Press, 1975], 148).

18. Woodhouse, C. M., "Contributions from Chios to the Classical Revival," in John Boardman and C. E. Vaphopoulou-Richardson, eds., *Chios: A Conference at the Homereion in Chios* (Oxford: Clarendon Press, 1986), 55–9.

19. Miller, "The Genoese in Chios," 311. In 1474 Andreolo's son would entertain here Christopher Columbus, then only a modest Genoese ship captain.

20. There was a shadowy and shady Fra Francesco da Pistoia who traveled in the eastern Mediterranean and sent back ancient works to humanists in Italy, including Cosimo de' Medici and Poggio, but as Poggio's letters reveal, the friar was not to be trusted.

21. Bracciolini, *Two Renaissance Book Hunters*, 166.

22. S. Rizzo, in Questa, C. and R. Raffaelli, eds., *Il libro e il testo: atti del convegno internazionale, Urbino, 20–23 Settembre 1982* (Urbino: Università degli studi di Urbino/Edizioni Quattro Venti, 1984), 231–8, pls. 1–10.

23. Scalamonti, *Vita Viri Clarissimi*, 121.

24. Ibid., 122.

25. Ziadeh, Nicola A., *Damascus under the Mamluks* (Norman: University of Oklahoma Press, 1964).

26. Flood, Finbarr Barry, *The Great Mosque of Damascus: Studies in the Makings of an Umayyad Visual Culture* (Leiden: Brill, 2001).

27. The urban fabric of Damascus is discussed by Bianchi, Francesco, and Deborah Howard, "Life and Death in Damascus: The Material Culture of Venetians in the Syrian Capital in the Mid-Fifteenth Century," *Studi Veneziani*, n.s. XLVI (2003), 233–300, esp. 238–42. On Damascus schools see Ziadeh, *Damascus Under the Mamluks*, 51–4.

28. Spufford, *Power and Profit*, 385; Ashtor, Eliyahu, "L'Apogée du

commerce vénitien au levant: un nouvel essai d'explication," in his *Technology, Industry and Trade. The Levant versus Europe, 1250–1500* (Hampshire and Brookfield: Variorum, 1992).

29. *Visit to the holy places of Egypt, Sinai, Palestine and Syria in 1384, by Frescobaldi, Gucci and Sigoli,* trans. Theophilus Bellorini (Jerusalem: Franciscan Press, 1948), 140.

30. Ibid., 183.

31. Ibid., 182.

32. Ibid., 143, 182.

33. Scalamonti, *Vita Viri Clarissimi,* 122.

34. Tafur, *Travels and Adventures,* 83–4.

35. la Broquière, Bertrandon de, *Voyage doutremer,* trans. and ed. Galen R. Kline (New York: Peter Lang, 1988), 32.

36. Pliny, *Historia Naturalis* IX, chs. 36–38; Jensen, Lloyd B., "Royal Purple of Tyre," *Journal of Near Eastern Studies* 22, no. 2 (1963), 104–18.

37. Famagusta was governed by the Genoese, and Cyriacus may have carried a letter of recommendation from Andreolo Giustiniani, which helped open doors. He clearly impressed these Italians, for they asked him to assume this post which entailed administering civil and criminal justice in the district. He used this as an opportunity to deepen his knowledge of antiquity. As he told his biographer, "he took pleasure in his first study of the rules and important opinions laid down in the Roman law books, thereby increasing his skill as a magistrate. He admirably pronounced judgments on the basis of ancient legal texts alone and skillfully devoted himself to the task of creating concord and peace among the citizens" (Scalamonti, *Vita Viri Clarissimi,* 122). Apparently he did such an excellent job that when Contarini's letter finally arrived from Venice, anxiously urging him to proceed to Nicosia and assume his duties there, Cyriacus had a hard time convincing the government of Famagusta to let him resign his office.

38. Scalamonti, *Vita Viri Clarissimi,* 123.

39. For the history of Cyprus and Janus in particular see Hill, George, *A History of Cyprus,* Vol. II, *The Frankish Period, 1192–1432* (Cambridge: Cambridge University Press, 1948), VII, VIII.

40. Ziada, M. M., "Mamluk Conquest of Cyprus in the Fifteenth

Century," *Bulletin of the Faculty of Arts,* Egyptian University, 1933–34, I, 90–113, and II, 37–42.

41. Scalamonti, *Vita Viri Clarissimi,* 123.

42. Ibid.

43. Ibid.

44. Ibid.

The Ottoman Threat

1. Cyriac of Ancona, *Later Travels,* 11.

2. Imber, Colin, *The Ottoman Empire 1300–1481* (Istanbul: Isis Press, 1990), 22–6.

3. la Broquière, *Voyage doutremer,* 108.

4. Inalcik, Halil, *The Ottoman Empire: The Classical Age 1300–1600* (London: Weidenfeld and Nicolson, 1973), 21–2.

5. Tafur, *Travels and Adventures,* 128.

6. la Broquière, *Voyage doutremer,* 114–5.

7. Cited in Babinger, Franz, *Mehmed the Conqueror and His Time* (Princeton: Princeton University Press, 1978), 61–2.

8. la Broquière, *Voyage doutremer,* 116–7. He added that "His people and his household are very loyal, for they do as he commands, without question, if it is possible . . . He is very just and keeps his country safe."

9. Babinger, *Mehmed the Conqueror,* 62.

10. Scalamonti, *Vita Viri Clarissimi,* 124.

11. Vryonis, Speros, "The Ottoman Conquest of Thessaloniki in 1430," in Bryer, A. A. M. and Heath Lowry, eds., *Continuity and Change in Late Byzantine and Early Ottoman Society* (Birmingham: University of Birmingham Centre for Byzantine Studies and Dumbarton Oaks: Research Library and Collections, 1986), 281–321, quote on 305–6, history of Thessaloniki before 1430 on 305–8, the taking of the city in 1430, 290–9.

12. Vryonis, "The Ottoman Conquest of Thessaloniki," 291.

13. Spufford, *Power and Profit,* 304–5.

14. On Murad's charitable personality and patronage of arts and learning, see Babinger, *Mehmed the Conqueror,* 5–7; Kazhdan, Alex-

ander, and Robert Browning, "Education," in Kazhdan, Alexander P. ed., *The Oxford Dictionary of Byzantium* (Oxford: Oxford University Press, 1991).

15. Cited in Vryonis, "The Ottoman Conquest of Thessaloniki," 293–4.

16. Ibid., 297.

17. On slavery in Europe, see Origo, Iris, "The Domestic Enemy: The Eastern Slaves in Tuscany in the Fourteenth and Fifteenth Centuries," *Speculum* 30 (1955), 321–66; Spufford, *Power and Profit*, 338–41; Verlinden, Charles, *L'esclavage dans l'Europe médievale* (Bruges: De Tempel, 1955); Malowist, Marian, "The Trade of Eastern Europe in the Later Middle Ages," in Postan, M. M. and Edward Miller, eds. *The Cambridge Economic History of Europe*, Vol. II, 2nd ed. (Cambridge: Cambridge University Press, 1987), 525–612, esp. 587–90.

18. Origo, "The Domestic Enemy," 337. Deeds of sale, drawn up by a notary, described the origin of a slave, her price, appearance, and health. Sometimes the seller guaranteed that she was not a thieving, quarrelsome, or vicious creature, and not prone to running away. If she proved otherwise, the buyer could return her and reclaim his money.

19. Klapisch-Zuber, Christiane, *Women, Family, and Ritual in Renaissance Italy* (Chicago and London: University of Chicago Press, 1985), 141.

20. Brucker, Gene, ed., *Two Memoirs of Renaissance Florence* (New York: Harper & Row, 1967); Niccolini da Camugliano, Ginevra, *The Chronicles of a Florentine Family, 1200–1400* (London: Cape, 1933).

21. Theoretically, Christians were forbidden by the church to enslave other Christians. But many slaves bought and sold by the Italians were Greek and Balkan Christians captured by the Ottomans.

22. Origo, *The Merchant of Prato*, 298.

23. D'Elia, Anthony, F., "Marriage, Sexual Pleasure, and Learned Brides in the Wedding Orations of Fifteenth-Century Italy," *Renaissance Quarterly*, 55.2 (2002), 379–433, quote on p. 382.

24. Ibid., 400.

25. He never became a branch manager of a foreign firm, as men of his experience and abilities tended to do, because he did not wish to be tied down to one location, and thus unable to explore antiqui-

ties all over the Mediterranean. The expenses of a wife—often hundreds of florins—included her wardrobe, jewelry, and furnishings for the house. Klapisch-Zuber, *Women, Family, and Ritual*, 220–1.

26. Slaves could be a more economic and reliable form of labor than regular servants, and one did not need to worry about preserving their honor. Klapisch-Zuber, *Women, Family, and Ritual*, 173–6; King, Margaret L., *Women of the Renaissance* (Chicago and London: University of Chicago Press, 1991).

27. A common form of enfranchisement, *manumissio sub conditione*, specified that the slave would be freed after serving his master for a specified number of years without a salary. This bound the slave to the family.

28. Claudius Ptolemaeus, a Greek born in Alexandria in the second century AD, was a celebrated geographer and astrologer. His famous textbook on astronomy, the *Almagest*, laid out theories and tables necessary for describing and calculating the positions of the sun, moon, five planets, and over one thousand fixed stars (Ptolemy believed in the earth-centered universe). His *Geography* attempted to map the known terrestrial world by giving lists of places and their longitude and latitude coordinates—which he may have been the first to employ systematically—along with brief descriptions of key topographical features.

29. Slaves were often insured against acts of God, perils at sea, wars, and pirates.

30. Vickers, Michael, "Cyriacus of Ancona in Thessaloniki," *Byzantine and Modern Greek Studies* 2 (1976), 75–82.

31. Scalamonti, *Vita Viri Clarissimi*, 125. The high-relief carvings from the portico depicted Ganymede, a Dioskouros, Aura, Nike, Leda, Ariadne, and Dionysos. The sculpture is now in the Louvre.

Spy and Diplomat

1. Cyriac of Ancona, *Later Travels*, 7.
2. Scalamonti, *Vita Viri Clarissimi*, 126.
3. Ibid.
4. Cyriac of Ancona, *Later travels*, 21.

5. Scalamonti, *Vita Viri Clarissimi*, 126.

6. Ibid.

7. la Broquière, *Voyage doutremer*, 83–4.

8. Tafur, *Travels and Adventures*, 149.

9. Inalcik, *The Ottoman Empire: The Classical Age*, 124–5.

10. la Broquière, *Voyage doutremer*, 85. In Turkish sources Canuza Bey is called Hamza Bey.

11. Scalamonti, *Vita Viri Clarissimi*, 127.

12. Ibid.

13. Ovid, *Tristia*, I, 10, 29–30.

14. Strabo, *Geography*, 12. 575–6.

15. Scalamonti, *Vita Viri Clarissimi*, 127.

16. Ashmole, Bernard, "Cyriac of Ancona and the Temple of Hadrian at Cyzicus," *Journal of the Warburg and Courtauld Institutes* 19 (1956), 179–91. Cyriac of Ancona, *Later Travels*, 73–81. Copies of Cyriacus's drawings are preserved in a manuscript by Bartolomeus Fontius in Oxford, Ashmole MS, ff. 132v-136v., published by Saxl, Fritz, "The Classical Inscriptions in Renaissance Art and Politics," *Journal of the Warburg and Courtauld Institutes* 4 (1940–41), 19ff.

17. Scalamonti, *Vita Viri Clarissimi*, 126.

18. Translated and adapted from Bertalot, Ludwig, and Augusto Campana, "Gli scritti di Iacopo Zeno e il suo elogio di Ciriaco d'Ancona," *La Bibliofilia* 41 (1939), 356–76, esp. 374. I am grateful to Ken Lapatin and David Brafman for help with translation from Latin.

19. Gill, Joseph, *Personalities of the Council of Florence* (Oxford: Basil Blackwell, 1964), 105.

20. Quoted in ibid., after the contemporary Byzantine historian Sphrantzes.

21. Cited in Bréhier, L., "Attempts at Reunion of the Greek and Latin Churches," *Cambridge Medieval History* 4 (1936), 594–626, quote on p. 619.

22. Tafur, *Travels and Adventures*, 145.

23. Various efforts at achieving a union between 1054 and 1453 are discussed by Bréhier, "Attempts at Reunion of the Greek and Latin Churches."

24. Pollitt, J. J., *Art in the Hellenistic Age* (Cambridge: Cambridge University Press, 1986), 233–5.

25. Scalamonti, *Vita Viri Clarissimi*, 128.

26. Cyriacus also offered Guarini some ancient gems for sale during a visit to Ferrara, where the humanist taught classics, and he showed ancient coins to Ambrogio Traversari in Venice.

27. Cited in Argenti, *The Occupation of Chios by the Genoese*, Vol. 1, 178. Argenti relates the whole story in detail on pp. 174–200.

Poised and Thwarted

1. Quoted in Ludwig Pastor, *The History of the Popes from the Close of the Middle Ages* (London: P. Kegan, Trench, Trübner & Co., 1906), 351.

2. Hibbert, *Rome*, 113–5.

3. Lanciani, Rodolfo, *Storia degli Scavi di Roma e Notizie Intorno le Collezioni Reomane di Antichità*, Vol. I (Rome: Edizioni Quasar, 1989), 54, 55, 57, 77, 79.

4. Manuel Chrysoloras, *Comparison of Old and New Rome* (1411), cited in Smith, Christine. *Architecture in the Culture of Early Humanism: Ethics, Aesthetics, and Eloquence, 1400–1700* (New York: Oxford University Press, 1992), 201–2, 159–60.

5. Grafton, Anthony, *Leon Battista Alberti: Master Builder of the Italian Renaissance* (New York: Hill and Wang, 2000), 255, after Cugnoni, G., "Diritti nel Capitolo di S. Maria della Rotonda nel età di mezzo," *Archivio della R. Società Romana di Storia patria* 8 (1885), 577–89, esp. 582–3; Modigliani, *Mercati, botteghe e spazi di commercio*, 95–106, esp. 100–3.

6. Biondo, Flavio, "Roma instaurata," 3.65–6, in D'Onofrio, Cesare, *Visitiamo Roma nel Quattrocento: la città degli umanisti* (Rome: Romana Società Editrice, 1989), 249. Biondo would later compose a literary reconstruction of the city, called *Roma Instaurata Libri Tres* (1482)—the first attempt at a topographical description of Rome based on the examination of its physical remains interpreted in light of ancient sources.

7. Tafur, *Travels and Adventures*, 36.

8. Vespasiano, *Renaissance Princes, Popes & Prelates* (New York: Harper & Row, 1963), 27.

9. Scalamonti, *Vita Viri Clarissimi*, 129.

10. Vespasiano, *Renaissance Princes*, 18.

11. The full history of this conflict is presented by Stieber, Joachim W., *Pope Eugenius IV, the Council of Basel and the Secular and Ecclesiastical Authorities in the Empire* (Leiden: Brill, 1978).

12. Waugh, W., "Councils of Constance and Basel," *Cambridge Medieval History* 8 (1936), 1–44, esp. 23 ff. on Basel.

13. Geanakoplos, Deno J., "The Council of Florence (1438–1439) and the Problem of Union Between the Greek and Latin Churches," *Church History* 24.4 (1955), 324–46, quote on p. 328.

14. Gregorovius, Ferdinand, *History of the City of Rome in the Middle Ages* (London: G. Bell, 1900–1909), Vol. VII, pt. 1, 26–30.

15. Baxandall, Michael, "Guarino, Pisanello and Manuel Chrysoloras," *Journal of the Warbourg and Courtauld Institutes* 28 (1965), 183–204, quote on p. 197.

16. Cecchielli, Carlo, "Roma e il pensiero della Rinascita: Il Castello degli Orsini e un dialogo celebre," *L'Urbe* 6 (1941), 2–10.

17. Macdonald, William L., and John A. Pinto, *Hadrian's Villa and Its Legacy* (New Haven and London: Yale University Press, 1995).

18. Dio Cassius, *Dio's Roman History*, trans. Earnest Cary (Cambridge, MA: Harvard University Press, 1925), 9.1-5, p. 441.

19. Ibid., 5.2-3, p. 435.

20. *Scriptores Historiae Augustae* trans. David Magie (Cambridge, MA: Harvard University Press, 1953–4), XVII.8–9.

21. Quoted in Macdonald and Pinto, *Hadrian's Villa and Its Legacy*, 207.

22. Ibid., 220, 221, 247.

23. Pius II, *Memoirs of a Renaissance Pope. The Commentaries of Pius II*, trans. Florence A. Gragg (New York: Putnam, 1959), 306–7.

24. Martial, *Epigrammata*, trans. D. R. Shackleton-Bailey (Cambridge, MA: Harvard University Press, 1993), 11.77.

25. Seneca, *Ad Lucilium Epistulae Morales*, trans. Richard M. Gummere (Cambridge, MA: Harvard University Press, 1925), Epistle 122, 15–16, 421.

26. Renaissance homes were also very noisy. See Dennis, Flora, "Sound and Domestic Space in Fifteenth- and Sixteenth-Century Italy," *Studies in the Decorative Arts* (Fall–Winter 2008), 7–19.

27. Stillwell, R., et al., eds., *The Princeton Encyclopedia of Classical Sites* (Princeton: Princeton University Press, 1976); Meiggs, Russell, *Roman Ostia* (Oxford: Clarendon Press, 1973).

28. In the interim Cyriacus heard of a rebel Anconitan ship engaged in piracy in southern Italy and hurried there to meet an expedition sent from Ancona to bring it to justice. Of course he also used this as an opportunity to examine antiquities in the region. In the end, the Queen of Naples shielded the pirates from law, as she needed them for her own purposes, and the Anconitan fleet, with Cyriacus aboard, returned home. But soon he was back in Rome.

29. Gregorovius, *History of the City of Rome*, 35–7.

30. Johann (also called Hans) Schiltberger, a sixteen-year-old soldier from Bavaria, was captured at Nikopolis and spent most of his life as a servant for various masters, traveling throughout the Middle East and Central Asia. In 1427 he finally escaped and returned home, where he wrote an account of his ordeals—*The Bondage and Travels of Johann Schiltberger*, trans. J. Buchan Telfer (London: Hakluyt Society, series 1, no. 58; 1879). Imber, *The Ottoman Empire*, 47.

31. Scalamonti, *Vita Viri Clarissimi*, 130.

32. Ibid.

33. Poggio Bracciolini witnessed this entry and described it in a letter to Niccoli. Bracciolini, *Two Renaissance Book Hunters*, 176–8.

34. This ceremony was also recorded by Poggio, who commented that "this custom of crowning the emperor as we now do it is not the ancient one but was started long ago by Charlemagne." Bracciolini, *Two Renaissance Book Hunters*, 178–81.

35. Scalamonti, *Vita Viri Clarissimi*, 131.

36. Ibid.

The Measure of a Man

1. Alberti, Leon Battista, *On Painting*, trans. Cecil Grayson (London: Penguin, 1991), 34.

2. Robin, Diana, "A Reassessment of the Character of Francesco Filelfo (1398–1481)," *Renaissance Quarterly* 36 (1983), 202–24, quote on 217–8.

3. Cited in Robin, "A Reassessment," 217.

4. Filelfo's tempestuous career is analyzed in Robin, "A Reassessment."

5. Setton, Kenneth M., "The Byzantine Background to the Italian Renaissance," in *Europe and the Levant in the Middle Ages and the Renaissance*, Vol. I (London: Variorum Reprints, 1974), 72.

6. Colin, *Cyriaque d'Ancône*, 393–4.

7. Traversari was a monk who rose to become the head of his religious order, but he was also a dedicated humanist who mastered Greek, translated the writings of church fathers, and would play an important role at the Council of Florence in 1439, doing all the translating for the deliberations between representatives of the Greek and Roman churches and preparing a draft in Greek of the decree announcing their union.

8. Colin, *Cyriaque d'Ancône*, 303.

9. Vespasiano, *Renaissance Princes*, 353.

10. Colin, *Cyriaque d'Ancône*, 303.

11. Schadee, Hester, "Caesarea Laus: Ciriaco d'Ancona praising Caesar to Leonardo Bruni," *Renaissance Studies* 22.4 (2008), 435–49, quote on p. 442, n. 33.

12. Schadee, "Caesarea Laus," examines in detail the philosophy behind Cyriacus's letter to Bruni.

13. Manetti, Giannozzo, *Biographical Writings*, trans. and ed. Stefano U. Baldassarri and Rolf Bagemihl (Cambridge, MA: Harvard University Press, 2003), 119.

14. On the construction of the dome, see a lively account by King, Ross, *Brunelleschi's Dome: The Story of the Great Cathedral of Florence* (London: Pimlico, 2000).

15. Vasari, Giorgio, *Lives of the Painters, Sculptors and Architects*, trans. Gaston du De Vere, Vol. 1 (New York: Knopf, 1996), 331.

16. For where the cupola construction stood in 1433, see Saalman, Howard, *Filippo Brunelleschi: The Cupola of Santa Maria del Fiore* (London: Zwemmer, 1980), 132–3.

17. Vasari. *Lives*, 304.

18. Ibid., 371.

19. Donatello's trips to Rome in 1432–3, 1400, and 1403–4 are discussed in Janson, H. W., *The Sculpture of Donatello*, Vol. II (Princeton: Princeton University Press, 1957), 99–102, 110.

20. Bracciolini, *Two Renaissance Book Hunters*, 167.

21. Scalamonti, *Vita Vira Clarissimi*, 131–2. The Florentines believed the baptistery to have been originally a temple of Mars constructed by Julius Caesar in celebration of his victory over the nearby town of Fiesole. In reality, the building was probably erected in the seventh century AD.

22. Manetti, *Biographical Writings*, 127.

23. Ibid.

24. Both passages are cited in Gombrich, E. H., *The Heritage of Apelle: Studies in the Art of the Renaissance* (Oxford: Phaidon, 1976), 97–8.

25. Manetti, *Biographical Writings*, 125.

26. Ullman, Berthold L., and Philip A. Stadter, *The Public Library of Renaissance Florence* (Padua: Antenore, 1972).

27. Manetti, *Biographical Writings*, 121, 125.

28. Ibid., 125–7.

29. Ibid., 127.

30. Alsop, Joseph, *The Rare Art Traditions: The History of Art Collecting and its Linked Phenomena Wherever These Have Appeared* (London: Thames and Hudson, 1982), 328–9.

31. Scalamonti, *Vita Viri Clarissimi*, 132.

32. Vespasiano, *Renaissance Princes*, 399–400.

33. Scalamonti, *Vita Viri Clarissimi*, 132.

34. Cyriacus of Ancona, *Kyriaci Anconitani Itinerarium*, ed. Lorenzo Mehus (Florence: Joannis Pauli Giovannelli, 1742, 1969 fascimile), 54.

35. Vespasiano, *Renaissance Princes*, 213.

Into the Greek Past

1. Quoted in Tsigaku, Fani-Maria, *The Rediscovery of Greece* (New York: Caratzas Brothers, 1981), 26.

2. Turner, H. L., "The Expanding Horizons of Christopher Buondelmonti," *History Today* 40:10 (1990), 40–5; Turner, H. L., "Christopher Buondelmonti and the Isolario," *Terrae Incognitae* 19 (1987), 11–28.

3. Cyriacus's diaries, or *Commentaria*, for the Greek voyage survive only in a seventeenth-century printed edition made by Carlo Moroni from an earlier manuscript. From this volume, *Epigrammata reperta per Illyricum a Cyriaco Anconitano apud Liburniam* (ca. 1660), and some remaining letters regarding this journey, Edward W. Bodnar reconstructed Cyriacus's travels: Bodnar, E. W., *Cyriac of Ancona and Athens* (Latomus: Bruxelles-Berchem, 1960).

4. Strabo, *Geography*, trans. Horace L. Jones (Cambridge, MA: Harvard University Press, 1966), 9.3.3.

5. Plutarch, *Moralia*, trans. Frank Cole Babbitt (Cambridge, MA: Harvard University Press, 1967), "The Oracles at Delphi no Longer Given in Verse," 401 C.

6. Strabo, *Geography* 9.3.4, 6.

7. Ibid., 9.3.10.

8. *La redécouverte de Delphes* (Athens: École française d'Athènes; Paris: De Boccard, 1992).

9. Bodnar, *Cyriac of Ancona and Athens*, 35.

10. Plutarch, *The Lives of the Noble Grecians and Romans*, trans. John Dryden (London: Encyclopaedia Britannica, 1952), 127–8.

11. Kiilerich, Bente, "Making Sense of the *Spolia* in the Little Metropolis in Athens," *Arte Medievale* IV (2005), 95–114, esp. 106.

12. Bodnar, Edward W., "Athens in April 1436: Part 1," *Archaeology* 23 (1970), 96–105, quote on p. 97.

13. Strabo, *Geography*, 9.1.16.

14. Bodnar, "Athens in April 1436: Part 1," 99.

15. Vin, *Travellers to Greece and Constantinople*, Vol. II, 616.

16. Beard, Mary, *The Parthenon* (London: Profile, 2002), 60–1.

17. Thus, it was Christians, rather than Muslims, who were responsible for all the damage to the Parthenon.

18. Bodnar, "Athens in April 1436: Part 1," 100.

19. An anonymous Venetian visitor who passed through Athens around 1470 identified the Parthenon as a Roman building. Cyriacus correctly dated it to the time of Pericles. Cyriacus foreshadowed

the tendency of some modern archaeologists to disregard the Christian life of the temple, which lasted as long as its pagan one, not to mention its Muslim phase, and focus solely on its fifth-century BC glory.

20. For the monuments of Athens as elucidated by modern archaeologists, a very clear survey is offered by Camp, John M., *The Archaeology of Athens* (New Haven and London: Yale University Press, 2001).

21. Bodnar, Edward W., "Athens in April 1436: Part II," *Archaeology* 23 (1970), 188–99, quote on p. 188.

22. Bodnar, "Athens in April 1436: Part II," 191.

23. Camp, *The Archaeology of Athens*, 178, explains how the water clock worked.

24. Bodnar, "Athens in April 1436: Part 2," 195.

Meeting of the Minds

1. Quoted in Geanakoplos, Deno John, *Constantinople and the West* (Madison: University of Wisconsin Press, 1989), 231.

2. A detailed, if biased account of the Byzantine delegation's sojourn in Italy (the author being an opponent of the union) is Syropoulos, Sylvester, *Les Memoires du grand ecclesiarque de l'eglise de Constantinople Sylvestre Syropoulos sur le Concile de Florence (1438–1439)* (Rome: Pontificium institutum orientalium studiorum, 1971). For the hardships of the voyage, see Syropoulos, IV, 1–15. The quote about the miserable journey is cited in Gill, Joseph, *The Council of Florence* (Cambridge: Cambridge University Press, 1959), 91. Gill gives the most detailed treatment of this congress.

3. Syropoulos, *Memoires*, IV, 25.

4. Bréhier, "Attempts at Reunion of the Greek and Latin Churches," 594–626.

5. See Loenertz, R., "Les Dominicains Byzantins Théodore et André Chrysobergès et les Négociations pour l'union des églises de 1415 à 1430," *Archivum Fratrum Praedicatorum* IX (1939), 5–61, esp. 5.

6. Syropoulos, *Memoires*, IV, 30–5; Geanakoplos, "The Council of Florence," 329.

7. Syropoulos, *Memoires*, VI, 3, 5.

8. Gill, *Personalities*, 4.

9. Syropoulos, *Memoires*, VI, 43, 44; Gill, *Personalities*, 112.

10. Syropoulos, *Memoires*, VI, 42.

11. Sevcenko, Ihor, "Intellectual repercussions of the Council of Florence," *Church History* 24 (1955), 291–323, 291 ff.

12. Setton, *Europe and the Levant*, 69–70.

13. Ibid., 70.

14. Sevcenko, "Intellectual repercussions," 291.

15. Syropoulos, *Memoires*, V, 3.

16. Setton, *Europe and the Levant*, 70.

17. Gill, *Personalities*, 7–8.

18. Geanakoplos, "The Council of Florence," 334.

19. Ibid., n. 80.

20. Gill, *The Council of Florence*, 254.

21. Setton, Kenneth M., "The Emperor John Slept Here," *Speculum* 33 (1958), 222–8.

22. Setton, *Papacy and the Levant (1204–1571), Vol. II: The Fifteenth Century* (Philadelphia: American Philological Society, 1978), 57–8.

23. Colin, *Cyriaque d'Ancône*, 319–20.

The Last Crusade

1. Julius Caesar, *Commentaries on the Gallic War* (Boston: Lee & Shepard, 1904), 99.

2. Cyriac of Ancona, *Later Travels*, is the diary of Cyriacus's activities in the East in the years before and after the Crusade. For the Crusade itself and Cyriacus's role in it, see Bodnar, Edward W., "Ciriaco d'Ancona and the Crusade of Varna: A Closer Look," *Mediaevalia* 14 (1988), 253–80; Dabrowski, Jan, "L'anneé 1444," *Bulletin international de l'Academie polonaise des sciences et des letters, Classe de philology, Classe d'histoire et de philosophie*, No. supplementaire 6 (1951), 1–45; Pall, Francesco, "Ciriaco d'Ancona e le Crociata Contro

I Turchi," *Bulletin de la Section historique, Académie Roumaine* 20 (1938), 9–68.

3. Cyriac of Ancona, *Later Travels*, 11.

4. Ibid., 17. There were actually six columns on the front of the Propylaea, but the two outer ones were concealed within the walls that closed it on either side.

5. Tanoulas, Tasos, "Through the Broken Looking Glass: The Acciaiuoli Palace in the Propylaea Reflected in the Villa of Lorenzo il Magnifico at Poggio a Caiano," *Bolletino d'Arte* 100 (1997), 1–32; Brown, B. L., and D. E. E. Kleiner, "Giuliano da Sangallo's Drawings after Ciriaco d'Ancona: Transformations of Greek and Roman Antiquities in Athens," *Journal of the Society of Architectural Historians* 42 (1983), 321–35.

6. Cyriac of Ancona, *Later Travels*, 19. A drawing of the Parthenon, either made by Cyriacus himself or by another person after his sketches, survives in Ms. Hamilton 254, f. 85r, Staatsbibliothek Preussischer Kulturbesitz, Berlin. It shows an octastyle, pedimental structure with baseless, fluted Doric columns. Unlike Giuliano da Sangallo's later rendition of this image, which turned it into a Roman structure with composite order columns, Cyriacus's version was clear about the distinction between Greek and Roman styles. On the Renaissance practice of correcting buildings, see Brown and Kleiner, "Giuliano da Sangallo's Drawings," 333–5. The Hamilton ms. was made for Pietro Donato, Bishop of Padua and a friend of Cyriacus.

7. Bergstein, M., "Donatello's 'Gattamelata' and Its Humanist Audience," *Renaissance Quarterly* 55 (2002), 833–68.

8. Cyriac of Ancona, *Later Travels*, 27–9.

9. Ibid., 35.

10. Ibid., 37.

11. Ibid., 43.

12. Ibid., 51.

13. Ibid., 51–3.

14. Ibid., 73–7.

15. The highest known columns from antiquity are at Baalbek in Syria—they measure about 63 feet.

16. Cyriac of Ancona, *Later Travels*, 85–7.

17. Ibid., 87–9.

18. Imber, *The Ottoman Empire*, 129.

19. Cyriac of Ancona, *Later Travels*, 11, 15.

20. Ibid., 99–101.

21. Saxl, Fritz, "The Classical Inscriptions in Renaissance Art and Politics," *Journal of the Warburg and Courtauld Institutes* 4 (1940–41), 34 ff; Lehmann-Hartleben, K., "Cyriacus of Ancona, Aristotle, and Teiresias in Samothrace," *Hesperia* 12 (1943), 115–34; Williams Lehmann, P., *Samothrace Reflections* (Princeton: Princeton University Press, 1973), 3–56, 99–115, 125–31.

22. Cyriac of Ancona, *Later Travels*, 127–31.

23. Babinger, *Mehmed the Conqueror*, 37–40, esp. 40.

24. Cyriac of Ancona, *Later Travels*, 143.

25. Ibid., 193.

26. Ibid., 247–9.

27. Ibid., 251.

28. Ibid., 167, 173–5.

29. Ibid., 197–9, 428, n. 3 to letter 26.

30. Vickers, Michael, "The Changing Image of Alexander the Great," in M. Henig and D. Plantzos, eds., *Classicism to Neoclassicism: A Collection of Papers in Honour of Gertrud Seidmann* (Oxford: Archaeopress, 1999), 29–37, esp. 30.

31. Cyriac of Ancona, *Later Travels*, 277–9.

32. Ibid., 355–7.

In the Balance

1. Quoted in Cyriac of Ancona, *Later Travels*, 191.

2. Ibid., 21.

3. Kiilerich, "Making Sense of the *Spolia*," 95–114.

4. Vickers, Michael, "Mantegna and Constantinople," *Burlington Magazine* 118 (1976), 680–7; Lehmann, Phyllis W., *Cyriacus of Ancona's Egyptian Visit and its Reflections in Gentile Bellini and Hieronymous Bosch* (Locust Valley, NY: J. J. Augustin, 1977), 13–17.

5. Cyriac of Ancona, *Later Travels*, 191.

INDEX

Page numbers in *italics* refer to illustrations.
Page numbers beginning with 265 refer to notes.